Presented by

The Grundy Foundation

in memory of The

Honorable Joseph R. Grundy

"The Pennsylvanian"

THE PENNSYLVANIAN

Joseph R. Grundy

1335

By ANN HAWKES HUTTON

DORRANCE & COMPANY
Philadelphia

Copyright © 1962 by Ann Hawkes Hutton
All Rights Reserved

Library of Congress Catalog Card Number: 62-21713
Manufactured in the United States of America

PREFACE AND ACKNOWLEDGMENTS

The term "Grundyism" has been used and abused for the past sixty years. It appears frequently in print, in conversations and in statements by state and national political leaders who hold strikingly different interpretations of its meaning.

Through political perversions, it is now repeated by young people who have no knowledge whatsoever of the term's correct usage or of the man for whose activities it was coined. "Grundyism" stands as one of the first *isms* to befog our national concepts on many issues. Unfortunately a jaundiced manner of labelling different schools of thought is all too prevalent in today's society. Such tags as "McKinleyism," "Hooverism," and "Grundyism" are sometimes used to castigate reputable economic and political philosophies which honestly differ from those of contemporary liberals. The effect of this calculated tactic has been to identify conservatives as synonomous with reactionaries in the public mind. Joe Grundy was a convinced conservative, but he was both dynamic and forward-looking.

As one of his neighbors throughout my lifetime, I found it difficult to reconcile the public image of this man with the dedicated citizen and thoughtful gentleman whom I knew personally. Consequently, I undertook a study of his lengthy and eventful career in an effort to establish what manner of man Joe Grundy actually was. The result—which I present in the following chapters—is a conviction that my distinguished fellow townsman was one of the most maligned figures in Pennsylvania and national politics.

This conclusion does not carry the imputation that Joe Grundy was impeccable. He definitely was not, nor did he ever pretend to be a paragon of public or private virtue. He was tactless, unyielding and earthy. He held unpopular views which he expressed openly and sincerely. He firmly believed that "it is the manufacturing industries and the allied activities which they sustain that create the greater part of the purchasing power of the United States."

Because of this belief he unabashedly lent his tireless efforts to lobby for a high protective tariff. Unlike lobbyists and political leaders of a later era, Joe Grundy did not surround himself with a retinue of slick public relations experts to create, protect and preserve a popular image. He was too busy in doing what he thought was necessary for the public good to worry about his own public image. In the rough and tumble arena of early twentieth century politics, he masterfully and refreshingly held his own by being exactly what he was.

The portrait of Mr. Grundy which has taken shape in this book is drawn from his background and his record as a young man, a business executive, and a public spirited citizen. In a contemporary editorial in the *New York Herald Tribune* at the time Senator Grundy assumed his seat in the United States Senate in 1929, it was stated that "in the Senate more intellectual and moral courage and more serious conviction were needed." Mr. Grundy brought just such qualities not only to the United States Senate but also to American politics throughout the first half of the twentieth century.

The country knows the figure of Joe Grundy as a famed politician and industrialist, but I knew him primarily as a sincerely patriotic American whose enduring accomplishments for the economic development of his state entitle him to be also remembered as *The Pennsylvanian*.

It is impossible to acknowledge adequately those whose assistance was invaluable in the preparation of a biography. First of all, I wish to thank the Trustees of the Grundy Foundation, its Chairman, W. James MacIntosh, Esq.; its Secretary, Edwin R. Rummler; Oscar M. Hansen, Esq., Thomas E. Morris, and the Fidelity-Philadelphia Trust Company. All have shown helpful interest and continuing cooperation and have made available various important diaries and documents.

Mrs. James H. Emack, cousin of Mr. Grundy, has given

gracious and extensive assistance in procuring and interpreting old documents and photographs.

Mrs. Charles Stauffer's help has been invaluable in presenting an accurate picture of the Senator throughout the last thirty years of his life, and her daughter, Sarah Ann Stauffer, has added revealing sidelights on his character.

My warm thanks go to Dr. William W. Hassler, author-historian; Dr. Frederick B. Tolles, historian and director of the Friends' Historical Library of Swarthmore College; and to Russell Landstrom of the Associated Press for their cooperation and constructive suggestions. For information on many phases of Senator Grundy's political activities, I am greatly indebted to Mr. S. Edward Moore, House Parliamentarian of the General State Assembly, Commonwealth of Pennsylvania.

The tedious business of assembling material, organizing notes, reading and typing would not have been possible without the valued and conscientious work of Mrs. Newellyn R. Adams and my efficient secretary, Mrs. Melvin R. Schmid.

Last but far from least I wish to express my deepest appreciation to my forebearing family, especially my husband whose constructive criticism, challenging comment, and helpful editing made this work possible.

"Shadyside"
Bristol, Pennsylvania
April 17, 1962

CONTENTS

LIST OF ILLUSTRATIONS

THE PENNSYLVANIAN

JOSEPH R. GRUNDY

MUST BE ONE OF THOSE BOOMERANGS OR SOMETHING

—*From the New York Herald Tribune*

Chapter 1

"CAMPAIGN PROMISES SHOULD BE KEPT"

It was hot in Room 212 of the Senate Office Building. The room was packed with people and charged with emotion.

On this day, October 24, 1929, the Senate Lobby Investigating Committee was set to examine Joseph R. Grundy, labeled by journalists as the "king of lobbyists" and the "perfect Republican." A later generation, given to quick and easy titles, probably would have dubbed him "Mr. Pennsylvania." His contemporaries, those who admired him, called him *The Pennsylvanian*, because of his zeal for and interest in his state.

The hearings were being held in the first session of the Seventy-First Congress "to investigate the activities of lobbying associations and lobbyists in and around Washington, District of Columbia."

Joe Grundy, a vigorous sixty-six, sat directly in front of the committee table an uncomfortably few feet away from his eager inquisitors. His thick white hair was parted smoothly. His round, china-blue eyes surveyed the committee members with amused calm while his mouth curved in the famed, shy smile that was feared by knowing adversaries.

The committee chairman was Senator Thaddeus Caraway, an Arkansas Democrat. The other members were Thomas J. Walsh, a Montana Democrat; Arthur R. Robinson, an Indiana Republican, the only one of the five senators who did not show obvious hostility toward the Pennsylvanian; John J. Blaine, a Wisconsin Republican; and William E. Borah, an Idaho Republican. The latter two had joined southern Democrats in a coalition against the east. Another hostile Republican coalition leader was Senator George W. Norris of Nebraska, chairman of the Judiciary Committee, who had appointed the five-man subcommittee to investigate the influence of the industrial lobby. Plans had been carefully mapped for what was expected to be the most dramatic senatorial inquiry in years.

Joe Grundy was duly sworn by Senator Caraway. Responding to the latter's opening questions, Grundy stated that he lived in Bristol, Pennsylvania, was a manufacturer of worsted yarns and combed wool, and had been in the textile business for nearly fifty years.

After several further questions about the amount of time Grundy had spent in Washington, Senator Caraway attempted to prove that the Pennsylvanian was a paid lobbyist.

Caraway began innocently enough: "You have been down here ever since the Dingley bill. What year was that?"

"1897," replied Grundy.

Caraway shot the next question abruptly: "Who pays your expenses down here?"

The response was prompt and emphatic: "Why, I do!"

The senator was sarcastically incredulous: "Nobody contributes a cent to your expenses?"

"Not a bit."

Caraway allowed a cynical smile to accompany his next question: "You expect them [meaning, presumably, the manufacturers] to do it later?"

Joe Grundy's answer was direct and stern: "Never."

The senator's smile froze into a sneer: "It is a work of love on your part?"

The Quaker witness ignored the sarcasm. He replied quietly: "Not a work of love. I feel I have some obligations in this proposition."

Tension tightened as Caraway bore in anew: "They put up the campaign expenses, and they ought to get results for their money. Is that the obligation that rested on you—to see that they got their money's worth?"

Grundy could not be goaded into a corner: "I think they have a right to see that the Republican platform adopted at

Kansas City is put into law, and if through that they get their money back—"

Before Grundy could finish Caraway cut in: "They put up the money to take care of the election, and you feel they ought to get it back in legislation?"

Replied Grundy: "I feel that the Republican Party should put into law the platform adopted at Kansas City, on which they went before the people and received what you might call the mandate of 23,000,000 voters."

"They put up the money to bring that mandate about, and they ought to get the legislation they bought and paid for," Caraway persisted.

To which Grundy countered: "If that platform was put into law they would get their money back."

"And you were down here to see that they got their money back?"

"Yes, sir, I was helping every way I could."

Caraway agreed: "Yes, I don't think anybody could accuse you of laying down on the job."

"I hope not," said Grundy, "I don't want them to."

The grilling continued in the oppressive atmosphere of the hearing room.

"That has been your activity every time a tariff bill has been up?" Caraway asked.

"That has been the principle on which I have been present here."

"You just laid aside your business to come here?"

"Yes, sir. I felt it was more important than any branch of my business."

Caraway was sarcastic: "And the most important thing in the Government?"

The sarcasm lost its punch as Grundy answered seriously: "Yes, sir, by far."

The senator tried to put over his point in another way: "You haven't assisted in any other part of the Government or

3

lobbying for any other legislation, except that which would put money in the pockets of the campaign contributors, have you?"

Grundy was ready for the new twist: "I wouldn't put it that way."

"How would you put it?"

"That the Government here is run by parties; that one of the parties is definitely committed to the protective policy, and when it has gone before the people and received a mandate to carry a certain principle into legislation, it is their duty to do it."

The Pennsylvanian then managed to express his protective tariff theories for the record: "Of course, I have been brought up on the creed that the application of this theory of protection has been the one thing that has made our country what it is. It has developed this $65,000,000,000 worth of industrial turnover which is the reservoir out of which our employment of our people, our local and our Federal taxes largely come."

The senators next tried to impute to Grundy improper lobbying activity in Harrisburg, his state capital.

"Well," the Pennsylvanian explained carefully, "there is an interlocking relationship between Pennsylvania and the National Capital, a very intimate one."

Senator Walsh of Montana requested clarification: "Just explain. How would there be any difference between that and Helena, Montana, for instance?"

Grundy resumed: "Well, I suppose Pennsylvania does as much business with the Federal Government as two-thirds of the States of the Union put together, and it is right within a few hours of the Capital, and there has always been . . . a very active intercourse between the State of Pennsylvania and the National Capital. Politically, of course, as well as in other ways, because a very large number of public office holders are Federal office holders in Pennsylvania, and since the administration is Republican the State committee has to have contact down here."

Fully aware of the committee's motives and techniques, Grundy asked permission to read a statement he had prepared on

4

Pennsylvania's relationship to the protective tariff principle. Probably anticipating that his written statement would throw an unfavorable light on their efforts, the investigators refused to allow Grundy to read his statement. They obviously hoped that by questioning and inference they could bring forth some dubious facts, trap the witness by some misstatement or goad him into a display of unpleasant temperament. They were doomed to disappointment; Grundy was unfailingly accurate and imperturbably polite.

In the statement which was incorporated into the record, Grundy made a convincing case for his conviction that "the entire industrial and financial structure of the United States has been erected upon the sound principle which Henry Clay so aptly described as the 'American system.'"

By including certain references to Senator Borah in the prepared statement, the Pennsylvanian was exhibiting the kind of courage few men in public life would have dared to display. The senator from Idaho was as articulate as he was argumentative. Like all politicians, he had a tender spot regarding "unkept promises." Grundy struck a sensitive chord when he quoted Borah's campaign utterance of November 2, 1928, for protective tariff and compared it with his reversed position in October, 1929.

Joe Grundy was a regular Republican in every sense of the word. With firm beliefs in party loyalty and the inviolability of campaign pledges, he viewed the coalitionists with uncompromising disapproval and believed that their word was as weak as their loyalties. Furthermore, he never permitted anyone to forget a campaign promise involving tariff.

President-elect Hoover, in Grundy's opinion, was guilty of the same kind of inconstancy attributed to Borah. Grundy had maintained that Hoover promised higher protective tariff in his 1928 campaign. The Pennsylvanian, relying upon that pledge, proceeded to collect more than $700,000 for Hoover's campaign.

Grundy thought the Republican tariff plank had made it

5

clear that tariff rates would be raised for industrial as well as agricultural products. The plank was not, in his opinion, an empty campaign gesture: "According to my code the framing of the tariff plank imposed upon many a certain responsibility. Although it may not be the universal view, I hold to the opinion that campaign promises should be kept."

Soon after the election, he learned that President-elect Hoover apparently favored increases principally on agricultural products. Grundy had persuaded Senator Reed Smoot of Utah to visit Hoover and find out what his plans were for tariff revision. Smoot's report verified Grundy's fears that Hoover intended to raise merely a small percentage of the tariff rates, all dealing exclusively with farm relief.

Some of the Republican congressmen from the west were anxious to avoid a special session of Congress and its inevitable consideration of the tariff plank. These "progressives" had disliked the Pennsylvanian ever since his opposition in 1924 to Robert M. LaFollette's presidential bid on the Progressive Party ticket, with a Democrat, Burton K. Wheeler, for vice president. Subsequently they banded together in a coalition with the southern Democrats to snuff out the intent of the tariff plank of 1928.

President Coolidge apparently was seeing things their way and even Pennsylvania's lone senator, David A. Reed, was against an extra session of Congress.

In early January of 1929, while Coolidge was still in office, Joe Grundy had begun intense activities in Washington which were to stir the nation for the next year. He seemed to be fighting almost alone for the tariff standards of the Republican platform of 1928.

Said the *New Haven Courier* of February 13, 1929: "Grundy was interested in establishing a new industrial wall, not in buttressing one already rooted in prosperity . . . Industries were now adult."

Less than two weeks after the presidential inauguration a Hoover-Grundy conference was held at the White House.

The tariff question was discussed for forty minutes. Although Grundy refused comments to reporters after his visit, he appeared to be a disappointed man.

In his efforts to obtain a blanket embargo on all foreign goods that might compete with Pennsylvania, Grundy was repeatedly thwarted. He did, however, win a measure of victory. Hoover at least called a special session of Congress, but specified its purpose was a limited revision of the tariff of 1922. The Pennsylvanian knew now that he was facing a real fight. He rented a small office in downtown Washington as a lobbying headquarters. It bore the name American Tariff League News Bureau and was maintained entirely at Grundy's own expense. The staff consisted of a stenographer and several tariff experts who helped him with research for committee hearings, speeches and press releases.

The Pennsylvanian haunted the hearings of the House Ways and Means Committee but by the time the tariff bill under consideration was reported out of committee on May 7 he was bitterly dissatisfied. A few increases had been given in agricultural rates but not one substantial increase on manufactured products!

Grundy was a man who kept his eye on the ball and the ball was still the tariff plank of 1928: "The rises that are in the bill fall far short of meeting the requirements . . . along the lines indicated in the Republican platform adopted at Kansas City."

With renewed vigor Grundy worked to influence the members of the Senate Finance Committee to whom the bill had been referred. Before the committee meetings ended on July 18 it appeared that the tariff already passed by the House would be revised for the benefit of industry. As a result of Grundy's conferences with every member of the Finance Commitee, the Smoot-Hawley bill, as reported to the Senate on September 4, 1929, was more in keeping with the tariff plank of 1928.

Hoover and Grundy met at the White House several more times but neither changed his position. When debate over the

Smoot-Hawley bill began in the Senate on September 11, the President's insistence on a limited revision was unmistakably clear.

As soon as the House-passed bill left the Senate Finance Committee, Senator Borah proposed that all increases be made only in schedules pertaining to agriculture and related products. To everyone's astonishment except Grundy's, Borah's resolution on this proposal was defeated by one vote and the angry senator from Idaho moved with some of his western colleagues to join a fighting coalition of southern Democrats. This group, led by Borah, Norris and some Democratic Progressives, joined forces to prevent the manufacturing industries of the east from procuring any upward adjustment of duties. This was the background of the battleground in Room 212 of the Senate office building.

Grundy had been courageously reckless in his prepared statement for the Lobby Investigating Committee when he pointed out that . . . "the Senator from Idaho [Borah] who speaks so eloquently for agriculture represents a state that has only one-fifth the number of farms that are in Pennsylvania, only two-fifths of the farm value of Pennsylvania, less than one-fiftieth of the industry of Pennsylvania, and which contributes to the national treasury the magnificent sum of five-hundredths of one per cent of the total income tax."

This stumped the western coalitionists who were trying to prove that Grundy was against the farmers. Throughout much of his lifetime, Grundy maintained that more than ninety per cent of all American farm products were disposed of in the domestic market and that this purchasing power was sustained by the manufacturing and allied industries. The logic of this viewpoint had been repeatedly demonstrated by the fact that in Pennsylvania the farm vote, more consistently than any other vote bloc, remained favorable to Republican interests. It was also illustrated by the farm vote in New York and Ohio.

Grundy's prepared statement also maintained that the value of Pennsylvania's manufactured products was about equal to that of twenty-five other states combined. To appreciate fully his candor, it should be kept in mind that the home states of three of the questioning coalition senators were included in this list of twenty-five!

The Pennsylvanian also had his say on tariff theorists. He called them "swivel chair economists who've never spent an hour in an industrial plant and never had first hand contacts with any of the practical problems which are the very essence of that opinion on which they assume to speak with authority."

Cheerfully admitting that he was a lobbyist and proud of it, Grundy insisted that his lobbying was done at his own expense on behalf of the protective tariff that made America industrially strong and financially powerful.

As many news observers reported, the first day of the investigation ended in a decided victory for the quiet Quaker who managed to blunt every imputation and allegation of the senators.

When the questioning resumed on October 29, the day of the notorious Wall Street debacle, the lionesque Borah was bristling when he entered the arena. He tried to justify the change in his position on tariff. Grundy parried each thrust and Borah's efforts appeared more ridiculous with each question. Unhappily, the senator from Idaho turned to the irrelevant subject of campaign contributions. Here he thought he would dig into what appeared to be Grundy's soft spot, his well known work for campaign contributions, and prove that the Pennsylvanian's activities were entirely on behalf of industry, and not agriculture.

"Was there any part of this money which you raised from the agricultural interests?" Borah asked with bombastic sarcasm.

"I don't think it was," Grundy responded.

Borah, very sure of himself, interjected: "Has any part of it been used in the interest of agriculture?"

The Pennsylvanian answered slowly: "Well, of course, I am not a member of the Republican National Committee, and I can't answer as to what they did with it. My job was to raise it . . . I know in previous campaigns it has been used in the states where agriculture is predominant."

Here Grundy turned the tables adroitly as he continued: "If you would like to have that question answered, I might add that it was in the campaign in which you last ran for the Senate. It was used in the State of Idaho quite extensively."

Borah, on the defensive, barked: "Well, it wasn't used for me."

"I don't know," Grundy replied smoothly. "You were on the ticket. And I might further add that if they used in Pennsylvania a sum of money in proportion to the population that Idaho bears to Pennsylvania, that probably would have brought about another investigation . . .

"On September 2, 1924, there was $10,000 sent into Idaho to Mr. John McMurray, who was chairman of the Republican State Committee. On October 18, $5,000 sent into the State of Idaho; and October 24, $10,000. That is $25,000. Idaho has 431,000 people. Pennsylvania had at that time 8,720,000, and on a population or per capita basis, therefore, the contribution of $25,000 to the Idaho campaign was equivalent to $501,400 to Pennsylvania."

Senator Borah's face turned a threatening purple. He sputtered feeble protests and attempted a few more irrelevant questions but he had been stopped cold. The senator glanced helplessly toward his colleagues.

Rushing indignantly into the battle with reinforcements, Senator Walsh attempted to trap the Pennsylvanian: "Mr. Grundy, in a statement which you prepared for us the other day . . . incorporated in the record . . . I find the amount of wages paid in Pennsylvania and the number of wage earners as compared with the same group of states . . . likewise the value of products of those states compared with the value of the products of Pennsylvania . . . will you just explain what you think that has to do with the tariff and just what your purpose was in instituting that comparison."

Grundy: "May I be frank with you on this?"

"Oh, entirely so," Walsh replied with elaborate politeness. "Yes. We hope you will."

Joe Grundy took Walsh at his word: "My reason was that these states that are enumerated here have been states that have been most vocal on the floor of the Senate and raising all possible obstructions to the carrying out of the Republican platform adopted at Kansas City."

"There will be some difference of view about that," Walsh said.

"Well," said Grundy, "you asked me and I asked permission to make a frank statement . . . Frankly, when you come to analyze what they mean in the national life of this country, they haven't got any chips in the game at all."

Walsh was nonplussed by such brazen candor and Caraway had to leap back into the fray with the assertion, "They found that out long ago."

"Now," Grundy continued, "for these men that represent so little in the national economy to find fault and to obstruct and to try to destroy a policy which has been responsible for building up these great reservoirs of taxation that have been for the great benefit and advancement of the country, it seems it is a tragedy almost to mankind. It certainly ought to be pointed out to the country some way."

He explained patiently: "If this was a problem that had to do with junior Red Cross work for backward states or something like that, they would have a right to get into that game, but when it comes to this great fundamental policy that has made this country what it is and has produced this great revenue, those seven states that have about 2.66 per cent of the taxes of this country and put up all of this holler against the states which pay about 64 per cent of the revenues of the country, there is something wrong down here somewhere."

Caraway thought he saw a way to trap the wealthy

11

industrialist: "It is your view, then, that wealth and not states ought to be represented in the Senate?"

Grundy was not to be caught: "I did not say 'wealth,' " he replied, "but the general interest that goes with the tremendous weight of population and the tremendous weight of everything that goes to make up—"

Senator Caraway broke in, "You spoke about how much taxes they paid. You mean that the rich ought to . . . control the Senate?"

Grundy retorted: "No; I don't want the rich to control anything. I want everybody to control, but this is the only way you can bring this thing home to the people."

Caraway thought he saw another way to trap the witness: "Yet I understood you to say you thought it was a tragedy that the smaller states had two senators."

In eluding the trap, Joe Grundy permitted himself a bit of oratory: " . . . not that they should have elected two senators but that they should use their power to try to destroy what has been for the great good of the country and for the good of the world and for the good of civilization generally."

Caraway hammered on another version of the same theme: "I understand you now that they should not have a vote when the tariff laws are being enacted?"

Grundy could not be stampeded into a damaging statement: "I do not want to say they should not have a vote, but they should not throw a monkey wrench into the machinery every minute of the twenty-four hours of the day."

Caraway, giving up on the vote point, settled for: "They should not be allowed to talk?"

"I don't want to say that."

"What do you want them to do now?"

Grundy's frankness delighted the spectators: "They should talk darned small . . ."

Caraway asked stiffly: "Will you please make out a list of

the senators that should be heard when tariffs are being considered?"

Grundy went him one better: "I would rather make out a list of those that ought not to be heard."

Caraway: "Well, make out a list of those."

Grundy was refreshingly tactless: "Well, I will begin right here."

"I should not be heard?" asked Caraway.

Grundy was polite, but firm: "Yes sir."

"I am to be silenced?" repeated the senator.

Grundy tried to explain: "I will tell you why—"

Caraway cut in: "Let us commence with the committee and cut them all out and then we will come back to the rest of them."

Grundy persisted: "Can I tell you why?"

"No," replied Caraway. "Tell us first the people and then tell us why. I know why," he added angrily, "because we won't take your money and vote your politics. But now begin and tell us. Commence with me. I ought to be eliminated. Who else? . . ."

Grundy said he would begin alphabetically and spoke of the delegation from Arkansas, pronouncing it as in Kansas.

"We call it 'Arkansaw,' " Caraway cut in.

"Well, when I went to school—" Grundy started to explain.

Caraway was sarcastic: "I didn't know that you did," and went on, "we should be excluded. Now, who else? Go down the list."

Grundy: "I do not think the Senators from Georgia ought to be putting up the roar that they do."

"They are silenced. Go ahead."

"I might go down the line with many others from these western states as well."

"Well, name them."

Grundy was ready: "Take the two Dakotas—the two States of Dakota pay about $600,000 apiece . . ."

13

Walsh interrupted, "Well, please tell us then briefly what these tables do mean."

Grundy shot back: "It was to develop that on an important piece of legislation like the tariff that is responsible for so large a part of the revenues of this country, the states where industry has been so largely developed and where it is absolutely necessary that a protective tariff should be continued in order to preserve them and under which they should continue to pay and support the Government—their understanding of the tariff and their wishes should control, as against states that are the beneficiaries of that; states that do not contribute enough to make their own upkeep, practically, and their roads and their public buildings and their irrigation schemes and their dams are taken largely out of moneys that come from these larger states."

Walsh: "That is, the rich states ought to control and the poorer states ought to keep still?"

Grundy kept his temper: "They ought to receive greater consideration from the Congress when this type of legislation is being considered . . ."

Senator Walsh: "But how would you silence Senator Borah and myself in the United States Senate?"

Grundy was imperturbably polite: "I think your great understanding ought to indicate the propriety of allowing those things to prevail."

Walsh's next question was contemptuous: "You would improve our intelligence?"

Grundy handled that one expertly: "No, I would only want you to exercise it."

Senator Walsh, once more bested by the Pennsylvanian, and stung by his "backward states" comment, asked, "What do you mean by backward commonwealths?"

Grundy was again painfully frank: "The State of Arkansas is larger than the State of Pennsylvania. It is on the greatest navigable river of the country. It grows the best cotton in the country. It has iron and coal and gas and oil and zinc, and I think lead, and yet it has not got a cotton mill in the state, and it has not got a blast furnace in the state.

Grundy warmed to his subject: "Its industrial turnover, with all of its natural resources, is somewhere around $175,000,-000 a year, and it pays out about $35,000,000 in industrial wages as against a state like Pennsylvania that has not got all of those natural resources, that has not got the climate of Arkansas; that by application of the policy of protection which is free to every state to avail itself of, where it employs a million people in industry and has a payroll of a billion and a half dollars and an industrial turnover of somewhere around $7,000,000,000 a year, and has increased under this policy of protection in one decade as much as the total population of the State of Arkansas as it existed at that period of time, which was in 1920—I call that a backward state."

The way the hearing was going prompted Senator Norris to recite on the Senate floor an embarrassingly unfunny parody of Shakespeare's *Julius Caesar*. He waved aloft a yellow woolen jacket and told the senators that this was Grundy's mantle, as he intoned,

> "In this place, ran Caraway's dagger through;
> See what a rent the envious Borah made;
> Through this, the son of a wild jackass stabbed,
> And as he drew his cursed steel away,
> Mark how the blood of Grundy followed it."

The hearings had ceased being hearings in any real sense. The dominant committee members became prosecuting attorneys or policemen dealing with a suspect and the investigation became a "star jammed proceeding." It was, according to the *Tariff Review* of 1930, "a cross between a Roman holiday and the Spanish Inquisition."

The candid star furnished some comedy lines and flawless timing. One comment amused citizens across the land, except, perhaps, in Wisconsin. Grundy, who had a long memory, never forgave the Wisconsin delegation for deserting the regular ticket

15

at the Republican Convention in 1924. Hence, when, in the process of the questioning, Borah asked sarcastically, "Now what would you do with Wisconsin?" Grundy replied with a grin, "Well, what I would do with Wisconsin, I would hate to tell you!"

In this line of questioning all roads seemed eventually to lead back to Arkansas. Borah asked, "You do place Arkansas upon the list of backward states?"

Replied Grundy: "I think with the opportunities Arkansas has she is certainly very backward, and I think a state that has got 1,750,000 people and only allows 33,000 of them to vote to send this gentleman here (indicating Senator Caraway), there is something rotten in Denmark."

The *New York Times* exclaimed, "At last—a genuinely candid man!"

The next meeting was held on October 30. Most of this hearing also was devoted to unrelated details, the Republican National Convention of 1920, the Pennsylvania Manufacturers Association, patronage power, and campaign solicitations. Before the hearing ended Grundy managed to chide the senators once more for the actions of the Wisconsin delegation in 1924.

Senator Borah asked Mr. Grundy if he would like to apologize to the states he called "backward" and he said "No." It was apparent that the committee had thus far proved nothing to the Pennsylvanian's detriment and had, therefore, seized upon the "backward states" label as a means of discrediting him. The committee asked him to reappear on November 13 to state who were the backward senators from the "backward states."

Grundy appeared on the appointed date and stated simply that it would be "not quite proper" for him to introduce a discussion of personalities. He remained firm in his refusal to draw up a list of backward senators. Again he presented a written statement, mentioning among other things that "so far as I can recall, or can discover from a reading of the whole of my examination, the Committee has not denied or disputed a single fact which I set forth, but has shown a most remarkable interest in that single expression, 'backward commonwealths.'

"I neither advocate nor seek any special privilege, but an equality of opportunity for all—for the country as a whole—to continue to advance under those principles which have charted our progress and development from the beginning . . ."

In his refusal to draw up a list of "backward senators," Mr. Grundy had frustrated the last hope of the coalition. The final scene was described in the Philadelphia *Evening Bulletin* of December 12, 1929.

"He (Grundy) was smiling and suave under the strongest fire. After Senator Caraway had called him a welsher and said he was yellow, the senator, at the close of the hearing, walked over to Mr. Grundy and apologized. Mr. Grundy smiled cheerily and shook hands, apparently holding no animosity."

Nevertheless, both Caraway and Norris later denounced him on the Senate floor and the final report of the committee was devoted solely to assailing him in every possible way. At best this was a meaningless victory for the coalition because the personal vindictiveness of the members had been spotlighted and their unsuccessful fishing expedition held up to ridicule across the nation.

As on every political issue, public opinion was sharply divided, but Grundy won many friends, even among those who disagreed with him politically and economically. The public responded to his kind of frankness and courage and for the first time in his busy life he became a nationally known figure. It was a surprising situation for the candid Pennsylvania Quaker who had an honest dislike of personal publicity.

Speculation grew about the possibility of Grundy's appointment to Pennsylvania's vacant Senate seat. Hundreds of newspapers echoed the sentiments of the Bridgeport, Connecticut *Telegram*: "We cannot quite comprehend the viewpoint which seems to pervade some of our so-called statesmen, that to be a high protectionist is sinister and ignoble if not depraved, while to be a free-trader is lofty, ideal and disinterested.

"Such a distinction is utter bosh. One might take the whole parcel of free traders in Congress, put them into one huge cider press, apply the power and squeeze out nothing but pure elixir of self-interest . . .

"Morally he is just as good as any of his fellows in the Senate, while in candor and intellectual honesty he stands head and shoulders above some of them . . . We'd like to see Governor Fisher of Pennsylvania appoint Joseph R. Grundy to the vacant Senate seat. And we'd like to see that little clique of holier-than-thou senators stop him, if they can . . .

"All these things are matters of offense to certain senators, the kind of men whom William Allen White characterized many years ago as 'human hoop skirts discarded on the rubbish heap of time.' Who couldn't make one-tenth of their senatorial salaries at any outside job, and who hated worse than poison any successful man whose hobby is to keep industry going."

CHAPTER 2

BACKGROUND OF A REPUBLICAN

In that tumultuous year of 1929, Mark Sullivan, the widely known columnist and historian, wrote: "Permanent esteem for Mr. Grundy in Pennsylvania arises from his standing, his high personal character, his family line."

The family line was indeed worthy of pride. His grandmother on his paternal side, Rebecca Hulme, was descended from one of Pennsylvania's oldest Quaker families. She was the daughter of William Hulme and great-granddaughter of George Hulme, Jr., who, before 1700, had migrated with his father from England to Middletown Township in Bucks County. When his first wife, Naomi Palmer, died, George married her sister, Ruth; as a result, the couple was "read out of meeting." However, they were later reinstated.

George's son, John, married Rebecca Milnor of Falls Township. He conducted a weaving industry in Fallsington for many years, but eventually traded his farm and business for the Milford Mills along the Neshaminy Creek. With his sons he founded the Farmers Bank of Bucks County, established several new industries and laid out the town later named Hulmeville in his honor. John Hulme has rightly been called "one of Bucks County's first successful industrialists."

A second break in the family's Quaker affiliations occurred when John Hulme's granddaughter, Rebecca, born in 1803, became the wife of Edmund Grundy, an Episcopalian. Marrying out of denominational faith was forbidden. Hence, a fortnight after the ceremony, a committee of Friends called on Rebecca to ask her to admit that she was sorry for what she had done. The happy bride replied with spirit that she was not one bit repentant and, for this attitude, was "read out of meeting." Her grandson, Joe, frequently used the plain Quaker language; yet he was never actively affiliated with any meeting.

Joe's Episcopalian grandfather came to this country from England as a young man and established a small exporting business in Philadelphia. He kept a diary, a practice followed by both his son William and his grandson Joe. In each case the entries provide insight into the character of the writer.

A few notations from Edmund's journals indicate a point of view that was handed down in the family:

"January 21, 1864—Heard of the death of Joseph Ripka. His life has been very eventful. Got rich so sued by manufacturers—ambition and avarice led him on. Reverses . . . and a great change took place. Suppose he died poor—alas, the folly of too much ambition."

The Grundys, like the Hulmes, were ardent supporters of the Union cause in the Civil War: "March 29, 1864—A body of cavalry, Samuel Hulme's, 200 men and horses . . . the quartermaster and four others supped at our house, lodged three of them and five horses."

A touch of cynicism marks Edmund's entry of October 5, 1864: ". . . Mother went to the City and returned, she went to see principally Daniel's daughter Lydia Love married to a Mr. Burridge of Boston—entertain nothing but bright prospects and a constant flow of unalloyed love and pleasure, never a ripple of unpleasantness to interfere."

The elder Grundy's notation a few days later expresses a point of view notably different from that held by both his son and his grandson: "Election held today—did not vote for either party."

Edmund's final entry for the year 1864 points up the irony of prosperous times during a war: "December 31, 1864— . . . This has been an eventful year for Government, State, County, City—debts created—war—and its horrid consequences, destruction of life and property by war—and to crown all, great prosperity."

Grundy's ties to the Delaware Valley spanned both sides of the river. His maternal line, the Ridgway family, was a most distinguished one. It reached back to Roger de Lacie who served under the banner of Richard the Lionhearted at the Siege of Acon in 1192.

Richard Ridgway and his family of Welford, County of Buckingham in England, arrived in America in September, 1679 on the Ship "Jacob and Mary of London." It docked at the port of Burlington, New Jersey; however, the Ridgways first settled in Pennsylvania near the Falls of the Delaware, in Bucks County. Here Richard purchased considerable land which included 218 acres situated about a mile below Morrisville at a little settlement then known as "Crewcorne." The first court house in Bucks County was erected on his property. This background was undoubtedly a factor in Joe Grundy's life-long pride in the Bucks County Courts. He delighted in pointing out that in 1692 while the Witch Trials were going on in Salem, Massachusetts, Pennsylvania already had an enlightened court system inspired by Penn's advanced ideas on trial by a jury of one's peers.

Two years after Richard Ridgway's first wife died he married Abigail Stockton, daughter of Governor Stockton of New Jersey. Now the Ridgway family moved across the Delaware to New Jersey where Richard became a prominent farmer. Like William Penn, he was convinced that one of the first needs of any community was a place of worship. Just as Penn gave land for a Friends' Meeting House at Fallsington in Bucks County, Pennsylvania, so Ridgway gave the land at Springfield, in Burlington County, for one of the oldest meeting houses in New Jersey. On it, Francis Collins, the builder, erected the Springfield Meeting House in 1698. Until that time the Friends had been meeting at members' homes. This first Meeting House stood on or very near the site of the present one, built in 1775.

Several Ridgway homes bordered the Rancocas Creek near today's Levittown, New Jersey. One was erected in 1773, by

Solomon Ridgway, direct descendant of Richard, and great-great-grandfather of Joseph Ridgway Grundy.

In 1833, Solomon's son, Benjamin E. Ridgway, great-grandfather of Joseph Grundy, acquired 171 acres of this land. The son of Benjamin E., known as Benjamin of Pine Grove, the grandfather of Joseph Grundy, became the owner in 1858.

The Ridgways operated grain and lumber mills as well as farms and Rancocas Creek provided both water power and convenient transportation. This creek was important for navigation from the days of Indian dugout canoes to the opening of a railroad from Mount Holly to Camden in 1867.

Joe Grundy's grandfather, Benjamin Ridgway, was one of the active members of the Select Literary Society of Rancocas, organized in 1862. The Ridgways had come to the colonies as Friends and remained faithful members of the Society until Joseph's great-grandmother, the widow of Joseph Ridgway, married his brother, Benjamin E. Since the rules of the Friends forbade such a union, the two could not be married in Meeting. They married nevertheless, and like Grundy's paternal ancestors, were promptly expelled.

The Ridgways eventually sold the farm and "moved to town," nearby Mount Holly, the Burlington County seat. The last Ridgway home still stands on Ridgway Street. Joe's grandfather Ridgway did not marry until the age of forty. He had two daughters, Mary and Lizzie, and a son, Joseph.

Of all the Ridgways, Mary's brother Joseph exerted the most profound influence on the public career of his namesake, Joseph Ridgway Grundy. The nephew's views on loyalty in everything from patriotism and public service to politics reflected the imprint of the uncle's supreme sacrifice to preserve the Union during the Civil War.

Although twenty-one-year-old Joseph Ridgway could have afforded a substitute to serve for him in the Army (a common practice) so that he could marry and comfortably manage the extensive Ridgway properties in New Jersey, the sole male

Ridgway heir felt a deep obligation to serve his country. He did not use the philosophical shield from military service offered by the Quaker faith. The Ridgway Quakers, like the Hulmes, followed Penn's principle that every individual is free to obey the dictates of his own conscience. Furthermore, Joseph held the family conviction that a Ridgway always handled his own obligations personally.

These were stirring times. In 1862 Lincoln called for 300,000 additional troops "to assist in defending the Union and Constitution." Governors of the northern states shortly thereafter issued proclamations which aroused the emotions of citizens of all ages. General George B. McClellan's Peninsular Campaign against the Confederate Capital, Richmond, had been a failure.

It was during this critical time in northern fortunes that young Ridgway offered his services to the Union cause. Joining the Twenty-Third Regiment of the New Jersey Volunteers, he exhibited leadership qualities that earned his rank as Captain of Company G.

On November 7, 1862, President Lincoln, weary of General McClellan's inactivity, replaced the cautious, diminutive idol of the Army of the Potomac with hulking, blustery General Ambrose E. Burnside. This bewhiskered commander quickly reorganized his 122,000-man-army into three Grand Divisions, commanded by Generals Franklin, Hooker, and Sumner. Captain Ridgway's Company was assigned to Franklin's Left Grand Division.

General Burnside, prodded by impatient politicians and editorialists, proceeded to break camp at Warrenton, Virginia, and quickstep his bluecoats down the north bank of the Rappahannock to Fredericksburg where he hoped to whip General Robert E. Lee and then march "On to Richmond" in time to enjoy Christmas dinner in the Confederate capital.

The Twenty-Third New Jersey Volunteers soon reached Stafford Court House, ten miles north of Fredericksburg. From this encampment Captain Ridgway faithfully apprised his family of developments at the front. On November 26, 1862, he wrote:

"Captain of Company G of Beverly, of the Twenty-Third New Jersey Volunteers— Camp near Stafford Court House

"Dear Father:

"Here I am alone in my glory, the only officer that Company G can boast of. Lieut. Perkins has been promoted to the Adjutancy of the Regiment, the former Adjutant having been forced to resign. (A very polite way they have here of getting a man that they do not want out of the way, is to order him over to Headquarters to be examined or else to send in his resignation.) The latter is always adopted as he gets an honorable dismissal. . . . I am entirely alone, making me a considerable to do . . .

"Major Thompson left for home on second day; thus three of our field officers have left us, who will be the next to leave us or in what manner, it is hard to tell.

"Lieut. Perkins has just written for his father to come down and see him and bring some extra arrangements he needs in his new position; he will need a horse and he would like thee to see his father and assist him. I would like thee to come down with him and get Will [William Grundy] to come if thee can. Lieut. sent the directions how to come here. It is only four hours' ride from Washington to the Landing that is only six miles from camp. Thus it is not such an enormous journey. It looks as if we would lay here some time if not all winter, for the Generals are building stables for their horses and allowing the men to stockade their tents, so thee can see Mr. Perkins and get the direction. If thee gets to Washington, Mr. Dunn would get thee a pass. Thee must come if thee can, it would do me good to see thee; tell Mother she can send me a box of anything that is good, if she will. A little tea would be very accept-

24

able. Thee might bring a little money as I have but thirteen dollars left and some of that is the gold thee gave me and I don't want to spend that. If thee don't come, send me a little, for we do not know when payday will come and I do not want to run in debt.

"We have a Brigade band from Newark, New Jersey here, so we have plenty of music. It brings up the spirits of the boys famously. There is nothing of interest to tell thee more than I have already told, except that I am growing fat and am in good health. Until thee hears from me again, goodby, with much love to you all, as ever, thy loving son,

Joe

"P.S.—Tell Mother if she wants to send me some paper I can make use of it. General Torbert will treat the Brigade tomorrow to a gill of whiskey. Each soldier is to have a gill. It is on account of his promotion. I hear this minute that he has been commissioned as General."

"Camp near Stafford Court House, Virginia, November 30, 1862

"Dear Parents:

"I have been exceedingly busy since I last wrote, not as yet having a Lieut. to assist me, and probably will not for some days to come; thus it keeps me tied close to my duties, yet I get along very well.

"I received a letter from Lizzie [Ridgway] on fifth day, was very glad to hear from home and find you all so well.

". . . How singular it seems to be here on the oft heard of road to Richmond! I cannot scarcely realize it at times: to think that I am here, after reading so much of the movement of the army (while at home) of the attacks on the Rebel Capital, and I now find myself mingling with those that are marching on again, with the doubts of the result; yet it is so! If my assistance will be of any good, it is all that I ask.

"Col. Rierson has received his commission as Colonel of our Regiment. He takes a great deal of pains to try and make the Regiment what it should be. I like him very much, but he is quick tempered, yet it is soon over and when not out of humor, he is pleasant, social and free. He does not get out of humor often. I will have to hurry for we will have to form soon for service and to hear the Articles of War read; this morning we had a Brigade dress parade and a little drill afterward, which occupied nearly the whole forenoon, thus first day is one of the busiest days we have, instead of being a day of rest, ordered both by the Bible and the President, but what cares the General either for the President or Christianity.

"I have succeeded in procuring an A tent and have fitted it up nicely; for me alone it is very comfortable. I keep a large fire in front of it and when it is cold, take the coals and put them in the stove that came in the mess chest, set it in the tent. Thus it clears me of the smoke and makes it very warm and pleasant.

"I am becoming so accustomed to sleeping on the ground that I don't believe I can sleep in a bed when I get home. My rest here is sweet and sound, but they tell I have got to snoring famously, no matter, it don't disturb me.

"The boys have their tents fixed up so that they are warm and comfortable. Some have them with fireplaces in the end so they do their cooking in their tent. It will be hard to leave them. I believe there is as much writing in a company as in a wholesale store, for it keeps . . . me busy a good share of the time.

"I have a tremendous job ahead of me, to make out the quarterly return of clothing, camp and garrison equipage and ordinance to the Secretary of War. What it is

26

for, I do not know, but I guess I can get through. They have a singular way of doing things here, different from any other business I ever saw. We must be ready for service, so I must close with much love to all, I am as ever, thy loving son

Joe"

"Camp on road to King Georges Court House
[Undated—postmarked December 6, 1862]

"Dear Parents:

"We are still in the same camp as when I last wrote. The snow is gradually going yet it keeps cold, there seems to be but little difference between here and home, it may seem colder because we are more exposed, but we are pretty well inured to it now.

"Yesterday we had the first funeral that has been in the Regiment. A man by the name of Gilbert and a brother to old Billy Gilbert, a member of Company P, Captain Burnet's Company. The Colonel got the band for the occasion, the coffin was made of three cracker boxes and was borne on a stretcher-bearer. At ten o'clock the funeral was assembled, first marched the band, then the body, next was a squad of men with their arms inverted, after them the rest of the deceased's own Company marched in regular order. Then all that wished to go followed after in any order they pleased. At the grave the Chaplain preached a short but appropriate sermon. When the grave was filled up there were three rounds fired over his last resting place, as if to aid in sending his spirit to its eternal home. The band played sacred music all the time. After all was over they marched back to their starting place and were dismissed. It was a very solemn affair. Several more men are very sick, two or three are not expected to live. Out of the one thousand men that left Beverly [New Jersey], there is but about six hundred reported for duty, however some have been detailed from the Regiment, but there is a great many sick. It must be owing to the great change they have to undergo. Our present position, I believe is between the Potomac and Rappahannock and some ten miles to the left of Fredericksburg. What we are to do is hard to tell, whether we are to wait and hold the enemy while Banks completes his expedition, or whether we are to cooperate with him, it is hard to tell. Something must certainly be done before long—we must either fight or quit it, for the expense on the Government is tremendous.

"There are men in some of the old Regiment that have not been paid for eight months. It is very hard for their families now that everything is so high . . . Lt. Stokes arrived on Sunday, looks very well indeed. In Washington he saw . . . Mr. Hornby who was trying to get down here but could not, the proper way is for some one here to send an order from General Franklin home. I can get one when thee wants to come, and if thee will send me word when thee is ready, I will send it home for thee . . .

"The Colonel just told me that we would be likely to move back to Bell Plains tomorrow—as soon as we get there, I will write again. With much love to you all, I am as ever, your son

Joe"

"Bivouac on road to King Georges Court House,
December 6th, 1862

"Dear Sister [Lizzie]:

"Thee will forgive me for not writing directly to thee, as I have written home so often and I intend it for all, for I guess you all know the contents of each. We are encamped ten miles from King Georges Court House, and six miles from Bell Plains. We broke up our encampment on Thursday morning at five o'clock, passed Bell Plains at noon, stopped and rested there about fifteen minutes; we marched from there to our present camp in two hours and a half without a rest. Yesterday it rained all day and at evening it turned to snow. There is two inches of snow on the ground now but it has ceased to fall, yet it is not entirely clear. General Bartlett's Brigade that encamped for the night by us was ordered back to Bell Plains yesterday in the rain—not very pleasant. It is reported that we have to fall back there also, it will be necessary for us to get closer to a depot of provision for the roads are in awful trim so that farther advancement is impossible at present, but as soon as the roads get fit, I expect they will move us on again—perhaps the interim is to cross the Rappahannock and flank the rebels at Fredericksburg. We passed the pontoon train at White Oaks, I suppose they will throw a bridge across the Rappahannock as soon as the roads are fit to move upon.

"Where we are, what we are going to do, or when we will leave here, I cannot tell. Lieut. Newold of Company D was very sick at our last encampment and the Colonel got him and also Lieut. Shin of Company E furloughs for twenty days' time. To show the kindness of our Colonel, the night before we left he rode until twelve o'clock to procure these two furloughs. He was back and forth to Franklin's Headquarters two or three times. He complained of the doctors, for it was their place to have got them away. Colonel said they must go, so he did get them to go, so if I get sick, he will see to having me sent home.

"Mother wants to know who Uncle Mahlon is. Tell her he is white and the most faithful and ambitious man I have seen lately. I believe he would try to carry a house if he had it to carry. There is nothing too much for him to do for me. He is a true and worthy friend to me; my little quarters of ten feet square is nice and warm, although outside it is bleak and cold. You must have had a nice time on your riding pony the other day. I would have liked to have seen you. I suppose your reading circles come this week. They will be very nice. Tell Father not to forget to send me a little cash and you may send me that box you have been talking about. Direct it the same as a letter. Adams Express runs all the way through. I must close for the present. Give my love to Father and Mother and remember me to John, Seth and Toni, and all the rest. With much love, I am as ever thy brother

Joe"

This was the last communication penned by the young patriot to his family. On December 11, Franklin's Left Grand Division, 40,000 strong, took advantage of a dense fog to begin crossing over the Rappahannock River on a pontoon bridge which the army engineers had quietly contructed east of Fredericksburg. The crossing was contested only once when one of "Stonewall" Jackson's long-range Whitworth guns struck a bluecoated paymaster's tent and scattered bills like feathers from a pillow.

Having gained a foothold on the south bank of the Rappahannock just below the historic town of Fredericksburg, Franklin's shivering bluecoats spread out in three long lines facing the redoubtable corps of Stonewall Jackson, ensconced behind earthworks on a wooded ridge half a mile away. Although the Federals could not discern Jackson's strength, it was at an unprecedented firepower peak of eleven muskets per yard! Even so, the morale of Franklin's troops was stiffened considerably by the roar of salvos from General Hunt's 147 friendly cannon which fired from Stafford Heights across the river into the dense undergrowth and woodland which concealed Jackson's men.

On Saturday, December 13, Franklin ordered his lines to move forward and assail Jackson as soon as the hazy winter sun dispelled the morning fog. In the ensuing fierce engagement,

Confederate cannon and musketry fire tore gaps in the blue lines. But despite fearful losses, the blue wave closed ranks each time and pressed ahead. In one unit the entire color guard with the exception of one color corporal was killed.

During this determined assault on Jackson's line, Captain Joseph Ridgway received a mortal wound in the head from a bullet shot by a Confederate sharpshooter. News of Joseph's tragic death—one of 12,500 Federal casualties incurred during the one-day Federal debacle at Fredericksburg—shocked the family which received the following letter of condolence, written on Christmas Day by their son's good friend, Sergeant R. R. Lippincott:

"In Camp opposite Federicksburg, Virginia,
December 25, 1862

"Benjamin Ridgway and Family:

"In forwarding the written lines to you 'tis with feelings of unfeigned sorrow and regret that I note the untimely death of my dear friend and your beloved son and brother, Joseph Ridgway, and that while we bow with humble submission to the all-wise decrees of Him that 'doeth all things well,' we cannot but deplore the loss of one that was endeared to all who knew him by every tie that endears man to his fellow-man:

"Therefore let it be known that in his death the Country loses a good citizen and a brave officer, one that was always willing to obey, yes, and one that was willing to lay down his life in defense of his Country's flag, and whose battle-cry was 'the Union, the Constitution, and the enforcement of the laws.'

"Respectfully
R. R. Lippincott"

Joseph's death brought heartbreak to the Ridgways and their two daughters, Mary and Lizzie. Mary, married to William

1335

Grundy and awaiting the birth of her first child, was prostrated. It is not surprising that her son Joseph, born a month later in the midst of this tragic family loss in the Civil War, would be affected by its implications. The horror of war, the bitterness of brother against brother, the mystery of battle camaraderie, the valor of lost causes as well as the victor's courage, inexhaustibly fascinated the young Grundy. He never tired of asking questions about his uncle's experiences in the war.

In years to come whenever anyone spoke about Grundy's feelings for his country, he became reticent, making light of his public service, taking refuge behind Quaker repose. Not until his ninety-sixth year did he tell this writer outright what he considered to be the basic core of his patriotic sentiment and endeavors. This is what he said: "Thee knows my Uncle Joseph, the only male in the family, gave his life for the Union Cause, just before I was born. How could I do less than serve my country when he had given his very life in its service?"

Chapter 3

YOUNG PHILADELPHIA QUAKER

The civic and political activities of William Grundy doubt-less explained his son's deep interest in the same pursuits. But it is in William's actions and reactions as a Philadelphia teenager of the nineteenth century that we can foresee Joe Grundy as a young man. Joe's zest for life, his ingrained sense of civic responsibility, quiet confidence and relentless ambition all stemmed from parental influence.

As boys both William and Joe kept diaries in which they reported their activities, aspirations and comments on the passing scene. Their observations may surprise that reader who is under the impression that Quakers are somber of spirit, austere to the point of cheerlessness, shun liquor, and forego fine clothes. To contradict this false impression, one need only consider William Penn, the most outstanding Quaker in the colonies. Throughout his life, the "Father of Pennsylvania" left ample evidence that he enjoyed a luxurious home, handsome clothes, and a gay and gracious social life which by no means excluded alcoholic drinks. In fact, he had his own brew house at Pennsbury Manor. Unquestionably Penn was a sophisticated man of the world.

Grundy came from just such a line of upper class, socially prominent Quakers. The truth of this is evident in William's diary which foreshadows to a remarkable degree the tastes and attitudes of his son.

William Grundy's diary begins with a description of the new year 1853 dawning in an atmosphere of good cheer and security. One day there is a mention of going to church or meeting, then an entry reflecting the joy of a skating party on the Schuylkill River. A notation such as "Pap and Mother went to a lecture in the evening" is commonplace enough in a day that knew neither movies nor radio nor television. Going to lectures was one of the leading forms of entertainment as well as of instruction. Typical entries for the rest of 1853:

"Pap and Mother attended a lecture at Spring Garden Hall by Horace Mann, on 'Woman.'

"Took a music lesson in the afternoon which finishes the first quarter—two lessons per week, $15 per quarter.

"Went to Cherry Street Meeting this morning with Mother and Joe. Had a good sermon from Lucretia Mott on the silence of worship.

"Uncle Joseph Hulme came today . . . He looks very feeble and has lost a great deal of his flesh. It is Pap's opinion that it has been brought on by high living, of which Uncle was very fond."

In April when a young man's fancy turns, he noted the visit of one of his sister's boarding school friends, Mary Ridgway, the young woman whom he would one day marry. The magic of May followed and he wrote: "Things in the country look nice and green—lilacs are in full bloom . . . Pap bought a new carriage of the Jenny Lind style at the bazaar."

Summer meant fun and on August 5th he wrote: "Fine day. Cut around as usual . . . In the evening went to Hulmeville with old Ben and store wagon and serenaded Ned Harrison. I have the violin, the rest sing."

There were always girls: "Took Lydia Love a ride around the turnpike square . . . [and] Mary Ridgway a long ride on horseback.

"Ned [William's elder brother, Edmund Netherwood Grundy] came up with me [to Walnut Grove the Grundy country home] in the afternoon so as to be ready to start to Fallsington Quaker Quarterly Meeting early in the morning."

September was enlivened by playgoing in Philadelphia. One of the attractions was "Pathinia and Ingomar" at the Walnut

Street Theater, starring Fanny Davenport. Another was "Uncle Tom's Cabin." The diarist did not record his opinion.

On October 20th it was noted that Philadelphia's famous Franklin Institute was opened and a month later: "Lectures commence tonight at Spring Garden Hall. George Wood and myself went up but couldn't get in, it being crowded."

William enjoyed his own music: "Harry Ackley plays flute, Joe Seal plays first violin, I play second violin and a darkie to whom we pay $1 plays on the violincello. We make good music."

On the 11th of December William "took Mother to Cherry Street Meeting in the morning, had some dry sermons from several Friends" and the next day he said without any embroidery, "I am 17 years of age [today]." Here are samplings from William's diary for 1854:

"Jan. 14 The steamer San Francisco that was disabled on the 24th by the storm has been found. Nearly 200 lives lost, 100 being swept off by a single wave. Over 500 lives saved. She was bound for Panama with troops, etc.

"Jan. 18 Went to the debate (on the Bible), made my supper on crackers and cheese along the road. Mr. Barker's argument contains a great deal of sound sense. Dr. Berg also treats the subject well. House very full.

"Jan. 19 Attended the debate with Pap and Mother last night. Great excitement. Berg spoke last, after his speech was over the audience cried, 'Infidel out! Turn him out!' etc. A large force of police kept the disturbance down.

"Feb. 22 George Washington's Birthday celebrated by the firing of guns, ringing of bells, marching of troops, etc.

"Mar. 7 Great preparation being made for the Consolidation Ball. The whole of Philadelphia County has been consolidated into the city. This ball is to celebrate it.

"Mar. 22 Took a music lesson this afternoon. Gave up the cornet on account of it not agreeing with me.

"April 18 Attended the Debating Society. Charlie

Eastwick read an essay. George Wood read a piece. Debate: Which is the rightful mother of a chicken, the hen that lays the egg or the one that hatches it? Decided on the hatching."

The next entries suggest another question for debate in 1854. Which was worse, the illness or the cure?

"April 23 Very unwell. Severe pain in feet commenced about the middle of the night. Couldn't bear my weight on my feet, got downstairs on my hands and knees. Very faint and weak. Dr. Comfort pronounced an imperfection in my blood as being the cause . . . must take half a teaspoon of preparation every two hours.

"April 24 Dr. Comfort changed the dose—two lobelia pills every two hours, teaspoon of saloratus dissolved in tumbler . . . also two dessert spoons of charcoal. Pain in my left shoulder today. Pap and Mother steamed me in the evening. After coming out of the steam I fainted, being very weak; but soon came to.

"April 25 Some better, played the violin a little in bed.

"April 27 My right foot seems to be rather crooked in not getting well faster. Doctor called and steamed me, then left. Mother gave me the emetic (which was awful strong and nasty to take) consisting of three teaspoonsful of three preparations and one of green lobelia.

"April 30 Spring clothes, new bonnets, etc., move about in large quantities today and make a great display. Foot great deal improved, walk much better.

"May 7 (Sunday) . . . Foot better . . . Mother and myself attended the meeting of the Spiritualists at Franklin Hall, some very curious facts presented.

"May 26 An eclipse of the sun came off this afternoon about 5:20, continued about an hour, was not total—we viewed it through smoked glass.

"June 3 Bought a linen dust coat at Sheperd's this morning $4. Straw hat $1.25.

"June 23 Didn't attend school today. Went up about 11:30 o'clock, bid all goodby, left the school for the season and for good. Intend entering business next fall."

In July he and his sister Sue visited Mary Ridgway in Rancocas, New Jersey: "Arrived at Mr. Ridgway's at 10:30 o'clock. Put the horse up, sat and talked with the family until dinner time which was 12 o'clock, then took with Joe Ridgway a nap on the parlor floor. Slept an hour and a half or two hours and got up refreshed and invited the girls to take a ride.

"All things being agreed upon, Joe and myself hitched Lady to the carriage and I took Mary and Lizzie Ridgway and Sue to Beverly. Drove around there hunting for refreshments which at last we found in a mean condition in Grifith Hotel. We all took sarsparilla, and returned home . . . In the evening took a walk with the girls . . . Beautiful moonlight, returned and spent the rest of the evening talking with Mr. Ridgway and family."

Summer evenings provided many opportunities for a pleasant mixture of music and fun: "In the evening . . . on a boat ride . . . I took the the violin along at the company's request, had quite a nice time, got out at the Flushing sawmill and had a dance. Cut around and astonished the natives.

"July 28 In the morning took Mrs. Alfred Love and Lydia up the beach shell hunting . . . In the evening we had a hop in the parlor which I enjoyed, danced every set."

In August seventeen-year-old William, "entered the store this morning with Pap to commence learning the dry goods business, very busy getting in goods. Felt quite tired in the evening, not used to such hard work. There is no aristocratic feeling in the store. We are all pretty much as one, as concerns the work from top to the bottom."

"Sept. 6 Our musical band met at Harry's this evening. The bass met with us but being young in the science, he could plug but one piece. Got home . . . past 11."

The modern day disposition toward quick, odd-combination lunches has been much criticized. Apparently the practice is not new: "On account of wishing to remain at the store until the middle of the afternoon, I did not go to dinner but made one with Pap on watermelon and crackers which probably sat much better than a hot one. This and cantaloupe is Pap's dinner when he takes them at the store."

The next day he tells of being in Wilmington, Delaware, on a hunting trip, but doesn't specify what he is hunting. He confides: "After talking over the news and getting our heads examined by a phrenologist at 25 cents per head, we started for Woods Delaware Iron Works (with George Wood and his brother Allen Wood)."

"Sept. 13 A new place of amusement called the City Museum in Callowhill Street above fifth, it's the Universalist Church altered into a theater, not of much account, kind of half-cut."

The end of September found the young man relating the satisfaction he got out of seeing a performance of "Camille, or the Fate of the Coquette," and proclaiming his enrollment in a dancing school to give him more polish at parties.

A question of health was raised again on October 8: "Took dinner on return which was an excellent one of beef roasted and all the vegetables. Those I enjoyed much but the beef I could not, having made a vow upon a vow that I would not eat any meat from the first of October until the last as my blood is much out of order and I am trying hard to get rid of my bad ring worm, that still keeps tight hold of my neck and face."

With delightful naivete William wrote on October 15: "This is the memorable day that I am publicly seen with a hat on. Adolph and Reen made it in the young men's style, narrow rim and middling high crown . . . Went to Cherry Street Meeting and heard an excellent sermon from Henry Ridgway on the importance of silent thought and worship . . . In the afternoon . . . I concluded to return home and take my ease at the parlor window and read a little and look at the pretty girls that pass . . . Didn't get rid of the ring worm yet."

"October 17 This evening I commence taking dancing lessons in company with seven others—we form a private select company of our own. The party are Ned Hawkins, Bill Jenkins, Samuel Chapman, Comley Mathers, Israel Parry, Charles Parry, Chalk Holt and myself. We meet three nights in the week and receive instruction. All of the party are Quakers' children 'but that makes no difference.' "

More sartorial confidences on October 21: "New suit of clothes came home tonight, the coat cut in the fashion really Shanghi—short waist, long tail, that's the style. Vest made in proportion and pants cut after nature."

William turned out in all his new finery for the first time on Sunday, the twenty-second ("My new suit made its first debut at Cherry this morning"), and was bored by "third-rate sermons and long-winded prayer" at Cherry Street Meeting. He said nothing about church-going the next Sunday, but wrote the following with a worldly tolerance of his own backsliding: "In the afternoon we amused ourselves with a game of Euchre, bad work on a Sunday, I will admit, and in a Quaker's house, but when boys get together they will be boys—very nearly as bad as girls."

On November 8 he had a toothache: "Mother poulticed my face with one made of Indian mush and green lobelia, composition powder and Cayenne pepper and applied it hot. Still ached so Mother put on a poultice of hops and whiskey stewed together."

William supplied a pleasant Thanksgiving day vignette: ". . . A beautiful day. The streets are alive with walkers or promenaders, it being set apart as the day on which thanks shall be given to the Almighty for the bounteous provision we have been gifted with during the past year; but there are as many ways practiced as gifts bestowed. Some attend church and listen to well composed sermons. Others attend the theater and other places of amusement. Others remain at home with the family and enjoy a day's retirement with wife, children, friends—and turkey."

In December the first entry again concerned clothes: "My new overcoat which came home yesterday is quite comfortable . . . The old fashion of ancient times has revived. No velvet collar, low in the neck, short in the waist fit tight and tail at or below the knees. They are called Shanghi's.

"Dec. 12 Mother says my birth happened upon this day of the year and as I have no other knowledge of the fact than its insertion in the old family Bible, we will have to take it for granted . . . Which concludes my eighteenth year."

Christmas week held gaiety for the whole family; "Start with Sis to visit Miss Nettie Potts, a very intimate friend . . . Liked Miss Potts very well—short and stout—as the Dutchman said, 'Not very high up but middling wide out.' "

"Dec. 30 In the evening Uncle (Joe Hulme), Ned, and myself went to the Chestnut Street Theater to see Christy's Minstrels. They were very comical and amusing."

The old year ended with Quaker worship and attendance at a watch service, "Methodist, the yelling order; they shouted the old year out and new one in, then we left satisfied."

This is the first entry of 1855: "Jan. 1 The store commences today under the management of the new firm E. Grundy and Company. Father has taken Edmund Netherwood Grundy, William H. Wardin and Edward L. Parker into the business, Pap furnishing the amount of money required to conduct the business and they pay interest for their share of investment, which is one-quarter each, it being divided into four parts. A fine chance for young beginners if they will conduct themselves rightly. Pap is still practical manager, but is slackening off from the minor duties of the business . . ."

The diary goes on: "Jan. 3 In the morning William Wardin and myself attended Spruce Street Meeting to see Sanderson R. Martin and Mary Anna Morris joined in matrimony." This is something William had never seen before and . . . he concluded "it was a long time to wait to get married by Friends ceremony. I think myself I should prefer to say simply the word 'Yes' to such a long lingo as they go through."

"Jan. 11 I commence taking French lessons . . . Fee $5 a month in advance.

"Jan. 14 Took a curb-stone ticket for the adjournment of Cherry Street Meeting. Fine display of fine young ladies and fine clothes."

In March he wrote: "Mother and I attended the Opera at Walnut Street Theater, conducted by the Dyne and Harrison troupe, 'Cinderella.' "

The end of summer meant fun under an August moon: "Aug. 30 Started for Walnut Grove—taking instruments along to serenade our country friends . . . Took a boat ride with instruments, excepting bass being unhandy to carry in boat, rowed up and down the creek and played, which sounded very nice and pleasant in the dusk of the evening with full tide. Started for Uncle Joe Canby's by 9:30 o'clock, arrived about 10:15, found all quiet except the dog. Played several pieces and retired not being able to see signs of human life . . .

"Our next move was towards Ned Harrison which admitted of a call in and treat to cold water and peaches which were very acceptable . . . after which we started for Newport to serenade Miss Boutcher and friend, but on account of two terrier dogs which kept such a continued hubbub, we found it necessary to abscond . . . to Tullytown to visit Em and Annie Shoemaker. Left at 12:30—beautiful moonlight could not have had a prettier one . . .

"Arrived at Mr. Joseph Burton's about quarter past one and there we found another watchful dog . . . We played one piece and were partly through the second when Joseph made his appearance. After finishing I being the best acquainted, advanced and introduced the party. We were all heartily welcomed and invited in . . . Mr. Burton is very fond of music and its rare occurrence in this neighborhood made it more delightful. He seemed to be perfectly elated, charmed, and danced around and in short order set us out pie, cake, Adam's Ale, etc . . . Arrived at Walnut Grove at three oclock."

The morning after was a "fine beautiful day" but he "got up this morn very reluctantly at 5:30 . . ."

"Sept. 15 Started for Walnut Grove . . . Spent the evening after a hearty supper of raw tomatoes cut up in vinegar, bread and butter, and baked apples and cream—a treat we only get once a week—in assisting Mother in picking hops . . . Alf Hayes . . . will be able to take a proposed pedestrian trip from Lewisburg to Niagara, he seems like myself to be high in for the adventure . . .

"Sept. 22 Spent the evening very pleasantly with the young ladies—became very well acquainted with Annie (Shreve), (the first time I have met her). She is a really lively piece—full of fun.

"Sept. 23 . . . Pap, Mother, Sue and myself attended an abolition-antislavery meeting held in the factory at Hulmeville . . .

"Oct. 1 Start on pedestrian tour to Niagara Falls. To Milton by train. By October 13th in Rochester.

"Oct. 18 Continuing on trip to Niagara Falls, reached on the 18th—distance walked 215 miles.

"October 24 Snowing hard, determined to 'pedestrianize to Williamsport.'

"Oct. 25 Boarded the train at Williamsport for Milton. Riding seems strange and out of place after so many days pedestrianizing. Distance 304 miles.

"Oct. 27 Returned to Philadelphia found Pap and Mother in the country . . . So with this day ends my travels and the pedestrian adventure—one that, I think, has done me much good both physically and intellectually. I feel better, healthier and stronger and the knowledge of the country could not be gained as we passed it by another means . . .

"October 29 Spent the morning with Sue at Cherry Street Meeting in silent meditation for one and one-half hours, broken only by two worthy followers . . . Jane Martin gave out this morning that she would speak in particular to the young people. She gave us much good advice, but as she says, the wicked ways of this world hold too many inducements to the young and giddy. We approved but could not promise to practice . . . She spoke at length upon party-going, gay company dancing, theaters, etc., classing them all upon the same footing . . .

"Nov. 15 Started for Walnut Grove . . . On arriving found Pap in readiness to serve up tea in real old bachelor style—he lives on his trips here on plain substantial food, bread, butter, cold scrapple, cold corn beef, pickles, apple butter, etc., having a cup or two of tea, not at all dispeptic or high living.

"Dec. 12 Birthday—nineteen years . . . Commence tonight our weekly music meetings. Have dispensed with Male the bass violin player, not being disposed to take the right interest to practicing and general improvement."

Now it was New Year's again, and William related that 1856 was "ushered in amid the firing of guns, pistols, etc., generally throughout the city, creating much noise and disturbance."

"This year," the diary went on, "brings a change to our own circumstances. Pap retires from the firm of Edmund Grundy and Company, leaving it to the younger portion, Ned, William Wardin and Edward L. Parker . . ."

A little more than a week later William described a sleighing party: "about 30 and upward on large six-horse sleigh to hold 20 . . . arrived at Walnut Grove at 10, danced until 11, when we sat to a fine supper of turkey, chicken, fancy fixings."

Late hours for young people are not innovations of the twentieth century. After the hearty meal they danced until 3:30 a.m., rested for a half hour or so before heading for home.

It was bitterly cold, with a cutting wind, said William, "but being all packed in and all in a bunch, we surmounted many such difficulties. Miss Knight from Byberry and myself were very comfortable under my large shawl—not to be wondered at. Arrived in the city at 6:30 as the men were leaving their homes for work. Arrived home, took cat nap by the stove until the folks descended."

The saga of that eventful month proceeded: . . . "Spent the evening with the folks . . . Ned beat me at checkers . . . Retired at nine in a room cold enough to freeze a 'pump handle.' Circle of ice gathering on the woolen blanket in front of my mouth—good proof of a cold room."

"Jan. 12 . . . by 9:30 was off for Jersey via Bristol and Burlington . . . With assistance constructed a slip to take the horse on the ice . . . Drove across [the Delaware] for the first time in my life. At Burlington had no difficulty in getting off . . . arrived [at the Ridgways] about 12:30, unrigged and sat to a fine dinner of pork steak and fancy fixings—the cider is worthy of much praise. Sat, chatted, talked, skylarked, played snowball, until three.

Two weeks later he again: "Called on Mary Ridgway in the afternoon, received her consent to attend the party of the Saturday Evening Circle on fifth of next month . . . Accident about five this evening. Horse, sleigh with five occupants went through an air hole on the ice, two of the five drowned, both ladies. Creates great noise throughout the city."

William is now "on his own,": "From the first ultimo I commence to support myself, minus boarding and washing, for all tailor and shoe bills, minor expenses and pin money, etc. My salary at the store I calculate to meet, which has not yet been decided upon."

Mary emerges a "star" of the evening: "The party given by the Saturday Evening Circle came off tonight. . . . Myself waiting upon Mollie Ridgway [William now frequently uses Mary's nickname, Molly.] . . . [She], good looking at any time, shone forth doubly brilliant, a 'star' this evening . . ."

"Last night," William recorded in mid-March, "an awful calamity took place upon the River in front of the City in the burning of the steam ferry boat 'New Jersey' with the loss of upwards of fifty lives . . ."

In the spring William's fancy wandered: "April 6 At eleven took a trip to Cherry Street Meeting . . . and then formed one of the line of young gents along the front pavement to gaze at the display of fine looking females and the fashions . . . [at] Cherry Street Meeting . . . spent one and one-half hours in meditation interrupted by a worthy follower giving much good advice to all kinds, both young and old, which theoretically I subscribe to, but practically, the wicked ways of this world will not allow me to."

In the middle of the month, an aunt spoiled some fun: "Aunty's (Hulme) Quaker foot would not allow us to dance, although Uncle was in mind favorable to it—so much for Woman's Way, and so much for marrying one so high strung . . ."

"April 20 Indications of approaching storm, wind northeast, Orthodox Yearly Meeting commences today, therefore stormy weather is not much to be wondered at . . .

"April 21 Attended Walnut Street Theater . . . 'The Indian Tragedy' . . . Not suited to my fancy . . . entirely too much blood and thunder . . . At my suggestion nourished up in some fried oysters and glass of ale which went 'tres-bien' . . .

"May 24 . . . On way to French stopped at the Academy of Arts and viewed the living as well as scientific arts . . ."

In mid-summer of 1856 he attended Mary Ridgway's party and was again inspired to try out his French: "Marie est comme belle que jamais, elle est une creature charmant—et une que je ai beaucoup de regards et amour . . . All hands with but few exceptions took a walk, each pairing. Mary and myself joined and filled up the rear . . . Partook of a series of refreshments, ice creams, cake, wine, etc., in both of which I did not indulge, but the usual gentlemen partake of two or three plates of cream with cake and lemonade and wash it down with a glass or two of wine. Awful mess!"

In November his older brother Ned became engaged: "Ned about getting married finds himself in much trouble—Mother remarks his trouble is only commencing . . ."

"Nov. 30 Pap goes in for keeping old relics. I see that on the end [of Walnut Grove mansion] facing east he has the old stone from the old house marked, 'This is called the Page house 1770' under it he has placed another stone, rebuilt ERG, 1856 (drawing)."

As William neared his twentieth birthday, his mind like his brother's strayed toward matrimony.

"Took Sue to a lecture by Fowler on matrimony, courtship, etc., quite interesting to the inexperienced mind.

"Dec. 10 . . . Smoked my first segar this eve after one month's abstinence . . . Think . . . we will smoke until the first of the year. I find it does not really agree with me.

"Dec. 12 . . . Today finds me twenty years of age, so ends the first score of my existence. How will the second turn out—will it ever come? Will it be for good or bad? Will I marry? Will I be as successful at forty as present appearances indicate—to these time will only reveal . . ."

He celebrated his first score of existence by visiting the barber and "engaged a cup and brush with him to take from the first of the year 50 cent per month, two shaves a week, with hair trimming."

On February 24, 1857, the Academy of Music was opened in Philadelphia, and what a gala occasion it was! William expected to go, one of a special party of young people. However, he became ill and had to remain at home gulping down a foul mixture of lobelia pills, anti-canker pills, composition tea, etc., which must have left him feeling worse than before.

Further evidence of maturity appeared in this entry on April 4: "Changed from whiskers to a long narrow goatee."

On May 9 the diary has this curious observation: "Yearly meeting commences today and calls lots of the 'drabs' to the city."

"Drabs" or not, attractive young ladies were present: "May 10 Found the meeting house, stood around with many others awaiting the adjournment. The young gents took line along the sidewalk to witness the young ladies pass—a fine display—it can be truly said the Society of Friends possess more neat, handsome girls than any other. The meeting unusually large and the display of beauty, fine clothes, was immense . . . took walk through . . . some of the uptown streets to witness the beauty at the parlor windows . . .

"May 14 A very great disappointment to many folks . . . rained faithfully all day . . . Today is general worship with Friends and a great many anticipated visits to the city . . . much disappointment for many calculated on spreading themselves and fine clothes."

By late May William was annoyed: "Jersey folks always noted for gossip take it upon themselves that I am engaged 'to be married' to . . . Mary Ridgway, a fact that I am entirely ignorant of—and talk about it to such an extent that makes it very disagreeable."

He was not yet ready to settle down. A sportive touch appears on June 23: "In Bristol while in waitance for the stage made acquaintance with Dan Kelly's wife's sister, mutual introduction, quite good looking, rather splashy, gay, will have to call on it for amusement's sake . . ."

"July 5 . . . Took walk [with Mary] down the Mt. Holly turnpike and had much sport hunting for cherries after dark in a neighbor's lane . . . At ten [we] . . . had a capital moonlight ride. Of all my lady acquaintances, I enjoy Mary's company the most. Sprightly and lively . . . Fine disposition, etc., moves in society, very well liked . . ."

In August the family moved to renovated Walnut Grove, shipping its belongings by canal boat. William took lodgings in a boarding house, in order to be closer to his work.

Throughout this period he speaks often of hard times—of the suspension of old and trusted companies, of the difficulty of getting loans, of extraordinary dullness in the wholesale business: "Those in need of money at present are badly off," he wrote. "Stock of all kinds are in bad repute and will not hear handling."

And again: "Not busy at the store on account of the general depression in all branches of trade."

The young businessman kept a voluminous scrapbook in which he carefully pasted newspaper clippings describing the hard times. William designed the neatly lettered title page— "Hard Times—1857."

"Early in the day the Pennsylvania Bank suspended payment (specie)—this created a great furor throughout the city and in a short time in other cities. The Girard Bank refused to cash checks until after ten o'clock and when ten arrived, deferred until tomorrow . . . The experience of older persons is that such times have not been since 1837. Business entirely prostrate."

Hard times or not, William did not lose his appetite: "Mother's fresh baked apples and cream are delicious." [Joseph Grundy's favorite dessert throughout his ninety-eight years.]

By October William wrote: ". . . I consider myself too young and dependent to fasten myself up by any moral agreement that should govern my future life."

Scarcely a week later he resumed the argument with himself: "Mary is one I admire a great deal and one that's not hard to love. My feelings were much in favor of explaining my position and asking a return, but something said wait a little longer . . ."

William's moment of truth was very near, however, as revealed in these words written the next day: "Toward the latter part of the evening, finding ourselves alone, the conversation turned to that of our acquaintance, and our situation. We have been silent, our thoughts probably the same. I could not resist. I truly love and told her so plainly. The answer to my question of return was quickly given. The story was short but none the less endeared. With promises not to speak of our confidence, we kissed good night."

"Nov. 4 By 11:30 all hands dismissed, the other folks retired. Mollie and self enjoyed ourselves in private until after one. Of all things keep me from the society of two persons (said to be lovers) manifesting their feelings publicly in society—nothing looks more disgusting and nothing a greater mark of illbreeding . . . I have an idea our friends suspect our situation—but know nothing."

"Nov. 22 Found Mary well pleased to see me. Tells me her parents have broached the subject of our situation. Mrs. Ridgway concurs with her, is very much pleased and hopes to overcome the prejudice of Mr. R. who not altogether relishes Mary leaving the country and taking up with city life. Mary wished me to speak with him, but concluded to defer until another time . . . Presented Mary with a plain ring marked inside 'Mary from Will.' Rewarded by a kiss and many thanks."

The day after his twenty-first birthday he wrote: "I shall broach the subject plainly and ask . . . [Mr. Ridgway's] decision in my cause . . . I think there will be but little trouble—my mind is made up, trouble, consent, or otherwise."

All the same he dawdled like a moonstruck Hamlet for nearly a month, meanwhile devouring a book called *Love and Marriage.* On January 11, however, he: "Requested an audience with Mr. Ridgway in the parlor. Spoke to him of my feelings toward Mary and thinking our situation a subject in which he should be consulted, requested his views . . . He would much rather Mary would settle in the country, but if her happiness depends upon it, had not objections in the least, a result that was exceedingly satisfactory for I had anticipated some diversity of opinion on the subject . . .

"We had a long talk. He remarked that we were both quite young . . . Mollie came to me laughing for the result—she made a good guess, a kiss was the response . . . [At Walnut Grove] Spoke to Pap about Mary . . . He said she seemed to be a girl of sterling worth . . . Impressed the truth of the necessity of saving, gaining a start, and becoming independent of the world, etc. . . ."

The ensuing days were filled with lovers' talk and lovers' joys—a simple walk in the winter chill, a few words exchanged on the veranda, the bittersweet partings.

"The more I see of Mollie the stronger the attachment grows," he glowed. "We truly love one another."

This was what William had to say on St. Valentine's Day, 1858: "With Mollie enjoyed a social chat in the parlor beside the grate with no other save its light. Mollie is one that can be truly loved and whose love is returned. I feel perfectly happy in my choice; that she esteems, respects and loves me cannot be doubted and is undoubtedly equal to walk the remainder of life along with me. We have by ourselves thoroughly canvassed the matter and feel contented. I only hope it will always continue, and there be no cause for a different feeling."

And on March 4 these sentiments were expressed: "Do not take as much interest in the club as heretofore. It is very pleasant to belong to a social club of its character to pass away an evening once in while, but as for making it a steady place of resort . . . I don't think it right. It's a waste of time that can be spent to a great deal better advantage. I have been wasting too much time heretofore. Must make better use of it."

March was a quiet month for William. He was much taken with a play called "Sara the Creole; or, The Snake in the Grass." Mary gave him a watch chain made of her own hair and finished with gold. He confided that he was reading "Reveries of a Bachelor."

William veered from the personal for a moment to set down on August 16th: "Queen of England's congratulations to the President of the United States were received this afternoon in reference to the completion of the submarine telegraph connecting England with America. In honor of the event bonfires are numerous throughout the city."

In the new year 1859 William wrote: "(Pap) . . . intends to have placed this year to my credit at the store his interest with an addition to equal 20 per cent of the profits. I am thankful indeed for this advantage and will try to merit it by economy and strict attention to business. I have [a good] start, a much better one than Father had at thirty. May I follow his footsteps."

Long engagements were an accepted practice of the times. After a year of betrothal he wrote: ". . . Mary is sweet bodily, morally and in disposition. The more I see her, the more I find to admire . . . After the family's retirement, Mary and self collectively and alone enjoyed a seat 'tout ensemble' upon that old 'sofa' in sitting room. It's old fashioned, straight back and appears to have been made for strict disciplinarians and 'courtiers' also 'military.' "

But there were new business responsibilities. In May his father sailed for Europe on business and William wrote: "I dread his going alone, would like to accompany him if it were not too expensive . . . Pap bade Mother adieu and started on the road, probably not wishing to witness her emotion . . . Mother I pity, and it was the best part of the way to Bristol before I could speak, she took the parting so hard."

"May 22 . . . Spent much time in perusing the war news by last arrival from Europe. Austria and France no doubt contemplate a collision—what the result will be no one can conjecture—no doubt by this time deep in the horrors of war."

In early June William became ill: ". . . I think these bad colds are taken by overloading the stomach, thereby throwing the system open to changes of temperature . . ."

By June 15 he was well enough to go house hunting: "a long walk to South Camden . . . visited some nice cottages . . . examining, commenting, etc., upon their suitability to our purpose . . . I would as leave live in Camden in consideration of distance from business, cheapness and pleasantness of situation than in the outskirts of the city. These desirable properties are for sale at $2800, a small amount of cash. The interest, expense and charges will not amount above $200 per annum while to get such convenience in the city, $350 would hardly cover; it's nearer to business and decidedly more healthy, quiet and more open from the restraint of fashion."

At the end of June William attended to the paying of state and county taxes for the Walnut Grove farm, $48.31 in all for the year. On August 1 his father returned from Europe, looking well and hearty after his voyage.

In the latter 1850's the crisis in America was moving to terrible upheaval with what seemed to be the inevitability of Greek tragedy. Forces were at work that no man could control. Here, it appeared, was the will of history, not of men, in action.

On November 21, at a time when the country should have been most concerned with the tranquility of Thanksgiving William wrote: "John Brown, the leader of the Harpers Ferry insurrection, a few weeks since and now sentenced to be hanged on December 2nd, is the all-engrossing topic of newspaper articles and private comment."

On the New Year of 1860 William viewed his expenditures for the past year and decided that their total of $600.16 was "most too much for a single man."

During the spring he was "initiated into Lodge No. 121 of the order of A.G.M. Masons in the Grand Lodge Room of the Temple . . ."

By midsummer after an engagement of two-and-a-half years, he and Mary decided on a wedding date: "Mary and self have been quietly talking about our marriage . . . the last week in October . . . is the most accessible time. Peirson Penrose

. . . unable to serve as groomsman . . . I have engaged the third story front room at Mrs. Gilliams which we will furnish to suit our taste. We have determined our marriage to be plain . . ."

Three days later they decided to wed a month earlier and settled upon September 27th as the day for their marriage.

It was a social if quiet wedding. Man-like, William neglected to describe his bride's attire. As for himself, he was arrayed in the style of 1860—dress coat, white silk vest, black pants, patent leather boots, choker collar with black tie and white kid gloves. His best man and other attendants were similarly clothed. His second groomsman was one of the Penrose boys, old family friends and neighbors.

The couple honeymooned at Niagara Falls.

It is not surprising that in late October he wrote: "My journal has been neglected since September 10th . . . one of the important changes in life has in this time taken place. Mary and self were married on the 27th ult . . . in sitting room at Pine Grove . . . one—until death shall separate us. We married ourselves in the presence of our friends assembled." [The typical Quaker wedding ceremony.]

Back on the job in November the young husband reported: "Dull indeed in business, prospect of a tightness in the money market. Election of Lincoln . . . has caused a political and likely too a commercial and financial disruption between the North and South . . .

"The payers of money have had a hard time . . . Worse than the times of '57 . . . The banks have stopped discounting and throw borrowers to the mercy of private capitalists . . ."

Even more grave is the mood of December 15: "The President of U. S. proclaims and desires the fifth of January to be set aside as a day of humiliation, fasting and prayer upon the state of the Union. It's good in its way but he had better send a force sufficient to suppress the South Carolina Traitors."

Thus ends the diary of William Hulme Grundy. Like his son, Joe, William apparently kept no diaries as he grew older.

Recorded comments by his father indicate that William worked hard in the family business. In 1876 he branched into his own woolen mills at Bristol and wool buying took him abroad several times.

On one occasion he traveled to Russia on an errand of mercy. That country, then plagued by severe famine, had appealed for help. Philadelphia responded with supplies, and loaded a vessel for Russia. William Grundy, known for many civic activities in Philadelphia and throughout the state, was asked to accompany the ship. He did so with Rudolph Blankenburg, a prominent Philadelphian appointed by the city to undertake the mission. After a long voyage the two men turned the needed supplies over to the Russians.

William enlarged the scope of the family's civic, political and social activities. In both Washington and Harrisburg he was a dedicated and unpaid lobbyist in the interests of a high protective tariff. His deep concern for the Union cause led to his membership in the Union League of Philadelphia and he encouraged his son to join at an early age. Thus Joe Grundy later was, for many years, the oldest living member of this patriotic organization, founded to give vital financial aid to the Union forces.

None of these major interests lessened William's efforts on behalf of his home town and he was twice elected its burgess. At the age of twenty-two he had written in his diary, "to be rich, extravagantly rich, I do not care for, to be above the world, to be free and independent is my desire. *It's my great wish to succeed.*"

And succeed he did—far beyond the dreams of most men. But neither his financial nor social attainments matched the enduring success of his relationship with his son. This survived William's sudden death at the age of fifty-six, a stunning loss to his family and his many friends. One of them wrote to Joe, ". . . Surely I never had the pleasure of knowing a more genial, kind-hearted man than your Father in my lifetime. I shall never forget him, nor will any of his friends, and his influence will not fade away from our remembrance while we live."

Nor did his influence ever fade from his son's remembrance.

Chapter 4

EDUCATION OF A CANDID MAN

Young Joe Grundy basked in the affection of both maternal and paternal grandparents as well as devoted parents. Such an atmosphere probably explains his life-long cheerfulness and imperturbability, qualities stemming from the warm security of a happy home life. How many fathers bother to write separate letters to a boy only three years old? William Grundy did.

"Pittsburgh, Pennsylvania, June 17, 1866

"My Dear Son:

"How is thee getting along, my dear little boy? I have thought of thee a great deal lately. How is thy rash coming on? I hope thee does not scratch. Mama writes to me thee has got a new cart. She does not tell me who gave it to thee. I hope thee thanked the one that was so kind. Thank again for me. Be a right good little boy, always, and try and see how good thee can be until Papa comes home. If Mama gets sick any time thee must try and not worry her and play out around with Maggie and be as little trouble in the house as possible. Does thee get all the strawberries thee wants to eat? Always eat one extra one for me. Kiss thyself for thy Papa. From thy dear Papa. (10¢ son —10¢ Maggie)" [Maggie was the housekeeper.]

Another affectionate letter arrived from Pittsburgh on August 6th of that year. It referred to Joe's new sister, Margaret, born on July 14th.

"My Dear Son:

"Mother writes me thee received thy express wagon all right and is very much pleased with it. I hope it will be a means of thee enjoying thyself very much and that thee will take good care of it and not let it get broken, for I cannot afford to buy thee so expensive gifts every day in the week. I have no doubt Grandpap thinks thy father too extravagant, but these are little home pleasures and if it only rationally pleases thee and keeps thee out of trouble and should save thy Mother, Grandma, or Aunt Lizzie [his wife's sister] one ruffling of their otherwise sweet dispositions, thy Father would be truly repaid, even unto 100-fold, and consider the investment only a duty. Kiss thy Mother and little Sister and thyself for me and do not forget next 7th day when thee comes to the station that thee is coming for thy Father."

As a small boy, Joe had boundless energy and a vast curiosity—two characteristics that never deserted him. A propensity for childish mischief was taxing, even for two such loving parents as Mary and William Grundy.

One summer they found what appeared to be a solution. While the Grundys were vacationing in the Catskills, they met Abraham Beck, headmaster of The Moravian Family School for Boys, and a nearby school for girls, Linden Hall, in Lititz, Pennsylvania. Mrs. Grundy was impressed not only by the school's academic program but also by the emphasis on physical fitness. Since she was not well herself at this time, she was inclined to worry unnecessarily over the health of her two children.

Mary and William passed on the information about the Beck school to the devoted Grundy grandparents in Bristol and Grandfather Grundy hastened to Lititz to look over the school. He found it satisfactory and Joe was enrolled there at the age of nine.

Although lonely and homesick at first, he overcame these feelings and remained at the school for three years. Here he made new friends and developed a life-long interest in the Pennsylvania Dutch country and its people. His first letter reveals early and persistent difficulties with spelling.

"Dear Mama:

"I though the[e] would like to hear from me. I am very well but not happy hear. I have been intenting to wright for some time as somthing has always stopet me. I am weighting for my overcoat to rech me and send me up two bats and send me up my chatterboxes to me and please hurry them up for I am weighing for they are neadid hear and pleas tell Grandpa to send the things to me witch he promesed me. I am coming along with my studdies very well and donte the [e] think I am coming on with my wrighting to very well ... As I have nothing more to say, I ever remane thy affecton sun

Joseph Grundy"

Joe's lonely family sent many "goodies" that varied from cakes to barrels of apples. They wrote that he "could have his pick" of Christmas presents and he hastily replied that he wanted a gun and "a three-wheel velosipead like Joe Cinnet's."

At Christmas vacation, Dr. Beck, the headmaster, wrote to William Grundy: "I think you will find Joseph improved. He is a good, clever boy, and we, Mrs. Beck, old Mr. Beck, and myself, think a great deal of him, even though he has given us unwittingly, much trouble by his nervous fidgety manner."

Christmas vacation! How wonderful it was to be back at home in Philadelphia, to visit his Grundy grandparents at Walnut Grove and his Ridgway grandparents in Mount Holly! Here he, his parents, and sister spent New Year's Day 1873. When the others went home on the afternoon train to Philadelphia, Joe remained with his grandparents and beloved Aunt Lizzie. His grandfather took him skating and he enjoyed going sleighing with his Aunt. On January 4th, Aunt Lizzie wrote in her diary "Went down to the city to take Joe home ... I was sorry to have him go back to school. I miss him very much ... Poor little fellow, I do hope he will be happy."

Joe had been frankly bored and homesick during his first

winter at school, but spring brought better days with baseball, kite flying and long, interesting walks. Studies, however, did not improve. His report card for the second semester of his first year told the story. He had demerits for carelessness in dress [a fault he overcame quickly and permanently] and for improper conduct in class. His grades would have discouraged a less optimistic lad.

		Number of Scholars in Class	Standing in Class
Reading	Defective		
Geography		4	2
English Grammer		5	4
Composition		10	8
History		10	8
Natural Philosophy		10	9
Elocution	Improved		
Arithmetic	Tolerable		
Mental Arithmetic		9	6
Penmanship	Improved		
Vocal Music	Good		
General Deport- ment	Good		

In early May William Grundy, following in his father's footsteps, sailed for England on a business trip. Young Joe wished that he could go with him but settled for a jolly summer at Walnut Grove and Mount Holly.

He was much happier during his second year at The Moravian School for Boys and when he returned home for Christmas 1873, his Aunt Lizzie wrote in her diary, "Joe came home for the holidays . . . very much improved."

On the day before Christmas that year Aunt Lizzie told of trimming the Christmas tree and setting out presents for the children. When the wonderful day itself came it was clear and not very cold. The good woman related that "the children were delighted with their things," and with simple gratitude recorded that "Mary gave me two pocket handkerchiefs and a nail brush."

Holidays meant much to these people. Christmas was the most festive of them all, but Aunt Lizzie's diaries make it clear that no anniversary date passed without gaiety, whether it be New Year's, St Valentine's Day or Easter. At school Joe missed the excitement of these occasions; on February 10th, 1874, he wrote to his father: "I have not received a letter from thee. Will thee please send me up some money for valintines as we cant get any from Mr. Beck. Please send it as soon as possible for next Friday is valintine day."

By late May he was anxious to see his mother and told her so by letter: "The next time thee writes, please tell me when thee is comming up to see me, for I am very anxyous to see thee. Mrs. Farr is comming up on the 25th of this month and I think it would be nice for you to come up with her. I received my box and was very much pleased with my ball, it is just the kind I wanted. Mr. Beck has had a bouling alley made for the boys, but we dare not roll for we have not got the pins yet."

After a happy summer Joe returned to school for his third year. His first letter home after his return reveals his complete adjustment to boarding school and a marked improvement in spelling: "As I promised thee that I would write . . . as soon as I had time, I will now do so. I arrived here safely on Wednesday evening at about nine o'clock, as there was some slight detention on the road between Philadelphia and Reading. Mr. Beck has bought a very large ship cannon, its weight is 500 pounds—shoots a six pound ball. We have not had very regular school since my return and I have had splendid times playing tenpins which I have enjoyed very much . . .

"We have in our school a candy shop and every year Mr. Beck gives it to the two boys which have been here the longest, so Harry Winston and myself have got it this year, and all the profit that comes from it is ours. Please give my love to all at home, I will close, from thy affectionate grandson."

Joe became the champion bowler, or tenpins player as the game was then called, of the school, a distinction he retained throughout the years. He loved to skate and go coasting. His pleasure in all types of athletics was reflected in his letters. Not especially interested in books, he did enjoy newspapers and magazines, saying in one letter: "I wish that thee would either subscribe for the *St. Nicholas* (magazine) or let me subscribe to the paper which I told thee of in my last letter."

During the spring of his third year, 1875, spring fever pops from the pages of his letter:

"The other day Mr. Beck took us to Millway a small town about three miles from here, to fish and swim. As soon as we had reached our destination we got out of the cars as fast as we could and shouted Harrah! Harrah! And the people who were looking out of the cars laughed to see us so happy. We then ran as hard as we could to the swimming ground, and as soon as we had got out of our clothes, we all jumped in and splashed about worse than so many ducks. After staying in for about half an hour, Mr. Beck called us out, and after we had dressed ourselves, we set about rigging up our fishing lines. On the whole we had very bad luck; but towards the end I succeeded in finding a place where I had pretty good luck till a tramp came along, whose bait was superior to mine, so that he caught all the fish . . . When we got home from fishing, we were very hungry, and I don't think I ever ate more in my life."

Joe did not return to Dr. Beck's school in the fall. His parents were grateful to that amiable headmaster who had done so much for their son's scholastic and athletic development. They felt that Joe, now twelve years old, had quieted down sufficiently to fit into the family pattern at home. He was sent to public school for the next two years and his social contacts widened under the loving tutelage of Aunt Lizzie.

On Washington's Birthday in 1877, she took him to a "Calico Party" at the Academy of Music. In her diary she reported, "It was a very fine sight—the ball was opened by a number of ladies and gentlemen in the old Continental dress dancing the 'minuet.' We had a private box and could see everything nicely. Joe was there and seemed to enjoy everything very much. It was his first appearance at anything of the kind."

He was also an interested spectator at the "gentlemen's tea" which William gave two days later. Lizzie and Mary spent an entire day preparing the terrapin. Helpful spinster Lizzie wrote, "We got along very nicely and everything was satisfactory. There were eleven gentlemen—of course Mary and I only got a glimpse of them."

But Joe, the handsome only son, was introduced by his proud father and enjoyed mingling with the men for a short time.

On Easter Sunday Joe went to First Day School with Aunt Lizzie and then on to a Temperance meeting with a friend. A week later he visited his aunt on her thirty-fourth birthday when she wrote in her diary, ". . . I am thirty-four years old today, may I with God's help be led into Christians' walk during the coming year, so that at the end I can say truthfully, 'Thy will be done.' "

She and her adored nephew could not know that the end for her was a brief two years away.

Aunt Lizzie spent the Christmas holidays of 1876 with Joe and Meta, as his sister Margaret was called, helping to arrange a party for them at their parents' home in Philadelphia. Lizzie, the dutiful, unmarried daughter of the Ridgways, typified the Victorian version of the good Samaritan. In her diary, the entries for December 31, 1876 and January 1, 1877 read: "Arrived at Mary's a little after five. In the evening we had a little entertainment for the children. It was real fun. After the children left, we all went out to see the illumination. Will illuminated their house. The old year went out with a great deal of noise and commotion.

"January 1, 1877—Our Centennial year 1876 has passed away and the New Year has been ushered in today with a heavy fall of snow. We say goodbye to the old year with regret. It has been all too short, and full of events, it has marked a great era in the 'world's history.'

"Our great Centennial will ever be remembered with pleasure by all for it brought all nations together and through it many lives have been affected and much happiness brought about, but we will wish each other a better and happier New Year, and may we live so that we will have nothing to regret when it is ended."

In the fall of 1877, while Aunt Lizzie was showing the first symptoms of serious illness, Joe was entering the secondary division at Swarthmore, then a Quaker institution serving as both a preparatory school and a college. He kept in mind the sage advice of his Grandfather Grundy who on October 8th wrote from Walnut Grove:

"We are pleased to find that you are pleased with the situation and the mode of instruction, and we do hope that you will improve and profit by the opportunity to qualify yourself for any position that may be your lot to be placed in.

"Pay strict attention to the instruction you can avail yourself of—don't for a moment fancy—that if, neglecting your studies, it is your instructor's loss, the loss will be your own—not his. Avoid all contact with the boys who may attempt to influence to do wrong.

"Be truthful, neglect not any advantage, avoid all means of deception; study to form a character and duties to make yourself a man, which will be a source of great satisfaction to parents and friends."

He noted his grandson's weakness in spelling and added: "Your letter was directed Edmond. The proper direction should be Edmund, instead of Edmond."

Joe had no difficulty in adjusting to his first term at Swarthmore's preparatory school. He retained fond memories of his years at The Moravian School for Boys and corresponded with his former headmaster Beck. A letter from Dr. Beck early in 1879 stated:

"Your letter of January 8 came duly to hand and I assure you that it afforded me much pleasure; for it was long, warm-hearted, and written in a manly tone. The card photo of yourself came just right for I had just begun to place my large collection of old boys' pictures in an album, and although I already had a capital one of yours—with seal-skin cap—this one, at a more advanced age, was very acceptable, and I send my thanks for it. It was too bad, however, that you had to go and coax it back from some of the young ladies at Swarthmore, just to give it to me!

"Since you left I once saw your name on some kind of programme of gymnastic exercises and I supposed at once that you must be pretty good at that sort of thing as you were, here, the champion tenpin roller, and no one has ever been here, teacher included, who did better.

"Last autumn I attended, for one day, the Teachers' Institute at Lancaster, and while there had the pleasure of hearing one of your Swarthmore teachers, Miss Maria L. Sanford (a history teacher). I was delighted with her lecture and almost wished that I could be one of her pupils. The young people in the back part of the hall—where I sat—who generally talk and giggle while others speak, were hushed and attentive, seemingly anxious to lose not a word of Miss Sanford's remarks."

We do not know whether the inspiring Miss Sanford was responsible for Joe Grundy's life-long interest in history but from this time on he showed a real enthusiasm for the subject, especially American history.

The spring of 1879 brought sorrow to the entire family. Joe's beloved Aunt Lizzie, after two years of intense suffering, died at the age of thirty-six. This was a second tragedy for the Ridgways. More than ever they centered their attentions on Mary's children—Joe and Meta.

During the summer following the completion of Joe's college preparation, the sixteen-year-old boy decided that he should keep a diary just as his father had at the same age. On

August 1, 1879, we have the first entry. The observations of the sixteen-year-old Joe Grundy give a clear picture of the Pennsylvanian at sixty or even at ninety-six. They are printed here just as written without editing:

"August 1, 1879, Friday: In Sharon Springs, after a journey from New York up the North River to Albany, thence by cars. Town not very gay but hope it will improve with acquaintance. Boarders mostly Cubans.

"August 2: After amusing myself playing billiards, attended weekly hop at Union Hall.

"August 4: Played games with the Cubans and found them agreeable.

"August 5: Played game of football with Cubans and found myself the best player.

"August 7: I escorted the ladies up to the pavilion to witness the festivities there. I enjoyed this.

"August 9: Enjoyed a ride to Prospect Hill from which point the view is very fine. The Mohawk River being dimly seen in the distance.

"August 10: (Sunday) Enjoyed a bath this morning but do not think it agreed with me, owing to the parched condition of my skin after coming out. Am getting tired of this perch—hope to be allowed to return home Tuesday.

"August 19: (Tuesday) Left Albany for New York, then to Bristol.

"August 20: Went to Mount Holly and found Mother sick in bed. Returned to Bristol with Grandpa's horse, which he kindly loaned me. I often think I am favored to have such kind parents.

"August 31: I broke the Sabbath by accompanying a party out fishing . . . for white perch. I was not very successful, but we all together caught about five dozen.

"September 1: I drove Mother out to Walnut Grove to get some things. In the evening I called on Miss Nellie Thomonas.

"September 3: Invited Miss Anna Peirce to accompany me on a trip today which we enjoyed very much.

"September 10: Went to the city this morning preparatory to going to school, to get some clothes . . . Came home, called on Miss A. Prince this evening."

At sixteen—three different girls in ten days—and this was only the beginning! A yellowed clipping from the *Chicago Tribune* which was found in Joe Grundy's wallet dated back to this era of his life. It was a specimen of comic verse that caught and held his fancy.

MAID OF ATHENS

"Maid of Athens, we must part,
I hear your father—I must start;
He's broken on his midnight rest;
Discretion on my part is best
I'd better flit.
"Maid of Athens, here I go
Kiss me once, for luck, you know;
Your Father's foot is on the stair—
None but the brave deserve the fair—
The gas ain't lit.
"Maid of Athens, just once more—
Little ships must hug the shore;
Hark! the dog has broken his chain,
Zounds I am in what luck again.
Great Scott! I'm bit."

In the fall Joe Grundy's future beckoned excitingly as at sixteen he entered Swarthmore as a freshman. In college he continued his diary:

"September 16: The President put me up in the freshman class without any examination.

"September 21: Spent a quiet day like most Sundays at Swarthmore are naturally spent, attending Meeting in the morning. In the afternoon a party of us went out to Ridley Park for ice cream.

66

"October 6: (Monday) Awoke this morning to realize the fact that I had to return home to school, a sad realization. Left Bristol at 8:21 and arrived at 11:36. Found we had two new girls at our table which makes it more pleasant for us all.

"October 16: Cricket is becoming a fashionable game at Swarthmore. There are several class elevens, the one representing the freshman class seems to be the most successful. I play on it.

"November 8: (Saturday) Went home this morning and was much pleased at being once more with my parents who are so kind and indulgent to me."

Another week-end, November 10th, at home prompted him to write: "Was with sorrow that I realized the fact that today I had to return again to Swarthmore.

"November 12: After dinner we walked over to Chester to play . . . football and am sorry to say was beaten one goal and one touchdown to nothing, also sorry to state we were caught but will not be much punished.

"November 13: Received this morning a long lecture from the President concerning our game of yesterday. This afternoon the faculty is to act on our case. Hope they will be pretty easy on us. Do not much admire being made to report.

"November 14: We are all getting anxious for the faculty to come to some decision in regard to our case, but they are silent.

"November 18: Have received today a letter from home criticizing very strongly my action in regard to the Chester affair, and begin to see myself that we did not do exactly right in going away and playing, although we can not do anything else if we want to play.

"November 21: Received a very severe letter from Mother today in which she criticizes very severely my action on Wednesday week."

Joe was so upset by the criticism from home that he forgot to record an important event of that day. He served as the affirmative leader of the debating team which on November 21, 1879, "Resolved: That the annexation of Canada to the United States would be beneficial to Canada." His first assistant was James E. Verree; second assistant, Manilius Seipt; with Henry B. Seaman as Censor. Grundy's college debating experience would come in handy during Washington investigations five decades later!

"November 23: Took quite a long walk this afternoon up to a place called Beddies Dam and witnessed the boys breaking the Sabbath in the way of skating on the Sabbath. They were not Swarthmore boys.

"December 1: Am getting along quite well in lessons.

"December 16: Today very pleasant indeed. Went to Phila. to see the parade in honor of General Grant. Was very fine, took five hours to pass one point and it is stated that 60,000 people were in it.

"December 17: Spent afternoon in Media. Am not entirely satisfied with my present conduct and think that there could be many changes made in it for the better. Am glad the Christmas holidays are so near.

"December 20: (Saturday) Today had our expected examination (English Literature) and I got 96 per cent in it. Consider that I did pretty well, spent the afternoon over in Media playing billiards and came out pretty well.

"December 22: Received from Mrs. Wood [a college dean] this evening a most thorough overhauling in which she expressed her most decided opinion of me. Am determined to show her that there is some good left in me.

"December 23: Arrived home about time for supper. Seems very pleasant to be at home once more. My trouble with Mrs. Wood worries me greatly.

"December 24: Woke up much to my delight in

68

Bristol and found everything quite natural. Went to the mill this morning.

"December 25: Meta and I spent most of the day in Phila. Was quite fortunate in way of presents. Received a pair of sleeve buttons, watch and chain and various other articles.

"December 26: Went to Phila. this afternoon and met there several of our Swarthmore boys and spent the afternoon in playing billiards with them. Was most sorry to see one of them become intoxicated."

Joe Grundy's diary of 1879 closed with a list of itemized expenses. The entry read in part: "Expense account items—Shoes $6.00, Dinner 50¢, For Self 50¢, Oysters 20¢, Theater $1.00, and New Hat $3.50."

He kept exact accounts throughout his life, a fact which always frustrated his political opponents. The careful habits of the sixteen-year-old forecast the cautious and candid politician of sixty.

During the second semester at Swarthmore, Joe's letters to his sister were filled with brotherly instructions and evidence of his never-ending pleasure in "going home." In February he wrote that "on Thursday next Louisa Wood and a little girl by the name of Lilian Benton [are] going up to Bristol to pay thee and the rest a visit, and in order to prepare thee for so grand an era in the history of the Grundy family, thought maybe it would be well to inform my sister of the fact.

"Now the aforesaid Lilian is a little girl about twelve or thirteen years of age, is very pretty, has blue eyes and golden hair, but like all Brooklyn girls, wears short dresses. I think thee will like her very much. I was talking to her this morning and told her to stay up in Bristol as long as she wanted for I knew she would have a good time.

"See if Papa will let Fanny [the mare] come in from the farm for you to use, or if not you can drive the sorrel. They are coming up in the afternoon boat from City so thee must meet them, also get Mother to let thee stay away from school on Friday, so as to be as agreeable as possible."

In late May he wrote a final note from college: "Am writing this in Chemistry class and it is as hot as the D——, and we all have got the spring fever.

"Yesterday I in company with another boy went to West Chester to see about a class supper at the end of the year. We are going to have one built to cost about $80, the biggest thing of the kind ever had here.

"I will be home Friday night in the 11:30 p.m. train as I cannot leave the college till the 10:40 train—I have to be present at the Class Society meeting in the evening, so somebody must try to keep awake and let me in."

Joe Grundy's college record was academically unimpressive. He made "C's" in each of his courses. But in debate and in athletics he had an outstanding year. He remained proud of his sports activities, especially of his early efforts to introduce football. Dr. Frederick B. Tolles, well-known historian and director of Friends' Historical Library of Swarthmore College, states that football was not permitted at Swarthmore until 1883. Hence, Grundy's efforts, although undoubtedly productive, were against the rules of 1879.

A treasured clipping from the college paper, in reference to his athletic prowess, reads: "The Swarthmoreian athlete J. R. Grundy whose muscles are the admiration of his fellows is no relation to the famous 'Mrs. Grundy.' "

CHAPTER 5

THE GRAND TOUR

Joe Grundy was to cross the Atlantic many times on business as well as for pleasure. During the period when his sister Meta was in ill health abroad, between 1894 and 1900, he visited her and his mother in Switzerland every summer. There in the Grundy summer cottage on Lake Geneva he enjoyed many pleasant times. With his blonde good looks, merry blue eyes and bubbling humor, he never lacked feminine companionship. The eligible daughters of prominent American tourists invariably met the attractive and highly acceptable bachelor.

However, none of Grundy's later trips ever held the excitement and promise of that magical first voyage to Europe during his seventeenth summer. Arranged by Mrs. Caroline S. Wood of Swarthmore College, the tour included trips through England, Scotland, Switzerland, France and Italy. She joined her party with one being directed by a Dr. Loomis of Washington, D. C., whom she described as "a gentleman of culture, and fully competent to instruct us in all matters of history, art and literature. He will give us interesting preparatory lectures on spare evenings on architecture, sculpture, early Christian art, The Renaissance, modern schools, the Great Masters and Masterpieces, etc."

Mrs. Wood had reassuring words for Joe's apprehensive mother: "Now we are to have a physician in our party and she must not be nervous about anything."

Grundy's diary of the summer of 1880 speaks for itself. Who else but the exacting young Quaker would refer to Europe as "the eastern shore of the Atlantic Ocean!"

"Trip to Eastern Shore of Atlantic Ocean on board the Steamer State of Indiana, June 17, 1880. Steamer is 326 feet long and about forty-five feet wide, has three masts . . . Party consisted of Mrs. Wood, her daughter Louise, Bessie Clark, Miss Setchworth and myself."

The seventeen-year-old traveler had been with the party of four women just twenty-four hours when he wrote in quiet desperation "I have at last come to the conclusion that if there is anything true in the Bible it is the part pertaining to the serving of two masters—and when it comes that there are four to serve, it is proportionately worse."

Joe's first night at sea "was a beautiful one, the moon being three-quarters full . . . The music made by the sailors as they hoist up the sails is something very amusing. It reminds me of the much heard of Indian War Dance songs . . ."

On the following night he wrote: ". . . I am getting to be the most sun-burnt fellow that can readily be imagined . . . and at this rate there will be very little left of me to visit my thoroughbred relatives in England . . . This is Sunday morning . . . We have divine services aboard at 10:30 A.M., but I don't believe that I want any of it."

The third day at sea held "a great scare. Bessie and I were promenading the deck when suddenly one of the men rushed on deck crying 'Fire.' This instantly caused a panic on board which was followed by smoke pouring out of the cabin windows and doors in a very reckless manner . . . Smothered out by the Captain with a wet sheet, much to the relief of the passengers. It was found afterwards to be Mrs. Wood's room and how it caught fire is a mystery to most all, but it is supposed to have occurred by something blowing over the lamp . . . The feelings which I had when the cry of 'Fire' was raised can't be described, but it did worry me immensely. Bessie and I after that walked the deck till almost ten in order to get calm."

The next entry in his diary disclosed the problems in his relationships with the four women: "As I stated farther back it is awful hard to serve two masters and proportionately hard to serve four, which at present I most painfully realize. I have since I have been on board, owing during the first part of the voyage to circumstances, paid some special attention to Bessie, she being the only one that had been spared the pains and trouble of seasickness; and having so begun, have continued my attention in that direction until yesterday afternoon. Bessie and I had come in from promenading the deck. Mrs. W. snubbed me and informed me that my conduct towards the rest of the party had been extremely insulting and I had not shared my times and attentions in a sufficient measure to looking after herself, Miss Setchworth and Louise, and for such conduct she had been considering the plausibility when we arrived at Glasgow of sending me back by the next steamer to America and so on.

"Now I am very desirous of finding out just how far Mrs. W.'s authority goes in regard to such matters, and to obtain such information I am intent on seeing Dr. Loomis regarding it, and then having a regular straightforward talk with the lady, and if she insists upon disposing of my time and attentions for me, I will find some way of getting out of it or bust."

The self-confident boy continued: "I have not been squarely beaten this year at anything I have undertaken and if it is possible for me to get ahead of her, I will break my neck to do it. She wishes me to fulfill Harry's place in the party by being a *son* to her and a brother to Louise, and in other words a soap to the whole business. Now I pay my money and take my choice, and won't play soap to anybody unless it exactly suits me."

On the following day Mrs. Wood apologized "for the remarks she made yesterday . . . and very gladly excused me and hoped that things would be all right; but as much as I try to overcome prejudices which not only her actions but her words created, I can not. But hope that I will soon forget them . . . Have resolved not to say a word to any at home (by letter) of the little misunderstanding we had for it would only worry them and probably put a stop to my hoping to be allowed to accompany Dr. Loomis on the Russian trip, which I so much desire doing."

Joe determined to do his part to keep things going smoothly. On the following morning when Mrs. Wood came through the saloon and interrupted him while writing with the question, "Will my son walk with me on deck?" the "son" thanked her for her kind invitation, and assured her that nothing would give him more pleasure and quietly stopped writing and went.

On June 26th he noted: "Have today sent in my final licks regarding my taking Russian trip. Do most sincerely hope to be able to go."

Joe's "final licks" to his parents shrewdly followed an amusing account of shipboard anecdotes: "How to begin a letter to you when, and what to put first is what bothers thy hairpin; but I will begin by saying we are all on deck, and nearly all well, Mrs. Wood being the only one that is at present out of step, she, poor mortal, has had a most wonderful hard time of it, and one which I bet she will remember for some time to come, to begin to describe the manner in which she gets to work is beyond my powers, but I will try to give thee some kind of an idea of her first attack.

"We had not been gone more than two hours when I came upon deck after making some arrangements in my state-room when suddenly from the depths of her steamer chair, the form of Mrs. Wood arose as if shot, she cleared the distance to the rail in about two jumps, and before she got fairly planted, there let drive, and my what a capacity she has for a small woman, and what a picnic she did provide for the fish, after working away in a most reckless manner for about ten minutes, she gave it up and retired to her chair at a more civilized rate of speed, amid the smothered laughter of all around. This was the first, but not the last of similar tableaux."

"The living on board is elegant, and the manner in which I get outside of my four-meal-a-day is something astonishing to the waiters. We have breakfast at 8:30, lunch at 12:30, dinner at 4:30, supper at 7:30, and I am, I assure thee, right there every time the bell rings." [Joe's intermingling of both "thee", and "you" persisted throughout his life.] "Thee knows that my appetite was never delicate and if thee would just multiply it by five, you would get at my present capacity.

"This is about the laziest life I think that I ever led. You seem to do nothing but eat, drink and sleep, and I do all these to perfection . . ."

After the pleasant introduction debater Joe waded into his "proposition":

". . . Now you may think it a little strange in my writing so soon on our voyage, but there is a matter . . . which I would like to ask you about.

"Dr. Loomis has on board with him what is known as his Russian party . . . consisting of about ten which in addition to the Swiss-Italian tour, . . . are going to leave London on September 1st and proceed to Hamburg, thence to Copenhagen where they run through Denmark, Stockholm, Sweden, . . . and Norway, thence via the Gulf of Finland [to] Abo Helsingfort, and Vibory to St. Petersburg . . . [proceeding] to Moscow, Warsaw, and back to Berlin, Dresden, Prague, and down to Vienna where" [here he slipped in a "we" instead of "they"] "we explore to a slight measure the beauties of Austria.

"They then wander leisurely back to London, arriving about November 1st to 10th and returning to America between the middle of November and the first of December."

You can almost feel Joe take a deep breath as he continues: "Now I feel as if it is not right for me to ask to be allowed to accompany this party for I really feel . . . you have allowed me so many privileges and pleasures already, but it is a trip which is as Dr. Loomis expresses, seldom made by tourists and though expensive, is by far the finest for it thoroughs you not only directly with the manner and customs of people upon whom the effect of American travel and civilization has not lended aid in changing their manners and customs, as has been the case in France, Switzerland, Italy and Scotland. The trip presents to us places of the rarest beauty which, owing to the lack of facility in former years for getting to them, have not been explored so thoroughly as yet, and also as Dr. Loomis has no allotted time for stopping at one place, they can travel more to suit themselves.

"Also in my case, it is very doubtful whether or not I will ever get another shot at this side of the Atlantic and while I am here, if I could by any means be allowed to, I would consider it an immense privilege for which I could not but always feel indebted . . . Also, if ever I was to take it, no better time could be selected, for Dr. Loomis has been over it before either once or twice and probably three times, and, the party being small, can give us individually more instruction and consequently the amount of knowledge would increase in proportion."

Joe had thought of all the angles: "Also, if ever I was to be allowed to take it, it would not be for several years, but if by taking it now, I would get the knowledge and benefit just so many years earlier, which in a money point of view would amount to the expense of the trip by the time I could be permitted to go again."

Joe's parents must have been amused by his next point: "Now if the argument is brought up that I was too young to go alone, I can assure you that I have as it is, not only myself but the rest of the crowd to look after and instead of Mrs. W. taking care of me as that extra fifty dollars was, I suppose, appropriated for, I have her on my hands like a dead beat to take care of.

"Also there is another argument—in the case of a war in Europe it would turn everything upside down and never could we see this country as it is now. (P.S. This is an original argument.)

"Now regarding the expense, Dr. Loomis takes this trip in

connection with the Swiss-Italian for $1,000, so I would have to pay some $500 yet to him . . . Now as for the expense on Papa, it will be just the same as if he had sent me alone, which if Grandpa had not kindly volunteered to assist, I think he might have done."

Joe's letter surely was one of the longest of its kind ever written. Much was at stake, of course, and the shrewd young man made certain that every possible argument was mustered in favor of his traveling as extensively as persuasion could accomplish. The epistle continued, "Now if this is explained to Grandpa, to whom it is owing that I got this far, he might assist in bearing part of the new expense incurred and in so doing would enable me to visit all the civilized and uncivilized portions of Europe.

"I think you will both fully agree with me that as far as opportunity and knowledge and benefit is concerned, that this is a most elegant trip and one which if the money can be obtained, you would like me not to miss. No one could be in better hands for safe traveling than in those of Dr. Loomis, who devotes all his time and attention to the welfare of his party, and who guarantees if the girls won't eat too much candy and the boys too much fruit, to bring them through all right.

"Now if you can be so convinced by anything I have said to permit me this great privilege, please write and inform me as soon as practicable, after giving it due consideration, and I will, till I hear, hope most longingly for a favorable reply.

". . . Do not be afraid but that I am perfectly able to take care of myself on this side of the Atlantic as well as on our own side and being as I will be with Dr. Loomis, I think it will remove all cause of doubt and fear from your ever-anxious and watchful minds."

Now came an appeal to family pride: "I do not wish to express any opinions [what, one wonders, did he think he had been doing?], but I think maybe that Papa can as well spare the money now as he ever can, and the advantage which I would receive from it now would be an everlasting benefit and blessing to me. And now you see that it isn't from any personal interests but for the mutual enlightening of the Grundy family to whom I hope to be able to impart much information when I will return to the shores of the United States."

To allay his mother's misgivings, he wrote: "Now Mother has been very much worried about what is known as Roman Fever or what is so dangerous to citizens in that country. I have at last found out the cause of it. Last night, Dr. Loomis in the stateroom was explaining it to us. He says that in Rome, in the hotels all the waterclosets are right in the rooms, and also that they have no water in them, and that the wells attached to them if there are any at all, are walled with porous bricks which absorb the moisture for a while. When they get clogged up, then the moisture and all goes right up through the house. He also stated that as soon as you enter one of these hotels you can immediately smell the waterclosets very plainly, and that the so-called Roman Fever is nothing more than typhoid fever, the same as we have in America.

"The hotel [where] we stop in Rome is run by a man from England, . . . [who] has his hotel arranged with all modern improvements; this is the advantage of going with Dr. Loomis, who knows where, why and what to do.

"There is no danger therefore for any accident or fever occurring for us; also there is as little or less fever and ague in Rome as there is in or around Philadelphia . . . In winter, although it is reported to be healthy, it is not, for the dampness and bad odors are kept indoors, while in summer the windows being up, allow the perfumes to pass out and off. So this is the explanation of Roman Fever."

Young Grundy ranged over a wide area of subjects. Even his personal appearance came in for a paragraph: "I have not been shaved since I left the other side for the simple reason there is no barber on board and I have not the necessary tools to do it with, and I am beginning to be the worst looking fellow you ever saw. Will have a full beard before we get to Glasgow, but I am not proud, so I don't care a cent. If the rest can stand it, I guess I can!"

Even unshaven, good-looking Joe was undoubtedly one of the ship's main attractions. He continued the marathon letter: "Last night, the 25th, we had an entertainment in the cabin consisting of musical and oratorical selections and also Mrs. Jarley's wax works. I was the orator and got along a sight.

"There are lots of pretty girls on board, and between the girls and writing my diary and letters, I have been right busy lately and have not had much time to waste."

The vastness of the sea overcame him at one point and he wrote: "The longer we are out, the bigger thing I think the Atlantic Ocean is, and the more respect I have for the great Christopher Columbus for his enterprise in crossing its broad depths."

He wrote that he looked forward to seeing the Passion Play at Oberammergau, the battlefield of Waterloo, the winter grandeur of the Alps, the scenery of Scandinavia. Over and over he accents the enormous educational value of his travels. In all, he wrote some 4,000 words, an epistolary feat at any age and in any circumstances. And as any debater would do, he wound it up by hammering home anew his arguments for what he represented as the economical and intellectual advantages of allowing him to round out his journeys as he proposed.

"Now . . . if I should take the [Russian] trip now, it would be done, and the information obtained at a much less cost than ever it could be done again by me alone and . . . now, time is nothing to me in comparison to what it will be in the course of five, ten, or more years; and if it could be so arranged *financially*, I would be most delighted as it would enable me to pass through and visit . . . countries . . . with scenery as surpasses all other in grandeur . . .

"I wrote to Grandpa concerning it, and you, I hope, will have a private conference regarding it—the result of which, I hope, will be favorable to the cause of knowledge, wisdom, pleasure and general education of your most humble son and grandson.

"Now I must close . . . your affectionate and *anxious son*,

Jos. R. Grundy

"Write soon!"

On the tenth day Grundy saw land, the northern head of Ireland and on the following night, June 28th, he landed in Scotland. At Glasgow he wrote: "The grass is beautifully green all over the Kingdom—is kept in fine condition with the aid of nothing but the scythe, which they wield with great skill, disdaining the services of the lawn mower . . . Our ignorance of the city (Glasgow) causes us continually to require a cab and driver which can be engaged for three shillings an hour. The beauty of the scene is greatly enhanced by the many mountain streams . . . We visited Lake Katrine in which is Ellen's Isle, where Rob Roy is said to have met Ellen. It is a most beautiful and lovely spot and exceedingly romantic. I could, I think, if I lived in such a country long, write poetry myself. After spending the day looking around Edinborough . . . Bessie and I went out shopping, nearly busting myself. After supper . . . we drove to Authors Seat and Salisbury Craggs. It was hard work to mount up and drag a girl, yet the view from the top fully repaid you."

Joe prided himself upon his thrift—"since we left America I have spent $25," but assures his family "that I have gotten about five times as much information as any others in the party."

Scotland impressed him, as this recording of July 1, 1880 discloses: "Tomorrow we leave Scotland, I am sorry to say, and a very good country it is. Beautiful beyond description, all well-kept. Labor is cheap and plenty. A skilled laborer gets about 25 shillings per week while the ordinary laborer gets about 18 or 20."

Manchester, the English industrial city visited the next day, did not appeal to him: "It is principally manufacturing and many of the mills are idle. They are not bright and clean like our American ones, and the houses for the working class are very poor and small affairs, and one at first is convinced of how infinitely better is the American workman than are the English."

Here he hunted up his English relatives, cousins John and Alfred Grundy, both solicitors for the Great Western Railway. Joe described them in a letter to his grandparents: "They are, I am told, very fair samples of Englishmen. John Grundy is a bachelor with neither chick nor child and is worth between two and three millions. Alfred Grundy is nearly as wealthy, the latter gentleman has excited much indignation among the Grundys by . . . engaging himself in marriage to a young lady of twenty-six years, while he is sixty-seven and has grown-up children older than his intended. He is a widower, the wedding is to come off this month . . ."

Joe, staying at the "mansion" of still another cousin, Herbert Grundy, was surprisingly observant for a seventeen-year-old and was obviously interested in money and material possessions. He described Herbert's "beautiful little place, furnished most elegantly and extravagantly with $15,000 worth of pictures and paintings, . . . good as an art gallery. In one room I counted twenty-three large paintings."

Grundy's cousins were the offspring of Thomas Grundy. Young Thomas and Edmund [Joe's grandfather] had in 1820 come from Lancashire to seek their fortunes in America. Here they found a severe depression. Joe Grundy's explanation was that after the Napoleonic wars, Britain was free to export actively, thus postponing the development of America's colonial economy. Thomas, discouraged by conditions here, returned to England, but Edmund had become engaged to Rebecca Hulme ("had got his feet in the flypaper," as Joe said) and was tied romantically to the Delaware valley.

Joe studied the English textile mills with interest and reported to his parents, "The wages paid the drawer and spinner are three to three-fifty per week, while the man in the warp room gets about the same."

He assured his mother that he found out all he could and added, "Tell Papa, I have got it down nearly to a science."

Joe was learning a great deal! He wrote: ". . . We took dinner at one of the principal hotels and . . . had some beautiful and elegant sparkling Burgundy for dinner. I have so far got hold of champagne, bitter, beer, port, claret, ale, hock, burgundy. Am learning fast. Today ends my stay in Manchester and here I have passed the brightest part of my trip, have met many kind friends and relatives who have treated me most handsomely, especially my Cousin Herbert. How thankful should I be for such kind friends!"

In London, Joe wrote: "Arriving here I found that a party of six ladies had gotten tickets for the theater, and also one for me and expected me to take them, to which I submitted as gracefully as the circumstances would permit."

All his life Grundy loved the theater. Apparently not the least of its charms were some of the "pert soubrettes." At least the following verse, clipped from the Boston *Courier* and kept over the years would so indicate:

"To Several"

> "Oh! the plump and pert soubrette
> She's a pet.
> She can ogle and coquette
> Then forget.
> Blond and flowing hair, and yet
> Only recently we met,
> And I say it with regret,
> It was jet.
> "Ev'ry night a seat I get
> Front parquette,
> There I worship her and yet
> Fume and fret,

At the matinees, you bet,
I am always to be met,
And for roses for my pet
I'm in debt.
"Oh, perfidious soubrette
To coquette
With my heart! My eyes are wet
With regret.
It was hardly etiquette
Your admirer to forget
For a fellow with a yellow
Clarinet."

The shops fascinated the young American who boasted: "Am getting to be a mighty good shopper, can Jew people down a sight."

On July 8th about twenty of the party left for Antwerp, and Joe, a bit homesick, went to the Opera Comique to see the "Pirates of Penzance." Now away from home for three weeks, he tried to forget his blues by shopping but admitted, "It is lonely wandering around alone."

From London Joe traveled to Antwerp. Enroute he checked up on his accounts: "Since I have been there I drew $47.00 from Dr. Loomis which I distributed in somewhat the following manner: $12.50 for clothing, $7.50 for shoes, $6.00 for umbrella, $7.50 on a deposit for clothes, $5.00 in theatergoing, about $2.50 in food purchased at Hotel and elsewhere, and about $6.00 gone in a way unknown."

He gave some thought to the English people whom he had met and concluded: "The English people as a class lack that same energy and quickness which characterizes the people of the United States. Their manner of conversation differs from ours also . . . Ends with a rising inflection which makes their manner lack that go ahead spirit which predominates with us."

At Antwerp he noted that, "On the road from Antwerp

to Brussels it is not unusual to see a pair of dogs hitched to a cart, drawing it along. The private yards of the dwellings are kept up to great style and would form fit examples for our American florists to follow."

At the Hotel Du Saxe he learned that his party had left before his arrival. Homesick and unhappy he drank a bottle of claret with his dinner and became so ill that he took a sleeping car "at about an expense of $5.00 extra," to Cologne to catch up with the party. There he dutifully "visited the cathedral which is the most beautiful Gothic structure in the world."

He enjoyed the Rhine scenery from Cologne to Coblenz, where he noted sadly, "were I well now, I would enjoy the fruit, but I am now paying the penalty for previous sins."

At Heidelberg he ascended to its famous castle on a donkey and "got swindled, never will take another donkey ride in my life if I can help it, am generally disgusted. We returned to our hotel in a carriage. More civilized."

At the next stop—Munich—the somewhat spoiled boy made this entry. "I wrote for money. Hope it won't be in vain. Never yet have failed in any attempt to get that article from Papa, and don't of all times, want to now. Don't think I have been extravagant."

On July 17th, Joe wrote: "Today we saw the Passion Play at Oberammergau. The train was densely packed with all kinds and classes of people, peasants with their short checque skirts of all colors and in most cases green aprons and all as ugly as sin. Saw hundreds of people praying before the different shrines of the Virgin. Our cottage had no carpets and no modern conveniences. Our waiters were three German women who could not talk a bit of English . . . We got plenty to eat, so I won't complain if we did have to use pewter spoons and two-prong forks and bone-handled knives . . ."

The Grand Tour continued then as it does now, to Botzeu, Verona, Venice and Florence. At Venice he wrote: "In the same house I stopped was also to be found a bar-room, grocery store, stable for horses and cows, a haymow, in fact they believed in mixing things up . . . We had breakfast served, as dinner had been, in our own private rooms, not wishing to mix us with the common herd . . . Saw many beautiful specimens of . . . glass for which the city is so famous . . . Saw also two palaces of the fifteenth century which were handsome in their way, but did not admire their way . . ."

Joe saw Venice as it should be seen—from a gondola, beside an attractive partner and beneath a moon: "That evening myself and a grass widow from South Carolina by the name of Mrs. White took a gondola ride by moonlight, had a delightful time floating around with a man to row you, listening to the music across the water from the concert gardens. Was full moon and if anything could be more delightful than a moonlight night at Venice, bring it along . . . It is useless for me to say that I have been having a perfectly lovely time, and I hope that when I return in the fall to go to work in a way which will convince you that I fully appreciate your kindness to me, and be of some use to you . . . Tell Grandma Ridgway that I have followed out her instructions as far as possible and not yet fallen in love with any of the girls."

The lengthy plea for the Russian trip paid off. Grandfather Ridgway offered to supply the additional funds and a grateful Joe wrote: ". . . I only wish that instead of your reading my miserable descriptions of these beautiful objects, you could all enjoy the same privilege I am, to see them for yourself . . . At Milan I received the most delighting news that I was to be permitted to continue my travels, which privilege I am well aware of, I am greatly indebted to you, and to you I wish to offer my most sincere thanks for the same. You have always been to me most generous and kind, more so than ever did I deserve and appreciate until I have been thrown among strangers whose only object is to get and see all themselves and let you do the same . . . Your most affectionate and grateful grandson,

J. R. Grundy"

In Rome he chose a gift for Meta and wrote in his diary: "Invested in two beautiful Roman sashes, I hope I am not too extravagant, but want Meta to have everything that is a-going for she is a good sister."

The pace of the Grand Tour was fast, even in 1880: Pisa, Milan, Bellagio, Como, "on top of the Alps," Lucerne, Geneva, all in eleven days! Joe sent a detailed description of Geneva to his parents: "The city is not as remarkably pretty as Lucerne, nor as pleasant; it is not situated directly on the lake, but on an outlet of the same. There is built a great stone wall from both shores, extending to a distance of about 150 feet of each other, and through this opening flows the water of the lake at a rate of speed equal to a mill race."

Seventeen-year-old Grundy was already an industrialist. He wrote: "This vast water power is, I think, not used at all, but had we such a one in America, it would be lined with mills."

There were many romantic interludes: "One evening while there, Bess took it into her head she wanted to go rowing and accordingly we started out, I as escort, Bess as courier. We promenaded the pier for at least half-an-hour vainly hoping to be tackled by a fellow who would hurl at us in his best English, 'Wantezee eine boate!' No such cuss showed up, and at last I meekly took a back seat while Bess, by a combination of French and gestures, impressed a fellow with the idea that we wished to row. He at last saw the true inwardness of her gestures and after beckoning to an assistant, we started out and had a beautiful row under the bright moonlight glistening on the still but rapid waters of the beautiful lake, bounded on one side by the brilliantly illuminated town, on the other by the mountains. As I before intimated, we had a pleasant row, but when we landed at the pier and the fellow said, 'Dix francs,' it took some of the romance out of things.

"The islands in the river were all converted more or less into beautiful parks, for the pleasure of the inhabitants . . . The river was divided off into small duck ponds, at least portions of it, and great quantities of fancy swans, ducks, geese, etc., were raised there. It was amusing to watch them. The river acts as a public wash house, in it are anchored wash houses to which the women of the town flock with their baskets of clothes to be washed here in this anchored house in a bountiful supply of water, always fresh, clear and pure. It must be hard on soap to wash this way."

From Geneva he mentioned his wardrobe: "I am now glad that I have gotten a new suit in London as both my others owing to hard travel are very shabby and now will have something to appear in before my grand relatives. My polo cap which heretofore was the pride of my heart was, I am sorry to say, lost by one of the ladies of the party . . .

"With the assistance of four ladies I selected a beautiful watch and chain for Meta . . . The watch is all frosted, the front case being enameled with forget-me-nots and pansies . . . the monogram M.R.G. is enameled in the form of a wreath on the frosting in the same flowers . . . stem-winder and of the best that could be gotten. Inside I had engraved 'Meta R. Grundy from Father and Mother, 1880'. . . Got it for $100 and think that I did very well."

In true tourist fashion he was photographed in the local costume: "Enclosed you will find a tintype of a party of us in our alpine costumes, consisting of the oldest clothes you own, broad straw hats with a great long crepe ribbon twisted around, an alpine stalk, a mule, 'one of Mark Twains,' and a riding whip."

"How to begin this letter, or how to break the information to you which has been foremost in my mind for the past few weeks, is a little more than I exactly know, but at any rate I . . . have decided not to go on the Russian and Austrian trip.

"This information I doubtlessly think will greatly surprise you but after giving you my reasons for so doing, I most sincerely hope that you will approve of my decision and actions. Now when I wrote my first letters to you asking for your permission to take that extra trip, I knew very little of the people with whom I would have to go, and I knew less of the extra expense which would be attached to such an expedition.

"Then I had not been separated from home and placed among people whose regard for me lasted just as long as my ability for gratifying their wishes went, for nearly three months . . . Now after thinking the matter over thoroughly and not acting on my own judgment only, but on that of both Dr. Loomis and Mrs. Wood, I have come to the conclusion that the best thing for me to do is to return on September 3rd, with the party.

"First . . . the Russian party consists simply of ladies, mostly all old maids, at least all of them are much older than I am, and to go for so long a time so great a distance to begin with is enough to scare one. It is very pleasant to travel with ladies for a short time, but when it comes to day after day and not being able to stir without going either with them or alone, it is not as you might imagine a very promising prospect.

"Second, in regard to the expense of such a trip, I have already spent nearly twice as much as you at first thought after making due allowances for all things, and should I take the longer trip it would necessitate . . . at some time again, drawing on Papa, which I do not think under the circumstances would be right . . . To start out under the conditions before named is not an agreeable prospect . . . Dr. Loomis considered that I had seen enough for one summer . . . in a few years come again . . . You have been very kind in writing . . . It has been the only thing by which I could imagine that I ever had such a thing as a home . . . Grandpa Ridgway . . . has been most kind and generous . . . in regard to assisting in bearing my expenses, which kindness I do most heartily appreciate, but when you explain the matter to him, as I trust you will, I hope he will not consider that I have not made the most of my opportunities.

"This volume of the trials, tribulations, joys and sorrows experienced by the author during the last three months I dedicate to the girl and the only girl whose lot it shall ever be permitted at her leisure, for it will, owing to the bad writing, have to be done at her leisure, peruse its scribbled pages."

Joe was dazzled by Paris, its great stores, shaded boulevards, and arts galleries. Obviously he had read his guide book. In fact, he sounded like one: "We visited the Louvre art gallery, seeing there the famous Venus de Milo, which is itself a very beautiful piece of statuary, but one which could not well be copied for the expression is the sole beauty of the figure.

"The little time that I spent in Paris . . . was occupied more thoroughly in shopping . . . than in sightseeing. Naturally in our driving around we received a very good view of things in general and also saw and appreciated how beautiful the city is; its streets are wide, at least all that pretend to be streets, well-paved, elegantly kept, shaded by beautiful avenues of trees; the sidewalks are wide also and afford ample room for the throng which moves continually on them to pass with ease.

"The building which took my time and admiration most was the Royal Opera, a most beautiful edifice of stone built in the grandest style . . . Bess and I took in the Racket one night (I mean went to the opera) and had a swell time.

"The marble staircase leading to it is one of great beauty and when you find yourself mounting it, it places in you an air of importance which is astonishing. We took in all the promenading on the moonlit balcony and in the beautiful, illuminated marble-floored room built for that purpose. The play was 'The Huguenots!' It was in French, so I understood it all in my mind."

The evening was not a complete triumph for Joe because: "Bess would not feed for some reason or other best known to herself, so I went home hungry."

Joe, like every Paris visitor, before and since, observed: "The parks are very beautiful, being laid out regardless of expense or cost.

"One evening I in company with Bess went to call upon

Sue Brown, or, excuse me, Mrs. Crawford and husband, but the aforesaid were not at home. I was not particularly sorry, for I do not think they particularly wanted to see me. Getting married does change some folks awfully.

"Paris by gaslight is a beautiful sight, too much so to be attempted to be described by me. How you roll along wide avenues of Rues (as the French prefer) . . . [the lights reflect] from the beautiful plate glass store windows and from the diamonds worn by the females on the street—an enchanting sight! No wonder fellows go wrong in a city like this where every temptation that we Americans would think to be wrong is set before him and is looked upon by the French as perfectly proper and correct.

"I invested quite profusely and recklessly while at Paris, I am afraid too much so for the size of the Grundy family of Bristol. The purchases were confined to articles not for myself, though, but for Mother, Meta and Papa."

From Paris Joe returned to England. Back with his kin, young Grundy couldn't get enough of the Gilbert and Sullivan comic opera, "The Pirates of Penzance" and saw it for the fourth time. [He retained this enthusiasm until his death.]

He enjoyed meeting other English cousins. At Windermere, he "was met by my cousin Mr. James Wrigley, a large bard of heaving, side-whiskered, jolly Englishman, with his pair and coachman, and was driven in style behind his large bay horses to his mansion, poetically known as Holbeck. It is situated on the side of a hill rising from the shore of Lake Windermere to the height of probably a thousand feet. It commands a most beautiful view of the surrounding country, overlooking the large hotel of Lowwood, . . . a celebrated watering place. The house is a stone one, the front very nearly is made up of three large bow windows, one being the parlor, the middle one, Mr. Wrigley's library, and the other end one, the dining room. It is quite a large house, but not as handsome a place as Walnut Grove, had it Holbeck's situation.

90

"The house stands back from the road some distance and the approach to it through the beautifully shaded avenue of trees is exceedingly picturesque. I was met at the front door of the house by my cousin Mrs. James Wrigley, an elderly English lady with fine features, dark eyes nearly black, with curls hanging down over her ears, rather stout—who has been evidently in her more youthful days an extremely handsome lady."

Joe had then, as later, an eye for pretty girls: "Of her three daughters, Mary, the oldest, a large dark-eyed, fair, rosy-cheeked English girl of about twenty-eight, is very lively and we had a fine time of it together. Sarcasm flew around a sight when we got together. The next daughter was Scholes Grundy Wrigley. She was also quite tall, having a darker complexion than Mary, owned very pretty black eyes and hair—she was very quiet, but nice. Maggie, . . . the youngest, . . . was a gay one, . . . about twenty-three and full of fun, not so pretty as Mary or Scholes. The whole three were about the same height, quite tall and good figures, and none of them wore corsets or Jersies which are so common over here and are awfully ugly."

He was a real competitor at seventeen as well as seventy: "The following day it rained and we spent it indoors and in visiting the greenhouses, poultry yard and school houses of the mansion. In the afternoon we played billiards and pool. I, much to their amazement and my own gratification, came out first nearly every time."

Then came the preparations for the trip back home, with the usual mix-ups in luggage, the lost parcels, the things forgotten, the jostlings from other tourists. There was the mixture of excitement and exasperation, the promises to write, the pledges never to forget, all highly sentimental and dear to the young.

Joe's journal gave an idea of the westward passage itself: "Our voyage home has been a very mixed-up and confused sort of arrangement. The first few days out it was extremely rough and stormy; most everybody was seasick, there being for one whole day only three of us passengers who were able to be at meals and our presence there was under the most heart-rending circumstances, such as eating with your dishes held in your hand and all that. Exciting as was the eating question, it was at the same time necessary.

"We have had some pleasant weather, no alarm of fire or alarms from other sources. Passed through several schools of porpoises and have nearly every day seen several vessels. We passed a wreck yesterday, turned upside down, and it was thought by the Captain that it had occurred but recently . . .

"Tomorrow we hope to be in New York where our journey will be at an end. It has been a very pleasant, instructive and agreeable one to me, and one which I can never be too thankful to both my parents and grandparents for allowing me the opportunity to go. I hope I have profited by it. I most sincerely can say I have tried to, but with what success, I must leave to others to judge. I have since starting formed many new and agreeable acquaintances, some of which I would like to continue.

"My expenses since leaving home have been much more than my ideas ever expanded to, but I have taken home with me several very pretty reminiscences of my trip to Europe, . . . for those who did not enjoy all the privileges which I have experienced during the last three months."

It was quite typical that Joe's diary on his Grand Tour should close with an itemized list of his expenditures:

Visit to English relatives—first dash	$30
Spent in London for clothes and umbrella	35
" for mosaics	20
" " pictures	15
" " scarfs	35
" " suit clothes extra not on deposit	20
" " watch and chain	100
" " ring for Meta	30

Spent for

"	"	sleeve buttons and scarf pin	33
"	"	present for Cousin Herbert	30
"	"	gloves	30
"	"	silk stockings	10

$388

CHAPTER 6

COMING OF AGE

Immediately after his return from Europe, Joe Grundy went to work as a wool sorter in the Bristol mill. He was no boss's son consigned to a comfortable office near his father. Joe was simply another employee learning his trade, and this particular employee became convinced that the woolen business was the most important in the United States.

The significance of this industry in Great Britain had been recognized for centuries and, through his English connections, Joe had developed a keen appreciation of its history. Before the emergence of cotton as the major textile, wool was the giant of all fibers used by mankind. It could easily be made into thread; furthermore the comfort of woolen clothing had long been apparent. Sheep-raising became one of the earliest occupations. As far back as the days of the Roman historian Pliny, there are descriptions of types of cloth that could be woven from various kinds of wool. Although sheep and the use of wool had existed in England before the Roman occupation, it was the Romans who carried the spinning and weaving of the fiber to the British Isles. The invaders introduced woolen factories to supply clothing for their occupying forces.

The British were quick to appreciate the value of the Roman advances in manufacturing. Eventually products of the Winchester looms, and the wool from which they were produced, achieved wide recognition abroad.

This status was maintained throughout medieval times. The English woolen fiber was in great demand in the Low Countries and other European centers where manufacturing techniques had developed. When troubles beset various industries on the Continent, many skilled workers sought asylum in England. At the time of William the Conqueror, hundreds of Flemish weavers went to Britain.

Henry II instituted the custom of holding cloth fairs in the church yard of the priory of St. Bartholomew. Weavers' guilds sprang up and the city of London was granted the exclusive privilege of exporting woolen cloth. Edward III was also interested in encouraging the industry. He brought many weavers and dyers from Flanders. Although English wool was extremely popular on the Continent, Edward prohibited wool export in order to encourage home consumption. His efforts resulted in extensive wool smuggling.

It was not until the reign of Queen Elizabeth that the free export of wool was permitted. From that time woolen manufacturing in England made its most rapid progress. In 1660 wool export was again banned and this decree was not repealed until 1825. So desperate were the efforts to use wool in the home market that a law was passed requiring the dead to be buried in woolen shrouds. The use of English cloth in the colonies was encouraged, but its manufacture was discouraged and even prohibited in Ireland.

Wool was "the flower and strength and revenue and blood of England" until the development of the cotton trade toward the end of the eighteenth century. That expression had been repeated frequently to young Joe Grundy by his English grandfather. But apprentice Joe was aware that he needed a great deal more than theoretical knowledge about the woolen industry. He must become familiar with the product itself and with the great variance in the types of wool.

At the Bristol mill young Grundy learned how worsted yarns, as distinguished from other types, are usually made from long woolen fibers, combed parallel to one another. After the spinning the worsted yarn is smooth and, when woven into cloth, does not need to be milled or felted—a fiber interlocking process used for short wool carding.

As a wool sorter, Joe Grundy was learning the business

from the bottom up, and he did not shirk either the long hours or the hard work. It was during his first year at the mill that wool sorters' disease was first identified as a type of anthrax, a usually fatal ailment which attacks cattle, and can be contracted by those handling infected hides.

Young Grundy spent months at each of the mill operations, including the unpleasant and difficult job of wool dyeing. It might be assumed that other employees would resent the appearance of the boss's son. Apparently, this was not the case. The author has talked to descendants of several mill hands who were contemporaries of young Joe. One of these, Miss Alice Smith of Bristol, said: "Grandfather, who worked in the dyeing process for many years, said that when the well-dressed young Grundy first walked into the plant the employees were skeptical and ready to be highly critical. He soon showed them that he would wear their kind of clothes, work the same hours, and mingle as a fellow-worker. Grandfather always said, 'There was nothing high-hat about Joe Grundy. He was a regular guy, and that is the way we all felt about him.' "

In winter he rode a bicycle from his home at 610 Radcliffe Street, Bristol, to the mill by the Delaware Canal. Summer meant a longer trip from Walnut Grove farm, but in spite of the two-mile bicycle ride he would reach Bristol by 6 a.m. He was invariably hatless, with his coat across the handle bars. Joe worked a sixty-hour week and more—was among the first on the job and one of the last to leave. He returned the friendliness of his co-workers and took an active interest in hardship cases. A former employee has said that these were handled more sympathetically and liberally than in many other mills of the time.

Young Grundy must have practiced the advice written on a faded clipping, dated from this period and treasured over the years. It read, "The conditions for success are these: first, work; second, concentration; third, fitness; without these no important achievements have been won."

In the year 1885, after five years of training in the various mill departments, he was promoted to the important job of buying the raw materials. During each clipping season he bought wool direct from sheep raisers in northeastern and mid-western states. While on his buying trips, he wrote conscientiously to his parents, just as he had on his foreign travels.

From upstate New York he wrote, "This must be a good country to get married in and among these little country heifers there are some very good-looking girls, but I did not mean the looks of the girls was so much of a special inducement as the cheapness of living. You can buy potatoes for 35¢ a bushel, butter at from 15 to 22¢, eggs 12¢ a dozen, and other things in about the same proportion . . . It being distinctly a farming community, the wealth all lies with them, some of whom are very rich and own several thousand acres, with one of these I stayed several days, . . . having bought his wool, and was very well entertained and had a very enjoyable time. They are very largely Scotch and Scotch descent, and consequently very frugal and saving."

A later letter written from Indiana to his sister reveals his deep interest in his Bristol home and its furnishings. ". . . How does the yard and lawn look since you have gotten it all sodded? . . . Thee wrote that the hall stand and glass had arrived. I hope they were a success for on them depended so much the appearance of the hall" [still to be seen at 610 Radcliffe Street].

Besides his buying trips throughout the east and mid-west, Grundy frequently accompanied his father to Washington in the interests of tariff. He differed in viewpoint from many of his well-educated young friends. They, like most others of college age, rebelled against parental conservatism and were, at least for a few years, opinionated reformers. Not so with Joe Grundy. This young man, from his first day in the Grundy mill in 1880, turned his energy and youthful enthusiasm into all industry generally, and the wool business in particular.

In the first presidential election in which Joe could cast his ballot, 1884, Democrat Grover Cleveland was elected after a Republican rule of twenty-four years. This change of administration was a great blow to young Grundy and his father, who now made dire predictions about the country's future. It is not surprising that the twenty-one-year-old businessman, who soon saw these predictions come true, became convinced that the country lost economic gains under the Democrats and would only prosper again under a Republican administration.

No sooner had Cleveland been inaugurated than serious trouble developed. During 1885-86 strikes in factories, mines, railroads and street car systems spread across the country. Prosperity suffered accordingly. This was the opinion not only of Republican businessmen but also of historians of the period. The then currently popular textbook, A. S. Barnes' *A Brief History of the United States,* reports: "Strikes and labor disturbances greatly injured prosperity. In many instances railroad traffic was suspended, switches were misplaced, trains derailed and valuable property destroyed. Dynamite plots added to the gravity of the situation. In Chicago on May 4, 1886, when the police were attempting to scatter a body of anarchists, a bomb was thrown among them. This resulted in the death of seven policemen and the injury of many others. Seven men were arrested for the crime, convicted, and sentenced to death. In the following July, three Chicago anarchists were arrested on a charge of conspiracy to murder the judges who presided at the trial and to burn the city."

In spite of generally poor business conditions, Joe Grundy, the young wool buyer, was quite successful in his transactions. In fact, he was becoming so adept at driving a good bargain that his father decided he was ready to try his hand in the European market.

In May of 1887 Joe sailed for Europe with his twenty-one-year-old sister. Fun-loving Meta had persuaded her parents to allow her to accompany Joe on his "business trip." She made elaborate plans to do extensive sight-seeing abroad with her close friend and Bristol neighbor, Annie Landreth.

Meta was apparently too busy for family correspondence but Joe dutifully reported to his mother on their social activities: From Devon, England, he wrote, ". . . I don't think I ever enjoyed a visit more, everything seems to run on so cheerfully, there being but one opinion about the place and that being the opinion of the head of the house . . . Meta keeps very well and seems to be enjoying herself very much . . . The Landreths go to Paris today to be gone some ten days, when we will join them in London. Mr. Landreth very kindly sent us passes to the American Exhibition, which makes us feel quite important."

Joe seemed particularly adept at combining business with pleasure. He enjoyed the companionship of Meta's friends, especially that of Annie Landreth. Nine years older than Joseph, she jokingly spoke of herself as "Mother." That Annie really understood Joe is apparent in her letter from Paris on May 28, 1887: "I should not call you Joe after the very formal business-like note you sent in reply to my letter about staterooms. Well, I suppose I did make myself very much at home, but . . . you have so quietly corrected me . . . I was glad to hear that you would return with us and that you really wanted to. I felt afraid that perhaps after visiting in England and having such nice times . . . you would give us the slip. We will be in London Thursday afternoon, then we can be together at last for a few days, if you do not go to visit friends until the 15th or so . . ."

In a letter from London on June 23rd, Joe omitted references to business but gave detailed accounts of his social activities: "The Landreths on their return from the Continent came to this Hotel where we joined them. It is full of Americans, among whom are many friends of the Landreths and some that we know. Meta has written you fully about the Reform Club ball we attended last week, a very grand affair . . . Had seats for the Jubilee . . . secured us by Mr. Landreth for nothing . . . such as sold for five and six pounds each. The Queen of course was the central figure and I think she was the ugliest woman I saw the whole day. She hardly received as much recognition from the crowd as did the Prince of Wales who seems very popular . . ."

Joe visited Cousin Herbert in Manchester as he had seven years before; but this trip included business responsibilities: ". . . Thursday I visited with several of the wool brokers whose acquaintance I will cultivate for business purposes . . ."

Joe Grundy was learning well how to "cultivate friends for business purposes," an art that was to make him the number one lobbyist in his own country. Under his father's expert tutelage he practiced the art in Harrisburg and Washington, D. C., immediately after his return from Europe in August of 1887.

As the next presidential election approached, the Democrats, who advocated a reduction of the duties on imports, renominated Grover Cleveland. The Republicans promised to help industry by higher tariff as a means of protection against European competition.

In 1888, a majority of the voters chose the Republican higher tariff platform and Benjamin Harrison, a hero of the Civil War, was elected. The following fall found young Joe Grundy and his father in Washington working on tariff recommendations, and the Republicans keeping their campaign promises by adopting the McKinley Tariff Bill which increased the duties on many imports.

The Grundys were great admirers of William McKinley of Ohio, another Civil War hero and a convinced high tariff man who had served in Congress on the important Ways and Means Committee and had been a leader of the House when tariff was the big issue. McKinley, like the Grundys, saw a connection between the tariff, the growing success of their own states and the rapid development of manufacturing.

Joe Grundy said, "My recollection as a very young man is of the making of the McKinley Tariff Act . . . Major McKinley [young Grundy admired his gallant Civil War record] lived

Joseph R Grundy, aged 24, in London, 1887.

at the Ebbitt House. In those days we did not have the House office building or the Senate office building. My father at that time was very active in tariff matters. I know he and others came down and met the Chairman of the Ways and Means Committee in Major McKinley's room at the Ebbitt House, and they sat there in that room, with his wife ill in an adjoining bedroom, and there the men who understood industry got together . . . and brought out that bill, which was one of the greatest bills the country ever had from a protective standpoint."

This measure had been a change from the Tariff of 1883 which, although it retained the protectionist principle, had lowered tariffs by five per cent. William Grundy and his son were elated to see the McKinley bill raise the average tariff level and provide for reciprocal increase of duties to meet discrimination by foreign nations. After this bill passed, a cry went up across the land that the legislature was "in league with the Capitalists!"

In the next presidential campaign the Grundys worked hard for Harrison's re-election. They vigorously opposed President Cleveland's candidacy for a second term out of sequence, and, with other Republicans, were greatly disappointed when he won. The Democrats now kept their campaign promise to lower tariff.

The summer following Cleveland's inauguration brought a repetition of the situation which followed his previous Democratic administration. There was a severe financial depression. Factory owners, banks and merchants could not collect their bills. Railway lines reduced employment. Strikes made the situation even worse. The years of 1893 and 1894 saw panics, riots and thousands of starving, unemployed Americans.

A majority of citizens associated the hard times with the low tariff and the Republicans once more offered to help the national economy and the manufacturers. Again the Republican promises were persuasive. The Party's presidential candidate, William McKinley, was elected and entered office in 1897. The

Republican Congress adopted the Dingley Tariff bill which increased the duties on many imports and removed wool and several other items from the free list. The voters had concurred in the Republican contention that a higher tariff made it possible for growing industries to pay higher wages and enjoy a higher standard of living. To quote from Thwaites and Kendall, *The History of the United States*. "During McKinley's term of office the prosperity of the United States was much talked about throughout the entire world."

As a result of increased trade, American-made tools, typewriters, sewing machines, steel rails, bridges and other revolutionary items appeared on every continent. Cities grew rapidly in north, south, east, and west. Small wonder that Joe Grundy became convinced that higher tariff enabled America to reach undreamed of heights of prosperity! He saw it happen, not only in his own business, but across the land.

In his mind the success of the Republican Party nationally and in his own precinct, in Bucks County, Pennsylvania, meant a greater measure of prosperity, not only for the industrialists but also for the industrial workers and the farmers. He saw a connection between politics and prosperity. Thus, soon after attaining his majority, he began to work at the polling place every election day. It was his father who placed a poll book in his hands and urged him to become a watcher at the polls. Consequently on every election day Grundy stood for hours and checked the name of each voter. This became his regular duty and he missed it only once in sixty-five years—that was in the year 1896 when he was buying wool in England. It was not until the age of eighty-six that he reluctantly relinquished this important and beloved post.

To Grundy, politics was the duty of every citizen and he was highly critical of those who did not exercise their right to vote, especially in the primaries. His father's convictions became his. "Your bread and butter," he would frequently say, "the price of the clothes your wear, the streets you travel on, the water you drink, all depend on political administrations; so, inevitably, everyone should be deeply concerned with politics. Every American should read the record before he decides which party he will give his vote to, and that record will show that the development of American industry and our resultant prosperity came about primarily from the policies of the Republican party."

Chapter 7

THE NOT-SO-GAY NINETIES

William Grundy's death on October 26, 1893, thrust new obligations on his ambitious thirty-year-old son. In addition to Joe's new duties as head of William H. Grundy and Company, he faced serious family problems.

His sister, Meta, an imaginative and sensitive young woman, could not face the reality of her first experience with the death of a loved one. Always close to her father, she was unable to cope with the sudden loss. Mrs. Grundy, also prostrated by grief, was worried about Meta's condition. Joe decided that they should both get away from the scenes of their bereavement and made arrangements for a trip abroad.

After their departure, he faced alone the problems of business plus the management of the house in Bristol and the family home, Walnut Grove. There his grandmother Grundy was in the throes of a terminal illness. His thoughtful letters related little of his problems but revealed deep concern for his mother and sister.

On April 20th he wrote to his mother: ". . . I am anxiously awaiting advices which will make me acquainted with 'where you are at,' as Meta's last letter written on your return from the Burning Sands of the upper Nile was not the embodiment of 'definiteness' . . ."

Meta's condition grew worse and on May 11th Joe again wrote to his mother about his contemplated trip to see her. "I have thy letter from Geneva dated the 1st and note that Meta is under the care of a doctor leaving thee so much alone . . . you do seem to be in the hardest kind of luck . . . anxious to see you . . . the 26th can't roll around too soon . . . Don't worry about me . . . have given up wine and don't eat desserts and consequently am feeling well . . . In business . . . from our economical running I think we must be making a little money . . . which considering the times is very gratifying . . . I have thy letter telling me . . . about Meta's illness that led up to her being taken to the clinique . . . Don't let Meta or thee worry about what people in the States think about your absence—it is none of their D— business . . ."

Just before sailing, in his usual good humor, he wrote a teasing letter to his mother about a young woman who was sailing on the same ship: ". . . I tell my friends it is like taking my life in my hands, as it were, to go off on a ten-day cruise with so sweet a girl as Miss Josie, but I have managed to stand up so far, will hope to struggle through this without presenting thee with a daughter-in-law. . ."

In Europe he found Meta suffering from mild but persistent nervous symptoms. He did what he could to cheer the unhappy girl but soon had to return home to the family business.

Back at Bristol he dutifully fulfilled the women's requests. "I found Meta's watch safe and sound . . . where I had put it for safe keeping after you departed in the winter. I will try to get out tonight that sealskin cape or coat of Meta's thee wants me to send to the Royal Tiger Fur Co . . . in Geneva . . . Give [Meta] lots of love and tell her to hump herself and get well."

But her condition continued and Mrs. Grundy suggested a doctor from home. Her anxious son wrote: ". . . Dr. Pancoast . . . would come to thee and would charge $30 per day and expenses . . . If thee thinks best to have him come . . . send for him because we can't leave any stone unturned to get our dear little sister back to health . . ."

A few days later he enclosed "two powers-of-attorney to sell the Pennsylvania Railroad stock and the Northern Pacific shares—the condition the country is to be in I am confident the next three years will see them lower and I want to be in a position if in the next month or so it looks best, to sell them. We can do so for I am not very hopeful of railroad investments under this reign of perfidy and dishonor."

Joe Grundy was rapidly learning about investments in connection with his new responsibilities as the principal stockholder in the Farmers National Bank, an institution founded by his great-great-grandfather Hulme.

At the time Joe inherited his controlling interest in the bank, its strong position, gauged by surplus and profits in excess of capital, was very different from the troubled times of its organization in 1814. Business then was all but paralyzed because of the costly loans to help the government carry on the War of 1812. City banks had been compelled to limit discounts, or even stop loans altogether.

By the end of 1814 the government could not pay its interest on the public debt and the treasury tried to get a loan at seven per cent. There was only one taker—Stephen Girard of Philadelphia—who subscribed the unsold balance and thereby saved the national credit.

Businessmen outside the big cities realized that in these difficult times they would have to "go it alone." Just the man to accept such a challenge was Joe Grundy's "go it alone" great-great-grandfather, John Hulme.

Surely the situation in the summer of 1814 would have dashed the hopes of a less determined man. The frugal farmers of Bucks County were not likely to hazard their small capital, already seriously impaired by the war, in some new venture at such a critical period. An old record antedating the establishment of the bank speaks for itself in reporting the discouraging efforts of the men who traveled through the county attempting to solicit subscribers for the first installment of "Capital Stock."

"1814		Shares
June 6	First Day's Subscription	
	Thomas Jones..................	2
	John Pugh.....................	2

Fidelity-Philadelphia Trust Company in Bristol, Pennsylvania, formerly The Farmers National Bank, founded by Grundy's great-great-grandfather, John Hulme.

	William Watts	2
	William Watts Hart	2
June 7	Second Day's Subscription	
	Septimus Evans	4
	Enoch Harvey	2
	Asher Miner	2
June 8	Third Day's Subscription	
	William Watts	2
	E. Morris	6
	Elizabeth Pugh	2
June 9	Fourth Day's Subscription	
		0
June 10	Fifth Day's Subscription	
		0

The first directors were elected at a meeting held on December 5, 1814, in one of the houses at Hulmeville. A few days later the directors convened and elected John Hulme president. They also reached an agreement whereby George Hulme, brother of John, rented to the bank for $100 per year as much of his house as might be needed for the accommodation of the bank. Desks and counters were constructed and windows and doors cast with sheet iron; window shutters being secured by iron bars fastened inside by keys.

An old brick cupboard served as a vault and an iron door with necessary bolts and locks was fastened across its front.

One of the first acquisitions was a sturdy iron-bound wooden chest 27x14x16 inches in size. It had huge handles, weighty padlocks, and an additional fascinating feature—a lock in the lid. When the key was withdrawn for the night, a flap was pushed over the opening on the theory that this would make it very difficult for a burglar to find the keyhole!

The salary of the president was fixed at $300 per year; the cashier, George Harrison, $800, and the clerk, Joseph T. Pickering, $300. The bank opened on December 17, 1814, at 9 a.m., with Tuesday and Friday of each week designated as the days of discount with public notice given in the papers published at Doylestown and at Newtown.

On November 6, 1815, the first dividend of eighty cents per share, equivalent to eight per cent a year for the time, was distributed to the 138 shareholders.

On October 25, 1823, the directors decided that the bank should be moved to Bristol. Its new location was a portion of a brick house at the corner of Mill and Cedar Streets. Removal of the assets presented no problem. President Anthony Taylor placed the strongbox and books in his one-horse chaise and deposited them in the new office. All that remained at the original location in Hulmeville was the four-inch brick cupboard with its sheet iron door.

By June, 1829, the directors were looking forward to an exciting new navigational program, the development of the new Delaware Division of the Pennsylvania Canal. On the 9th of the month a loan was made to the Commonwealth of Pennsylvania for $15,000 at five per cent to be expended on the new waterway.

As deposits increased, it was obvious that the present office did not offer adequate protection, so a committee bought a house on Radcliffe Street for $5,000. This was a beautiful colonial mansion of that early nineteenth century period so influenced by Grecian architecture. It had twenty-four-inch walls and massive columns front and rear, supporting porticos. The former owner, James Craig, was a nephew of Nicholas Biddle, who in 1823 became president of the Second Bank of the United States in Philadelphia. This bank had promoted sound methods and furnished currency that—according to congressional reports—was "as safe as silver" and "more convenient." However, the Philadelphia bank failed in the Panic of 1837.

Many other banks followed suit, but Hulme's Farmers Bank of Bucks County showed a comfortable surplus. Its directors felt entirely capable of handling all business because they declined an application from a Bucks County attorney for a position on the grounds that "the bank has no business at present which requires legal attention and hopes not to have for the future."

However, for most people these were hard times. The bank clerk, Benjamin Swain, lived in a portion of the bank building and served as night watchman. One night he heard hammering on the stone wall outside the vault. It was the kind of emergency for which he was ready. A heavy log lay on the window sill above the vault. The gentle Quaker cautiously raised the sash and called out, "I don't want to harm thee, friend, but I am about to drop this log on thee if thee don't go away." The would-be robber vanished before the log crashed to the ground.

Banking was fascinating, if informal in those days. One of the directors of the Farmers Bank, while a young man, bought cattle in the west. He frequently took along on his trips all the western notes which his bank had accepted at a discount. On one occasion he stopped at a farmhouse to ask the location of a bank that had issued some of the notes in his possession.

"Stranger," said the farmer, "this is it. You are at the bank."

The farmer declined to elucidate until his guest had shared a hearty country meal. Afterwards the host went to a barrel in the kitchen, lifted the lid and took out what eastern notes were required, giving them to his guest at the current rate of discount and redeeming the notes of the barrel bank at par.

Exchanges of this kind were fairly common with profits ranging from ten to fifty per cent according to the locality. Such transactions formed the foundations of the fortunes of the Drexel partners and others, who conducted business through correspondents. These were the "wild cat" days of banking when one lived in exciting uncertainty whether the bank that issued the note one was carrying would be solvent at the time the note was used to buy something or to pay a debt.

One committee of the Farmers Bank had a simple and

pleasant task—that of burning the redeemed circulating notes. This was done in an open fireplace in the directors' room. On one occasion, some notes, while only partially destroyed, blew up the chimney. A few days later, tinmen engaged in roof repairing found them. Those still showing enough printing to be available for redemption were passed about and for several days the officers received and redeemed hundreds of dollars of notes that were claimed to have been accidentally burned in different shops or houses. Although the fraud was discovered, the bank suffered a considerable loss and the directors resolved to be more careful in the future.

On October 25, 1864, at a stockholders' meeting, the bank voted unanimously to convert the institution from a state bank to a national bank under federal law and the title was changed to Farmers National Bank of Bucks County. Joe Grundy always spoke with pride of the fact that of some thirty "Farmers Banks" established under the laws of the Commonwealth of Pennsylvania, only six or eight had survived under their original title or a substantially similar type. The Farmers National Bank of Bucks County was one of these.

Young Joe Grundy's conscientious work in the family bank helped to develop his astute business judgment. He became highly proficient in buying and selling stocks as well as wool, a trick that was to build his inheritance of something less than a million dollars to nearly eighteen million at his death. The Pennsylvanian's uncanny knack for timing was a key factor in accumulating his fortune.

For his wool buying he traveled to distant parts of the world, visiting New Zealand a number of times. At one point, according to local legend, he cornered the Australian wool market and had wool bulging from warehouses, freight cars and even empty Bristol houses.

But in 1894 Grundy was concerned with rumored romances as well as business responsibilities. He lightly reproached his mother for what he apparently feared was her encouragement of a hopeful and perceptive girl. He wrote, "I enclose . . . a letter from Sallie—destroy it when thee reads it. I hope thee did not arouse any false hopes in her palpitating heart . . ." The letter read: "My dear Joseph . . . I suppose you are happy and busy and that you are holding your world in your hand—making it do what you wish towards that end. Shall I see you sometime? I hope so . . ."

On his birthday in 1895 he expressed his deep sense of family duty in a letter to his mother. In it he used the third person as a modesty device: "Today her son is thirty-two years old . . . He had her letter from Paris—about the money part, don't worry. As long as he can go on and make it there shall be no want of the necessities and some of the luxuries as we have had them in the past, for whatever he has got is 'hern' and sister's. She stood by him when he was a little kid and ever since and now it is his turn to return what he can of it."

His letter the following month was revealing. At thirty-two he was definitely thinking of marriage and children: "While thee is sitting around Paris . . . why don't thee look up some good portrait painter and in the interest of thy grandchildren have thy portrait painted . . . I know the little devils will so like to know how Grandma looked at *forty*, to say nothing of the pleasure its possession or existence would give those more closely related to thee now . . ." His next statement illustrated his innate shrewdness. Quaker thrift and Episcopalian sophistication complemented each other: "I would not go to some great high priced fellow because thee does not need that kind of talent to make thee beautiful. Nature has, thank God, had an inning ahead of art."

By late October of 1895 his mother and sister were still abroad. He wrote: "There are no end of inquiries after thine and sister's health and I have from constant practice a regular stereotyped speech which covers the whole subject in a thoroughly non-committal way, which pleases yet does not enlighten." This was a practice he also used expertly in both business and politics!

111

Grundy's next letter informed them "of the death of Grandmother Grundy which occurred yesterday . . . [Oct. 26, 1895]. Passed into deep stupor just as Grandma Ridgway did . . . We cannot but view it as a happy release to all her long and tedious suffering . . . Episcopal service read by Mr. R. G. Moses . . . Four pall-bearers shall be her grandsons . . . Her death involves the question of what will be done with Walnut Grove. It had always been Grandmother Grundy's wish that the property should remain in the family, and Meta had always wanted that we should hold on to it and . . . it would seem if that is to be considered alone, that among us we should be quite able to hold it at any reasonable valuation . . . As Grandmother's affairs would settle up—say Walnut Grove sold for $15,000, my share in the estates would be from $10,000 to $12,000, so it would take but little money to buy it . . .Now there is a lot to say on the other side about the expense of holding real estate; of our not wanting to become any more heavily involved in this neighborhood . . . Should Meta not improve and it was thought best another summer to bring her home, a more quiet place could not be found for her, especially as she always expressed a wish that we should hold on to it."

Apparently Grundy's mother and sister were not seriously concerned about family funds. They enjoyed spending money and Joe was amazingly tolerant. In the following February of 1896 he wrote: "I want to tell thee to get just what thee wants and sister wants, as I know neither of you will be extravagant. As for your past overdrafts, they are all right, I have made them good and forgotten all about them and thee and sister do the same. I am only thankful I was able to do so and while these sad conditions of sister's illness surround you, will wish and expect to the full extent of my ability to stand behind any excess in your expenditures, over and above your joint incomes. Thy income came in to the extent, I think, of $6,000 and Meta's about $2,000 more . . . It is a very good scheme the painting of the miniatures. Thee knows how I struggled last year for thee to have thy picture painted in Paris." And Joe switched to the third person as he added, "He would so like it for his art gallery at Walnut Grove, in order to point it out to his grandchildren."

The young Pennsylvanian led a busy social life, but his engagements never overlooked civic and patriotic interests. Young or old he did not forget those who had served their country. In August he wrote: "We are working on a Regiment Reunion which occurs on the 16th of September and all looks as if the occasion would be a success. It is the only Regiment sent to the [Civil] War from Bucks County and the first time Bristol has ever done anything to honor the memory of these survivors."

Five years after William Grundy's death, Mrs. Grundy and Meta were still abroad. In the spring of 1898 Grundy wrote to his sister about one of the few illnesses in his lifetime: "Had thy letter written from Cairo about the 14th of March . . . Just recovering from mumps . . . L'Annie [Landreth] insisted on the nurse being gotten . . . The threatened row with Spain has had everyone on the anxious bench and has very much retarded business, but we keep pegging away . . ."

In April he wrote to his mother: "I had yesterday sister's letter written on the 'Cuzco' and posted from Marseilles . . . I wrote you a week or so ago about coming home this summer. This I only meant if you cared to and there was nothing better offering over there . . . I can't but realize how dull you would find it after the first flush of excitement wears off . . . At this writing there does not seem to be much doubt but we will have a row with Spain . . . The feeling here is very bitter against the Spaniards, especially in connection with the Maine affair . . .

". . . I feel much concerned . . . of Meta's not being so well, . . . It may be her trouble comes from weakness after her attack of influenza . . . Try Divonne and the baths there to brace her up . . . Spent the evening with Mr. and Mrs. Wildman. Miss

Runyon, one of the belles of the town (developed since you left) was also there so we had a busy evening."

He became a bit impatient with the women's anxiety about the war: "Letter came this afternoon from Meta telling of your unsettlement and distress over the war situation with Spain . . . I cannot see how in the world it can affect you so long as you keep out of Spain . . ."

His loneliness in his family's long absence abroad, especially at Christmas time crept into his letter of December 1898 to Meta: ". . . It seems this year (at Christmas) we will be quite scattered . . . Thee in Munich, Mother in Paris and myself here at home; last year we were a little nearer together . . . Although thee and Mother were at Katoomba and I was on the way back from New Zealand. Then the year before we were all together at Meran where they did so much Christmas celebrating . . . We have gotten the white curtains out for the rooms and all hung up and also gotten the bed hangings up in her room and it looks very sweet and 'purty' and all it wants now is his little sister to hump herself and get back in the early summer and occupy her old apartments and help him run things."

He gave many dinner parties, occasionally describing one for his mother and sister: "My dinner Wednesday evening was a great success, about the most successful one I ever gave. All my guests arrived and from start till finish, which was nearly four in the morning, the thing kept going. There were eleven of us sat down and beside Mr. Blankenburg and Mr. Doak and Mr. Ingham, were the newly appointed collector of the Port of Philadelphia, Senator Thomas, the Naval Officer of the Port; Mr. Holland, the Republican boss of Montgomery County; the District Attorney of Bucks County, Mr. John C. Swartley, Mr. William R. Ellison, Mr. Farr and Mr. William P. Baltz. They were mostly a very bright lot of men and after the dinner was served we had a very interesting and entertaining time with the speeches and discussions that followed. Mr. Ingham is especially good, as is Senator Thomas and Mr. Blankenburg. They all said they had a most enjoyable time and I think they meant it—the only trouble about getting the reputation of being a host is to maintain it, especially when each affair seems to go better than the former one . . ."

Joe had some good financial advice for his mother: "Thee wrote me about your investments . . . Lately about $20,000 of estate money has been paid off and I have let it stay here in the business at six per cent. There is nothing you can buy in stocks at current prices that would pay that interest . . . I think we have done very well with your estates during these recent years when so much invested money went wrong. You have had from $7,000 to $8,000 each year, last year there was some $8,500, and this year your income will be quite as large . . ."

There were many girls. An old favorite was losing ground: "Called on Sallie, had quite a talk, and it was either the wear and tear of time or the gas light that made her look very much older . . ."

By March of 1899 he wrote: ". . . I note what thee says about sister's aversion to coming home while she is ill and in this decision I do not especially blame her . . . If sister should sufficiently improve to be left with her nurse, then thee could come back and spend as much time as thee would feel right about being away from sister with me [at home], and get some of the good eating that is going to waste hereabouts . . . I do not set my heart too firmly upon this possibility . . ."

The following month he was still faithfully reporting: "While I am writing thee Mr. Thomas is here varnishing the portrait of Uncle Joseph [Ridgway] which he is turning over to us today. We all about here feel very much gratified today at the verdict in favor of Senator Quay which was rendered today, acquitting him of the charges which for political purposes have largely been lodged against him . . ."

In May of 1899 he wrote a realistic note to his mother: "Thy letter from Aix came . . . telling of thy being settled in the family of defunct aristocracy . . . I wonder just how long thee will be able to stand the dropping of tableware about thee and on thy clothes before there is a row and thee seeks the surroundings of an establishment where they have less of the atmosphere of the past ages . . . and more of Anglo Saxon thrift and cleanliness . . ."

In optimistic mood, Grundy wrote: "We are having a very active business indeed and it looks as if in a short while we in the textiles will share in the same measure of prosperity that has come to iron and cotton which has been so extraordinary as to make fortunes so rapidly as to rival the tales in the Arabian Nights."

Joe Grundy was on the way! He still worked twelve hours a day, riding to the mill on a bicycle, a tin box holding his lunch propped by the handlebars. Lunches varied, except for the daily, shining apple for dessert. He rode to work at 6 a.m., and left the mill at 6 p.m.

But there were pleasures mixed with business—the theater in Philadelphia and New York, dinner parties and attractive women, many women, whose names will always be Joe Grundy's secret.

Why did the good looking and popular bachelor remain single? Was it a Victorian sense of responsibility for his frail sister, an all-powerful love of politics, or a continuing pleasure in "playing the field"? It was probably a combination of all three.

He was the epitome of discretion in his love affairs. But there was one slip in otherwise publicly impeccable deportment.

Joe was in his early forties and his mother and sister, who had returned to the United States in 1900, were living in Bristol. Meta's health had been restored and she enjoyed an active social life and many civic activities. Her brother had given her a handsome platinum and diamond pin which she unfortunately lost. Disconsolate she reordered another from Tiffany's in New York where her pin had been purchased. There the reliable firm was embarrassed by the fact that it could not tell which pin Grundy had ordered for his sister. He had purchased three at the same time!

Joe Grundy and his sister, Margaret (Meta), on a gala occasion.

CHAPTER 8

PENNSYLVANIA–THE KEYSTONE STATE

Grundy's unshakeable belief in the importance of Pennsylvania's place in America's industrial development was based on historical fact. Until the end of the War for Independence the economy of this province was colonial in character. What capital there was developed from the export of limited products from both farm and forest. Naturally, Pennsylvania's foremost trade center developed at the site of its busiest port, Philadelphia. In the last decade of the eighteenth century, Philadelphia was not only the capital of the United States, but also its major seaport.

At the time more people were attracted to the land of the Delaware Valley than to any other colony. In Joe Grundy's opinion the primary reason for this was the far-sighted and broad-minded government established by William Penn.

The Pennsylvanian's later work on behalf of Pennsbury Manor, Penn's Bucks County residence, was an outgrowth of his interest in Pennsylvania's founder. Grundy's knowledge of history gave him great respect for Penn's success in applying broad new theories of government in the beautiful Delaware Valley.

The "Father of Pennsylvania" had demonstrated his ability in his work on the Concessions and Agreements for West New Jersey, the enlightened governmental plan for that colony. In both this work and in his later planning for Pennsylvania we first see the impressive example of a person with unlimited power voluntarily limiting this power for the benefit of all the people. This inspired concept was later developed in our Constitution and Bill of Rights as the thrilling recognition of man's

117

right of freedom to worship as he pleased, vote as he pleased, and have his day in court.

Penn combined a good promotional sense with his idealism. His advertisements for the area would give pause to many a Madison Avenue copywriter:

"Of living creatures fish, fowl and the beast of the wood, there are divers sorts; some for food and profit and some for profit only. . . the elk—as big as a small ox, deer bigger than ours, beaver, raccoon, rabbits, squirrels. Some eat young bear and commend it. Of food of the land there is the turkey, forty and fifty pounds weight, which is very great; pheasants, heath birds, pigeons and partridges in abundance. Of the water: swan, goose—white and gray—brant, ducks, teals, also snipe, curlew— and that in great number. But the duck and teal excel, nor so good have I ate in other countries."

As more hopeful settlers came to this enticing colony, Philadelphia emerged as the largest and most important city in the new land. Much of the city's capital from commerce was available for investment in the infant industries which were popping up throughout the country. One of the earliest was iron.

Dr. S. K. Stevens, State Historian of Pennsylvania, pointed out in his work, *Pennsylvania, Titan of Industry*, that: "Our Commonwealth may well claim to have been the mother of the Industrial Revolution.

"Moses Brown's factory (in Providence, Rhode Island) is often acclaimed as the birthplace of the Industrial Revolution in America—but it should be clear that earlier evidences of factory enterprise in textile manufacturing can be observed at Philadelphia."

From the beginning, Pennsylvania's agriculture and manufacturing developed hand-in-hand: the money made from the sale of agricultural products provided some of the capital needed for industry. Furthermore, the early manufacturing evolved from land sources such as grains and timber.

Grundy's home town, Bristol, exemplifies this development.

At the turn of the seventeenth century, it consisted only of Mill Street—named for the mill erected by Samuel Carpenter, largest landowner in the town. Its location on the west bank of the Delaware attracted industries from the moment its first mill was erected. Here the water power of the creek made it possible to saw the lumber which the colonists were clearing from their lands. Here, too, was ground the grain raised in the newly cleared fields. Eventually—as crops increased—ships were needed to carry goods to distant points. Thus, in Bristol, the Delaware River's shipbuilding industry was born. However, this early leadership in shipbuilding was short-lived. Although Bristol was an older seaport than Philadelphia, it was rapidly surpassed in importance by Penn's carefully planned city, twenty-two miles to the south.

There was also need to transport the variety of Pennsylvania products by land, so the country's first turnpike connecting Philadelphia and Lancaster came into being in 1794. Philadelphia quickly became the center of the leather industry and of the new food processing and manufacturing plants. It was also the hub of the printing and publishing industry, and the heart of the engraving and bookbinding business.

Within the earth the Keystone State had bounties of which William Penn did not even dream. As early as the seventeenth century, Dutch mining engineers had been on the track of the colony's mineral deposits. Iron and coal provided the state with these additional riches beneath its surface.

Following the mineral discoveries, new techniques established here revolutionized the process of producing iron and steel commercially. This advance encouraged a tremendous growth in various manufactures based on iron. The machine age was on its way and the oil necessary to keep its wheels humming was found in August, 1859, at Titusville, Pennsylvania, by Colonel Edwin Drake. Thus Pennsylvania had the raw products, the manufacturing equipment and the oil to operate it. Now came the necessity for swift transportation of the many commodities. To answer this need the first steel rails for railroad use were rolled in 1867 at Harrisburg, on order of the United States government.

By this time Pennsylvania was emerging as the leader in technology and industrial management. No state equaled it for the variety of its manufacture. Such developments explain Joe Grundy's conception of Pennsylvania as a "forward state." They also indicate what he had in mind as a comparison when he referred to certain other states as "backward," the adjective that haunted him forever.

Admittedly, Pennsylvania's natural resources were an important factor in its swift growth. But this should not detract from the state's achievements for two reasons. First, it showed the forward-looking concepts of those early residents who settled here and invested in agriculture and manufacturing; and second, it took foresight and energy to develop so quickly and exploit so successfully the natural resources in fields, mines, and manufacture.

Pennsylvania was ready with industry and leadership at the outbreak of the Civil War. In fact, Lee's decision to invade the Keystone State was based upon the objective of crippling the heart of northern industrial strength. This strength was decisive in giving victory to the north over the south and it is easy to understand why southern legislators later found the Pennsylvania leadership hard to forgive.

Joe Grundy, the historian, offered his own explanation of the general economic situation at the time of the Civil War, in a paper read before the Bucks County Historical Society in 1910:

"The year 1860 found our country in a condition of great turmoil and alarm. A man had been elected President of the United States who was not in sympathy with southern traditions, and the south, which for many years had been in charge of the government, was upon the verge of secession. With the control of the government thus far in their hands and with secession in their minds, it was but natural that ships, arms and munitions of war should have been transferred by those in charge, to points south of Mason and Dixon's line, in anticipation of the coming struggle.

"Thus when Abraham Lincoln subscribed to the oath of office as President of the United States, he found the government of our country confronted not only with secession and civil war, but also stripped of means to enforce by force of arms the laws of our country and cope with the rebellion which was then before him. In order to provide and equip the armies and navies of the United States, large expenditures confronted the government; as the treasury was as depleted as were the arsenals, large sums of money had to be borrowed on the faith of the government, and to provide for the interest and principal of these obligations every method of taxation was, in the course of the struggle, resorted to, including heavy import duties upon all kinds of manufactured products into our country.

"The import duties on manufactures from abroad, high as they were, were not the only drawback to procuring goods from foreign lands. Many enterprises of a privateering character were entered into by men taking advantage of the condition in which the government of our country found itself and harassed in the name of the Confederacy the shipping trade of northern states, and so our foreign trade relations were not only made difficult by high tariff duties, but hazardous by the fear of capture by those engaged in preying on our commerce.

"The effect of the government being a very large purchaser of all commodities, such as clothing, boots and shoes, arms and armament, to say nothing of the general equipment necessary to maintain large armies in the field, coupled with the requirements of our people, also the great abundance of money due to the large expenditures on the part of the government for war purposes, created great opportunity for domestic manufacture of all classes of merchandise. Under this stimulant domestic industries to meet these requirements sprang up and flourished on every side, and the industrial strides made by the north during the Civil War reflect their most prosperous period in American history.

"The close of the Civil War, in 1865, brought many problems to those in charge of our government, but none that they approached with more serious consideration than that of restoring the revenues of government to a peace basis and yet not disturb the splendid industrial development which had been created by the conditions before described.

"To prepare for this the Congress of the United States appointed a Revenue Commission consisting of David A. Wells, of Connecticut; S.S. Hayes, of Massachusetts, and Stephen A. Colwell, of Pennsylvania. The work of this Commission covered a period of two years and proved to be a masterly review of the revenue laws of the land. In the latter part of 1866, this Commission made its report [which became] . . . the basis of what has since been known in history as the Morrell Tariff Act of 1867. The passage of this law brought continued confidence and encouragement to our industrial development as a country and formed the basis upon which every protective tariff bill has since been constructed."

Grundy concluded this account with an oft-repeated tribute to the valor of those who served on the side of the Union in the Civil War: "In all ages the valor and bravery of men who have borne arms in the defense of their country has been the subject of grateful appreciation by their fellow man. If this is true in a general sense, when applied to those who fought on the side of the Union in the Civil War, it should have a double significance, for did not the bravery and patriotism of these men preserve our national integrity, deliver unto freedom millions of men who had previously been held in bondage; but unknown even to themselves evolved and developed in the minds of our patriotic statesmen of that day, out of the necessity and circumstances of the war, what has since been known as the American Protective Tariff System. The advantages and benefits of this system are directly evidenced by the development and prosperity of the community and our entire country during the past fifty years, and the example set has led to the adoption of this system as part of the fiscal policy of every civilized nation in the world but one. Surely can it be said of the patriotic soldiers of '60 to '64, 'they built more wisely than they knew.' "

Perhaps Grundy's continuing expressions of partisan sentiment were partially responsible for the antagonism of southern senators and some from the western states. At least this is one plausible explanation for the coalition's eagerness to see both the Pennsylvanian and his state lose power and prestige.

Eventually with some help from other sources, the critical senators were to succeed. However, during the years of Grundy's childhood and up to the beginning of his middle age, Pennsylvania was in its most powerful position industrially, second only to New York. It took the lead in the development of the types of progressive concerns which prevail today. By 1900 the country's largest number of big business combinations was based in Pennsylvania.

However, later in the century the trend started the other way, with steel moving westward, textiles southward, and the new automotive industry beginning elsewhere. One person above all others in American life, Joe Grundy, saw the trend, knew some of the reasons for it and spent his life trying to overcome them. One explanation lay in the increasing tax burdens within the state. Other states, by now aware of the value of manufacturing, offered enticing inducements—cheaper ground, lower taxes and lower wages.

Although Pennsylvania continues to be one of the most important manufacturing areas in the country, it no longer has the keystone position in the industrial development of the nation that it held in the colonial period. But it can never be said that Grundy didn't devote his whole lifetime, his work and his fortune to trying to keep it at the very top. He remained convinced that as long as welfare issues provide unbeatable political fodder—and these must be paid for primarily from industrial taxation—Pennsylvania was not likely to enjoy the resurgence of its former power.

Joe Grundy labored unceasingly to prevent the same trend from occurring in his home town of Bristol. When as a small boy he first came to the town, it held the glamor of the past and the glow of a still promising future. Although he had spent many happy days at his Grandfather Grundy's farm, Walnut Grove, near Bristol, he did not live in the town itself until 1876 when his parents moved into a house on Jefferson Avenue, residing there a short time before settling permanently at 610 Radcliffe Street.

His lifetime pride in his Radcliffe Street home, now a museum, is best understood when one knows that its purchase was one of his very first business transactions. He had been working in the Grundy mill just four years and was twenty-one when his parents and sister left for a European visit. Final clearance of the former owner's title had been made and the long-postponed purchase was at last ready to be consummated. In his father's absence it became Joseph's proud duty to present a check for $10,000 and to assume ownership for the family.

The first written record of the land on which the dwelling was later erected deals with its sale in December, 1818, from John Caldwell of New Castle, Delaware, to William Heiss, a "coppersmith of the Northern Liberties" in Philadelphia. Apparently the original house was a small brick dwelling. Heiss, an artisan with imagination, enlarged the original house into an eight-sided dwelling sometime during his sixteen years of occupancy.

In February 1834 he sold the house and lot to Captain Joseph B. Hutchinson, a prominent sea captain of the period. Hutchinson further enlarged the octagonal brick house and purchased the adjacent tract to the south.

The dwelling attracted widespread attention at the beginning of the Civil War. It was then rented to Robert Tyler, son of ex-President John Tyler. Young Tyler had served as his father's secretary throughout his term as President of the United States. Robert Tyler's wife was Priscilla Cooper Tyler, daughter of Thomas A. Cooper, the great tragedian who lived just north of the Hutchinson house.

Cooper was the first American matinee idol to be well accepted socially in this country at a time when theatrical personalities were generally frowned upon by the more socially prominent citizens. The actor maintained his Bristol home in a magnificent fashion and his daughter's marriage to the son of the President was a social triumph for the ambitious gentleman. When Tyler's wife died, Priscilla, as a young bride, had been called upon to preside as hostess at the White House. She fulfilled her task with grace and charm until President Tyler's second marriage in June of 1844. At this time the Robert Tylers came to live in the Hutchinson house on Radcliffe Street and young Tyler became Prothonotary of the Superior Court of Pennsylvania, with his office in Philadelphia.

His loyalties were torn during the Civil War because he was a Virginian by birth and dedicated to the south. He had also been indiscreet in the expression of his sentiments which were well-known to many Philadelphians. When word reached the city that Fort Sumter had been fired upon, an angry speaker at a citizens' town meeting in Independence Square charged that Tyler was continually speaking in defense of the south. At that remark a shout went up from the crowd, "He ought to be lynched."

One of Tyler's friends, present at the rally, heard this with misgiving. He rushed to Tyler in his Philadelphia office, warning him to leave the city at once. It was fortunate that Tyler hastily boarded one of the daily steamboats bound for Bristol where Priscilla waited. The word that "a mob in Philadelphia was after Tyler" had reached his family in Bristol. Although influential friends reassured Tyler that he would not be harmed, he took no chances and left early the next morning for New

York City. It was a wise move because shortly afterward feeling ran so high in Bristol that he was hanged in effigy.

Joe Grundy always enjoyed recounting this story, often concluding with the remark, "Thee knows traitors were apt to find shelter in New York City. Over there they didn't have our loyalties to the North. Why, even back in the American Revolution, New York City was a great place for traitors to the American cause." Typically, the Pennsylvanian overlooked the Tories in Philadelphia.

Eventually Tyler wrote from New York to Mayor Mayo of Philadelphia asking whether he could have protection if he returned. The mayor said the excitement against him was so great that "the authorities could not promise protection from personal assaults."

Tyler's position was made even more difficult by the fact that his eldest daughter, Letitia, was visiting in the south. Because of the friendship between her grandfather and Jefferson Davis, she had been accorded the compliment of unfurling the first flag of the Confederacy in Montgomery, Alabama, then the southern capital. As these circumstances became known, hostility against the Tylers intensified and there was nothing left for the family to do but return to the south. Captain Hutchinson moved back into his Radcliffe Street house, remaining there until his death. The next owner of the property was William Hulme Grundy, who had been renting it before purchase. Joe completed the sale for his father, on March 24, 1884.

Grundy was now residing on the Delaware in one of the fabulous river mansions that had been synonymous with success and glamor for more than a century. His was the exciting experience of living in a house and on a street identified with one of the most culturally important periods in American history. The town of Bristol was situated in an area which had been favored by the Indians for centuries before white men discovered America. It was a spot where river and creek met

Indian path. Close by were the healing waters, later known as Bath Springs, and endless forests of hickory, walnut and white oak.

Joe Grundy loved Bristol, with its natural harbor curving southward toward the meadows between a rise in the land that became Mill Street, and an island known today as Maple Beach— loved the colorful heritage which stretched back to the arrival of the first settlers in this area.

It is not surprising that the early Dutch explorers found this spot to their liking. Captain Mey first ascended the Delaware in 1614. The first Dutch settlers were soon followed by the Swedes who, after 1638, dominated the colonist groups.

A map of the Delaware in the Bristol region was made in 1654 by a Swedish engineer, Peter Lindstrom. The river population between Wilmington, Delaware and Morrisville, Pennsylvania was then around eight hundred—mostly Finns, Swedes, Dutch and French, with a sprinkling of English. Then within a year the Dutch fleet ended Swedish possession.

For the next nine years the Dutch dominated, only to be dispossessed by the British in 1664. This coup was accomplished by Charles II, who had granted the area to his brother-in-law, the Duke of York.

The original site of Bristol was a tract of 240 acres granted to Samuel Clift in 1681 by Edmond Andros, governor of New York. This grant occurred three years before application was made for a charter for Philadelphia.

Bristol retained its colonial importance throughout the eighteenth century. In 1765 Charles Bessonett built an inn which he named the "George the Second Hotel." During the Revolution he hastily changed the name to the "Fountain House." According to the old ferry record, "the hotel was a favorite with Presidents Madison, Tyler and Fillmore, and Joseph Bonaparte was a frequent visitor."

In 1773 Bessonett started the stage coach line between Philadelphia and New York. He advertised "unparalleled speed from Philadelphia to New York in two days: $4.00. Comfort and safety assured."

During the Revolutionary War, General Cadwallader was posted at Bristol with 3,000 men in December, 1776. Radcliffe Street swarmed with soldiers. The wounded were cared for in private homes and in the Friends Meeting.

The humblest citizen knew instinctively what George Washington confided in secret only to his brother, "The game is almost up." Even Philadelphians were fleeing their homes and Bristol was much closer to the expected invaders.

It was a frightened, oddly expectant Christmas Day. A sleet storm moved in, worsened after dark. Cadwallader was to cross at Bristol with his three battalions and a New England brigade. Their mission was to engage the British near Bordentown and thus divert them from helping the enemy at Trenton. Cadwallader persisted in his attempts to cross at one of the nearby ferry points, though the ice-choked current made a crossing impossible.

But, twenty miles north of Bristol, General Washington crossed and marched to a swift, brilliant success at Trenton. It was the turning point of the American Revolution. Cadwallader sent the first report of the great victory to Philadelphia from Bristol on the morning of December 26.

Excitement along the river front did not end with the war. There was the trial run in 1787 of John Fitch's first steam-propelled boat. He had previously invented, within Bucks County, the first successful model steamboat.

One of Bristol's most colorful developments of the eighteenth century was Bath Springs. This famous spa brought Bristol its first taste of "high society" and the patronage of an early "international set." Named for the famous mineral waters at Bath, England, Bath Springs was located just half a mile northwest of Bristol. By 1720, the spa was known for its medicinal qualities, but these did not receive widespread

Grundy, aged 95, with the author, in front of the famed painting, "Washington Crossing the Delaware" by Emanuel Leutze, now on loan from the Metropolitan Museum of Art to the Washington Crossing Park Commission, Washington Crossing, Pennsylvania.

popularity until 1783, when Dr. Benjamin Rush read a medical paper on their healing powers.

In 1807 the springs were purchased by Dr. Joseph Minnick, who built the celebrated Bath Springs Hotel. In 1810 he added a race track and the resort became the nation's most fashionable watering place. The track played a big part in the town's exciting history. The owner of a farm near Bristol imported the immortal horse "Messenger" which he purchased from a brother of the Duke of York.

When Philadelphia became the nation's capital in 1790, it was natural for ambassadors and foreign representatives to look outside the city for a relaxing and social atmosphere. They found both in fashionable Bath Springs and a glamorous era followed.

Don Francisco Sarmiento, Spanish ambassador to the United States, settled here. He married Catherine Craig, the aunt of James Craig, who had built the colonnaded house that became the central part of the Farmers National Bank Building, later merged with the Fidelity-Philadelphia Trust Company. The ambassador's successor, Senor de Onis, lived at 235 Radcliffe, the brick house now owned and charmingly restored by Miss Georgine MacMichael.

De Onis had two beautiful daughters. One provided the town's most discussed social event. Her wedding date had been set when her fiance, a Spanish officer, was ordered into active service and could not be present. The harried father of the bride found an unusual solution. He represented his son-in-law at the wedding here while the sister of the groom substituted for the bride in Spain!

Several of Bristol's colonial homes are still in existence. The one generally regarded as the oldest is the Stanford K. Runyan house at 910 Radcliffe Street. Built in 1768 it has been superbly restored by the Runyans.

Other interesting old dwellings along the Delaware are the Morris house at 722 Radcliffe Street, once owned by Thomas

A. Cooper, the English actor; and the Keene home, built in 1816, a residence visited frequently by Joseph Bonaparte. He traveled to the mansion by sailing down-river from his Bordentown home on a splendid barge rowed by four oarsmen, with both the American and French flags flying.

In October 1830 Bristol celebrated the opening of the Delaware Division of the Pennsylvania canal, running from Bristol to Easton, and in 1834, the first railroad, the Pennsylvania, came to town. On February 21, 1861, President-elect Abraham Lincoln passed through Bristol on this railroad en route from Trenton to Philadelphia. A large crowd gathered at the station to see him.

This was Bristol, the town of gracious history, that Joe Grundy called "home."

Grundy's love for his community did not end with his death on March 3, 1961. The millions left to charity under his will including the establishment of both the Margaret R. Grundy Memorial Library and the Radcliffe Street home as a museum, are simply extensions of his interest in good citizenship in general and in his home town in particular.

This "side" of Joe Grundy had always been known to his close friends and neighbors, but it had remained largely unknown to the general public who met the man only through myths and sensational headlines. He always supported the cultural and recreational as well as the industrial development of his home state. His philosophy of public service is summed up in a worn clipping, carried by him for sixty-eight years and before that by his father. It reads, "Citizenship brings with it duties not unlike those we owe to our neighbor and to our God. He who cannot spare time to public concerns will perhaps find that he may become the prey of public plunderers, and he who indolently cares not who administers the government of his city will be living falsely and in the neglect of his highest duty as a citizen."

Although Senator Grundy had many interests of national

and international scope, it was his home town, Bristol, that came first. He served as a member of the Borough Council for more than thirty years. As the active head of the two Bristol banks he gave wise counsel as well as financial advice to many a local family.

How much does the town of Bristol owe to Senator Grundy? His gifts were quiet ones, his good works slipping by almost unnoticed and with matter-of-fact acceptance.

A reporter for an independent Bucks County newspaper interviewed Joe Grundy in 1909 and commented, "His life is a fine example to young men. Wealthy and influential . . . he gives patriotism and good government to his fellow citizens by consistently raising the standards of quality and executive efficiency of candidates. Never has there been a contest after election nor a ballot box opened . . . He is a millionaire and maybe more—and a life of ease and divertissement would seem to beckon. Perhaps it does—but he doesn't yield. Instead his life is one of service.

"And Joseph Ridgway Grundy, asking and receiving nothing—and refusing honors other men plan and struggle for, fights and spends because he loves his country, state, county and neighbors. He is a . . . . refreshing character to contemplate. An example to give pause to idle and wasteful scions and a monument and lighthouse for those who wish to know how."

Grundy was anxious that Bristol be modernized and, since such developments were costly even in 1909, he personally spent the then very large sum of $76,000 for improvements of roads and bridges, and acquiring rights-of-way for new streets. There were many $25,000 gifts for parks, for a new post office, for civic projects; $60,000 for fire fighting equipment, and a quarter of a million for the municipal building.

In getting things done quickly and well, Joe Grundy was apt to be tactless. When he became convinced that new fire fighting equipment was a real need in Bristol, he ordered it without consulting anyone, and paid the bill himself. Such a gesture inevitably ruffled the feelings of the fire chief and his volunteers. This type of action accounted for much of the opposition to the generous gestures of the Pennsylvanian. Whether it was fire engines to protect his town, or legislation to protect the industries in his state, Grundy following his own counsel, decided what should be done, did it, and paid the bill. Unfortunately for him and fortunately for his opponents, he serenely, even contemptuously, disregarded the public relations aspects of such ventures.

Years of experience left him with little respect for the efficiency of committees. He concluded that the best way to get things done was to do them himself. This conviction explains the obvious weakness of some of his political appointments, the "yes" men he could manage. He had learned, the hard way, that many of the other type, the strong-minded candidates, would win his support by agreeing to carry out his policies. Grundy, relying on their promises would use his own money and political power to put them in office. This they invariably forgot.

Gratitude, Grundy concluded, was something you might hope for but should never expect. Certainly the Pennsylvanian felt it in abundance for his family, his home town and his state. He expressed this by a continuing effort to convince the world that Pennsylvania's emblem, the keystone, was the literal representation of the state's place in American history.

Grundy's Bristol residence, 610 Radcliffe Street, the Margaret R. Grundy Memorial Museum and proposed adjoining library.

CHAPTER 9

THE POWERFUL PMA

The provocative initials of the Pennsylvania Manufacturers Association evoke sharply different reactions for many a Pennsylvanian. The high standing of the organization throughout its early years has been whittled down by several factors. One was the questionable activities of a few of its employees; another, the growing success of the Democratic Party in Pennsylvania. Perhaps it was inevitable that any association so successful and so powerful would be feared, envied and criticized. And of course, bigness invites attack.

From the first, PMA bore the stamp of Joe Grundy's political and economic philosophy, and its rise was in large measure due to the driving energy of this one man. He was convinced that the strength of unified action by the manufacturers was necessary to combat the growing power of the "reform" groups. These first sprang up across the country around the beginning of the twentieth century as the result of criticisms of monopolistic tendencies of big business during the lusty 1890s. The highly vocal groups, although comparatively few in number, had articulate leaders whose controversial charges gained widespread publicity. At first their protests about labor conditions made little impression upon elected officials who looked to the industries involved for the funds necessary to secure their elections.

However, toward the end of the first decade of the twentieth century the impact of these complaints was finally being felt in the legislatures of most states. New child labor laws had come into being; investigations to study working conditions had been organized, all with good intentions and many to good effect.

Joe Grundy, aware that reformers sometimes go too far in their zeal, decided that Pennsylvania's industrialists had better do something to protect themselves from excessive welfare efforts. He believed that they should support any measure which would "promote industry or improve the conditions of industrial workers without endangering that first essential to their comfort and happiness—wages." He insisted "if the source of wages be impoverished, the flow of wages will be diminished." In other words, as he frequently repeated, "the 'uplifters' were about to kill the goose that laid the golden egg."

Grundy concluded that an association was necessary not to resist the needs of the workers but to try to prevent excessive legislative burdens from hindering the further expansion of industry or causing it to leave the state.

Out of such convictions developed a temporary organization, headed by the Pennsylvanian, "to consider the advisability of forming an association of manufacturers of Pennsylvania for the purpose of promoting and protecting its members."

No one is justified in being critical more than fifty years after the fact, but if on the afternoon of October 19, 1909, the seven industrialists who met at the Hotel Senate in Harrisburg had decided also to promote an association for the political education of Pennsylvania citizens as to the benefits derived from the state's industrial growth, the PMA and the Republican Party in Pennsylvania might be in a much stronger position today.

It is apparent, by hindsight, always an easy form of perspective, that Senator Grundy's singleness of purpose made him overlook one important fact. That is the necessity for doing a public relations job for the man in the street, as well as the men in the legislative halls. Some of his opponents, less candid than he and, to put it bluntly, frequently less honest, dressed up their political ambitions in the glamour of so-called "nonpartisan groups," and "good government" reformers.

Grundy considered these moves hypocritical and scorned

those who used them. However, he ignored the well-meaning but uninformed citizen who took the impressive words of all "reformers" at face value.

The motto of the newly formed PMA was simplicity itself: "Manufacturing is the keystone of the Keystone State." On January 10, 1910, at the first annual meeting of the organization, Joe Grundy was elected president and the members unanimously agreed on a resolution which explains the purpose, action and achievements of the Pennsylvania Manufacturers Association. "The secretary shall notify the joint committee of the Senate and the House of Representatives of the Commonwealth of Pennsylvania which was appointed to consider and report upon a revision of the corporation and revenue laws of the Commonwealth that a committee of our Association would like to appear before said committee to be heard on matters affecting the interests of our Association."

There were two classes of membership in the organization—individuals, and firms and corporations directly engaged in manufacturing in Pennsylvania. Also admitted were trade and local associations which represented manufacturing interests in the state. Dues were 10 cents per employee. "The entire management and control of the Association [is] invested in the Executive Committee who shall appoint and fix the compensation of all employees and discharge the same at will." Each committee member was to serve for one year with elections taking place at annual meetings. The amount of annual dues paid determined the voting power, each member having one vote for every dollar of dues paid.

Grundy lost no time in appointing a special committee to make a study of the issue of a capital stock tax. This, in essence, was the concern of the Association and Grundy, throughout all the years of his connections with it. The tax has a long history within the Commonwealth. In 1849 a supposedly temporary law to tax the capital stock of industrial concerns for a five-year period had been passed by the legislature. Forty years later the tax was still in operation and many businessmen considered the condition of the state's industries deplorable. This was the situation which Joe Grundy had heard discussed by his father throughout his childhood. He listened to stories about the number of industries that had left the state in order to escape this tax burden, while some others simply failed.

Joe's father had been a persistent Harrisburg visitor in his lobbying efforts to improve the tax situation. Finally, in 1881, a revenue commission was established by the legislature to study the problem and make recommendations. Two years later the commission did recommend a repeal of this levy on manufacturers. However, nothing more happened for six years.

Meanwhile a new face appeared in the legislative halls at Harrisburg. It was that of twenty-one-year-old Joe Grundy who started his weekly visits in 1884, the year of his majority.

One cannot believe that our youthful, dedicated manufacturer was in any way responsible for what happened in 1889, but this is known. In that year capital engaged in manufacturing was exempted from the five-mill levy by the state legislature when Democratic Governor Robert C. Pattison signed the measure. From that time on, manufacturing flourished. Old industries expanded; new concerns appeared in the Commonwealth.

Two decades later with "reformers" demanding huge sums for social legislation, Grundy foresaw where officials would go to pay for these programs—the industries. Hence his interest in preventing the possible repeal of the tax exemption.

Some critics, in their eagerness to emphasize only the self-serving motives of such an organization as the PMA, are more comfortable in assuming that there were no humanitarian interests among the members of the manufacturing association. The fact is that industry was the prime mover of a law vesting the government with authority to appoint an industrial commission to investigate the causes of accidents in industry and to recommend improvements and adequate compensation for the injured worker.

In the year 1911, one of the bills which the Association worked to defeat was the eight-hour bill. This was in 1911 when the eight-hour-a-day work period, taken for granted today, was an innovation. The device which the Association used to defeat this bill was one which they resorted to time and again to defeat proposals. It is an accepted technique today, practiced by all types of groups for various purposes. The Association notified manufacturers throughout the state that the bill was coming up. It pointed out the adverse features and urged an expression of protest. This resulted in the flood of telegrams and letters that, then as today, persuades legislators to act on proposed legislation.

Another feature of the Association's work was to keep appraised of those proposals which, although temporarily defeated, would inevitably come up again. For example, in 1913 it was known that the industrial commission was working on a workmen's compensation measure for presentation to the session, so the Association's executive committee appointed another special committee to draft its own compensation bill for submission to the industrial commission. Experts were hired to draw up its terms and frequently such experts were paid by individuals. One suspects that the individual who often footed these bills was Joe Grundy.

The Pennsylvanian has left his own account of labor legislation in the state:

"In Pennsylvania the first serious mention of workmen's compensation legislation was heard during the John K. Tener campaign for Governor in 1910. I was in Washington very frequently in 1909 and 1910, and was in constant communication with Senator Boies Penrose, who was naturally interested in the protection of Pennsylvania's labor and industries. Senator Aldrich, chairman of the Finance Committee, was on the eve of retirement and had delegated to Senator Penrose, ranking member of the committee, the direction of that committee's affairs. Congress being almost continually in session, Senator

Penrose was able to give very little time to matters in Pennsylvania, relying upon his associates of the Republican Party to prosecute the campaign for Mr. Tener.

"The platform of a political candidate or of a party is virtually a promissory note, payable within the period of service of the successful candidate or party, and as I have said, it was agreed by those upon whom Sentor Penrose relied that the platform upon which Mr. Tener and his associates stood should contain a guarantee of legislation granting compensation to workmen killed or injured in the course of employment. As a representative of the industrial interests which had made Pennsylvania pre-eminent among American states, and also as a Republican interested in the success of Mr. Tener's campaign, I was in complete accord with that thought.

"After Governor Tener assumed office in 1911, he named a commission empowered to study the proposition of compensating victims of industrial accidents. The chairman of that commission was David A. Reed, of Pittsburgh, now United States Senator, and one of the members was George C. Hetzel, of Chester, representing the large labor and industrial interests in his district and who was named at the suggestion of the Pennsylvania Manufacturers Association.

It is not amiss to say that the Pennsylvania Manufacturers Association was the only organization in the State which really interested itself in the proposed legislation, other than organizations and associations devoted to labor. In support of that statement I present the fact that our association engaged and paid not only Miles Dawson, an actuary of wide reputation, but several lawyers, who went thoroughly into a study of compensation and drew up a bill.

"At that time there were two lines of thought in the matter of compensation, the German and the English, and while after their exhaustive studies our experts believed that the German plan met the Pennsylvania conditions more satisfactorily than the English, we agreed to go along when the Commission chose as its model the New Jersey Compensation law, which followed the English trend.

"The report of the committee was submitted to the 1913 session of the Legislature, and a bill prepared under the committee's direction was passed speedily by the Senate and sent to the House, where it was passed after changes were made which necessitated the appointment of a conference committee so that differences of the two bodies might be ironed out. These were not serious differences, and it was the consensus of opinion that they could be speedily adjusted and the bill passed. From a clear sky, however, came the declaration of the late Senator William E. Crow, of Fayette County, that the bill in its then form was objectionable. The end of the session was close at hand, and because it was impossible to satisfy Senator Crow's demands, the bill fell. It should be mentioned, however, that the representatives from Bucks County, in which I live, voted favorably on the Senate and House roll-calls, and would have voted favorably had the bill come up for final passage.

"Before going on with the story of the Compensation Bill. I should refer briefly to other humane legislation. Pennsylvania's statute books prior to 1913 contained no completely adequate laws covering the employment of women. During the 1913 legislative session an organization known as the Consumers' League interested itself in enactment of legislation of that kind, its affairs at Harrisburg being under the direction of a Miss Sanville, an estimable woman, who accomplished a wonderful work.

"Pennsylvania manufacturing interests were not opposed to what were then popularly known as 'women's laws,' and our representatives sat with Miss Sanville in one of the ante-rooms of the Senate chamber at Harrisburg and wrote a bill which became a law with scarcely a dissenting vote, and was acclaimed as being one of the most perfect and constructive pieces of legislation enacted in the United States, affecting the employment of women. And it is a matter of record that the Senator and members of the House from my county voted for the measure.

"The administration of Governor Brumbaugh came to an end and that of Governor William C. Sproul began. Mr. Sproul and I had always been the best of friends and I supported him, of course, in his campaign for election. During one of our casual meetings he volunteered the information that he was quite satisfied with the workmen's compensation law then on the statute books, and therefore I was more than a little surprised during the 1919 legislative session to learn that a member of Mr. Sproul's official family had submitted an entirely new bill. This bill raised compensation rates all along the line, particularly as to the anthracite industry.

"The Pennsylvania Manufacturers Association, of which I was president for many years, was not against compensation, nor did it oppose a fair revision, and the differences which developed at that time were chiefly the results of misunderstandings between industrialists and public officials. Had greater frankness and candor been evidenced on the part of those who backed the bill, all friction would have been avoided. However, the bill was finally passed, and legislative records will show that among those whose votes put it over were those of the Senator and Assemblymen from my home county of Bucks.

"From the 1919 session until that of 1925 no additions of moment were made to compensation legislation in Pennsylvania, but other States had gone ahead very materially. Aware of that fact, I suggested a revision of the Pennsylvania law. However, the same interests which had knifed the original bill in 1913 were antagonistic and nothing came of my efforts along the lines indicated.

"In 1927 all factions and interests were committed to revision in advance of the session, and a really meritorious bill became a law without difficulty.

"In brief, this is the history of labor legislation of Pennsylvania. More often than was necessary the real issue was fogged and clouded because of the injection of political irrelevances.

"No cause of disturbance to the general welfare of a people is so destructive as industrial warfare. It is a two-edged sword, cutting both ways. As an employer I have never pursued a course inimical to the interests of labor, and for years have favored the granting of greater benefits to men and women and children in industry. For information along this line I can do no more than refer inquiries to present and past employees of the manufactury I conducted at Bristol for so many years. Long before Mr. [T. R.] Roosevelt coined the 'square deal' phrase I conducted myself upon the infinitely older theory of the Golden Rule. I defy political opponents to prove otherwise, but suggest that proof does not lie in material issued by my enemies."

CHAPTER 10

LOBBYING IN HARRISBURG

Over the years an astonishing amount of material was issued by Grundy's enemies. The term "Grundyism" was successfully parlayed by the political opposition into something sinister and evil. In fact, Grundyism, or more properly the Grundy credo, stood for one thing, the protection of industry with special emphasis on the welfare of those manufacturing concerns within the Commonwealth of Pennsylvania.

Grundy was whole-heartedly convinced that two things were needed for industrial protection—low taxes in the state so that industry would not be overburdened, and high protective tariff on the national level. To achieve these ends, he counted on campaign contributions toward helping to get the men favorable to industry elected to office and to accomplish the lobbying needed to educate those in office to see the over-all importance of encouraging industry.

Grundy's techniques are today recognized as the most effective means of achieving political victory. Labor copied the unity idea to find its greatest power in such an organization as COPE. It has seen the effectiveness of campaign contributions and efforts to elect men in favor of labor to political office.

To learn first hand about Grundy's activities as a state lobbyist, the writer sought an interview with one of Pennsylvania's most distinguished Democrats, the Honorable Hiram G. Andrews, venerable Speaker of the House. Andrews was gracious and articulate.

"Joe Grundy," he said wonderingly and smiled. "I remember when I was a reporter for the Philadelphia *North American* and on the prowl for Grundy. In those days lobbyists had the run of the floor in both Senate and House, whereas today they must sit decorously on the sidelines. One time Grundy was unusually busy on the House floor, talking to various members. I did some lip reading, made some good guesses and wrote a critical article about Grundy's apparent comments and activities right on the floor of the House. He got the point, all right, because he never appeared on the House floor for the rest of the session."

Speaker Andrews gazed out the window. "Funny thing," he went on, "I didn't see him again for years. Then one day during the Pinchot administration, we met outside the Governor's office. I was surprised that he remembered me, even more surprised by his cordiality. He had an amazing memory, asked me to sit down and have a talk with him. I did. Joe Grundy," he said, thoughtfully, "was a man without malice." He repeated the phrase softly, "a man without malice."

Andrews said that as an editor in Johnstown, Pennsylvania, and a Democrat, he, like many another upstate editor, used Grundy as a "bugbear."

"Why," Andrews grinned, "around 1910 all we had to do to win an upstate election was use the name 'Grundy' to describe 'that predatory man' way down in Bucks County."

The format remained the same throughout the next forty years. For example, in 1930 the *Sunday Dispatch* of Harrisburg carried an editorial on the front page. Above the heading was printed:

"There is ONE ISSUE and ONLY ONE issue, in this year's campaign, an issue transcending in importance every other and minor issue. THAT ISSUE is

G R U N D Y I S M"

There followed half a column of irrelevancies, then came the usual climax.

"Grundy is the idol of organized money. He is the choice of all those dark and sinister forces that operate in the background of American life. He stands for, typifies, personifies all of the things that the wage earning masses of Republican Pennsylvania oppose and condemn."

Reminiscing in the fall of 1961, "Hi" Andrews, as the Speaker is affectionately called, spoke quietly and with the unruffled calm of years and wisdom:

"Grundy antedated Madison Avenue. He created an image although they didn't use the term in those days. He was the man who represented Pennsylvania's industrial potentials, represented all manufacturers large and small. Today's lobbyists are individual operators for a single industry or profession. Many of them think with a small brush. Grundy represented them all."

"Tell me frankly," I asked, "Do you believe that Joe Grundy profited personally from his political efforts?"

Senator Andrews answered slowly. "His knowledge undoubtedly gave him access to investment opportunities—but I don't believe Grundy ever took a crooked penny in his life."

The Grundy Speaker Andrews saw, in the maturity of his own eighty-odd years, was a different figure from the man he had visualized in his early reporting days for the *North American*. At that time Grundy was the target in all child labor issues and as he described himself, the "pet hate of the *North American*, a stormy petrel newspaper whose career ended when it was purchased and abruptly discontinued by the *Public Ledger*."

In 1930 Grundy made a statement on his child labor position and pointed to his county's voting record (admittedly dictated by him) to back up his points: "A great deal has been said and written on the subject of child labor legislation in Pennsylvania, and many individuals and agencies have taken credit for its enactment. It is of record that as industrialists we went to Harrisburg in 1905 and urged the Legislature to raise the minimum age of employment from thirteen to fourteen years, it being our belief that no matter how badly handicapped they may be in life's circumstances, children are at least entitled to a grammar school education. It is not out of place for me to say at this juncture that I consider Pennsylvania's school system a most important factor in this State's development.

" . . . The 1905 Legislature increased the minimum age to fourteen, as we requested, and thereafter matters drifted along until the session of 1913, when the National Child Labor Association interested itself in modernizing laws relating to children in industry. Representatives of our organization conferred with women representing the association and the result was a piece of legislation which, we had reason to believe, would encounter absolutely no opposition in the Legislature and would give to the children everything asked by the National Association. But this bill did not go through with the ease characterizing the bill covering women in employment. Mysterious opposition developed.

"Our co-operative efforts having made us joint sponsors of this meritorious measure, the Manufacturers Association was naturally interested in learning who or what was luring away votes and organizing resistance, and our investigations revealed that one of the turbulently violent advocates of the bill had suddenly changed front and for reasons of its own was working secretly for defeat."

Then Grundy added his own comment on the subject of Grundyism. He wrote:

"As long ago as the year 1900, if my memory serves me correctly, the *North American* flailed me upon any and every occasion. Its editors were sufficiently astute to know that to be virile a crusade must have a living objective. They knew, too, that if they adopted the role of a 'benefactor of mankind' they would sell more newspapers, and to sell more newspapers is to procure more advertising and more money for that advertising. The editors coined the word 'Grundyism,' which means very little to Pennsylvanians of today, but at the time the *North American's* attacks were most virulent it was construed by that newspaper to cover the entire gamut of political and industrial sins."

Grundy was modest. The term "Grundyism" continued to be used in political campaigns into the 1960s. As late as March 9, 1962, *Time* magazine, in an article on the approaching Pennsylvania gubernatorial contest, defined the term as "stiff-collared conservatism." However, throughout the first two decades of the twentieth century it symbolized all the political sins, including the employment of child labor.

Questioning any aspect of child labor was certain to be regarded as wicked. The phrase evoked strong emotions. It was in a class with "cruelty to children." It still creates an intolerable image—a picture of a helpless child being abused by an inhuman boss. Few politicians in the world would be foolish enough to question any phase of a child labor program.

Yet Joe Grundy both individually and through the organization he headed, the PMA, dared to question the wisdom of some aspects of child labor legislation. The fact that he questioned them at all provided the fuel its proponents needed. They fanned the flames by heart-wringing allegations that kept the public mind away from certain basic facts.

Grundy recognized some very practical problems involved in the sixteen-year-old age requirements. In any current consideration of this subject, we must remember the viewpoint during the early years of this century. Most people, like Grundy, worked ten or twelve hours a day. Today's readers can recall their grandfathers' reminiscences about how they had "started to work at twelve or fourteen" and it "never hurt us a bit."

In all mill towns there was a large percentage of foreign born. Bristol was typical. Joe Grundy knew personally most of the Italian-Americans and Irish-Americans who worked in his mill. They had been accustomed to going to work at a very early age "in the old country," and expected their children to do likewise here. They came to America for an opportunity to make more money. Now they wanted to do exactly that. And the best way to do it was to see that all the children got jobs—the sooner the better. Grundy maintained that each child should be judged by health and mental age, rather than solely "by the clock and the calendar."

Was he motivated by a desire to exploit cheaper labor or by a conviction that each, employer and employee, had the right to make his own decision as long as bodily harm and cruelty were not involved?

Discussions with many who once worked in the Grundy mill have convinced the writer that the latter was true in Grundy's case. However, Grundy's weakness, his refusal to compromise, hurt his position. His faith in the conditions in his own mill, model for the times, blinded him to the existence of child exploitation and the regulation needed in many another plant.

There were a few others who braved the protests of the crusaders. One of them was a judge from Schuylkill County, Senator Snyder, who on May 3, 1915 said in the Pennsylvania Senate:

"You know we hear a great deal about boys, [in summer] being denied the right to [go] swimming, etc. That is very beautiful, but on the other hand, not an uplifter, not a philanthropist in this state has stood up in the Senate or House providing a place for these boys and girls to go to school. One fourth of them can't go because there are no schools . . . Now, they say Pennsylvania ought to build schools . . . [that] is a poor business proposition and the uplifters won't help . . . the newspapers won't help—no exploitation there . . . Not a single person, not a woman interested in this great uplifting movement has a dollar of interest in this great and magnificent wealth that has made this state . . . [They say] Let the state do this . . . This was the condition of Rome, which fed its citizens out of troughs. Now when these uplifters are willing to feed the people, but want to do it at the expense of the state, I am against it . . ."

Senator Snyder said that he was speaking not for the

manufacturers but for boys and girls and their families. He added:

"Let me say to you unless you instill the habits of industry into boys and girls before they are sixteen, unless you keep them employed in school or at work, that boy or girl will amount to very little afterwards . . .

"The accomplishments of men who have revolutionized and made the progress in this country were people who did not attend college and most of them had no school advantages after they were ten years of age. Washington, Jackson, Lincoln, Edison, Wanamaker . . . Education procured by self-effort is a blessing, but education forced is frequently a curse because education can only be appreciated by self-effort after a boy works and realizes the hardship of toil. Then he gets a taste for education and then only education will do him the good that education is intended for. Education to make a drone, which is the intention today, is the curse of our people. Gentlemen, we are getting too many drones in this century. What do I mean by drones the people who want to live at the expense of the producer."

Senator Snyder thundered on: "They say a boy can't work before he's sixteen and yet under the latest census 35,000 boys and girls were married under 14 . . . [In] the war of 1860, out of 2,785,000—845,000 were only sixteen . . . They were able enough to go down to Gettysburg and defend the Constitution of the United States so that you and I could be here and legislate that boys of their age could not work before they were sixteen years of age!"

Senator Snyder, who served as the Chairman of the Judiciary Special Committee, added an observation on Grundy's mill:

". . . It has been urged and strongly proclaimed in the newspapers that the Chairman of the Judiciary Special Committee represents the manufacturers. He does not represent the manufacturer in the person of Joseph Grundy any more than you do . . . The activities of Mr. Grundy, I find upon investigation, were altogether at the request of the combined manufacturers in this state. The conditions in his mill . . . as far as health and sanitation and the welfare of every person in that factory are concerned [are] better than any other . . . . ."

Senator Snyder's viewpoint is borne out by J. H. Hoffman, Superintendent of Schools of Bucks County in 1930, who wrote:

"In my administration of the schools of Bucks County, Mr. Grundy has been ever anxious to have schools and politics kept separate. I have always been able to count on his moral support for every forward step taken in our schools. His welfare work for public education in his own town of Bristol is . . . well known. Upon numerous occasions he has given liberally and aided materially in providing for better school facilities. His welfare work there is of common knowledge. A model continuation school is operating [in] a most efficient and practical way in his Bristol mills. This is a definite contradiction to the charges that Mr. Grundy is opposed to the Child Labor Laws. I know that this is absolutely untrue from what he does for the children of his town . . . [His] leadership can be trusted at all times to do the right thing for the children of Pennsylvania . . ."

He certainly "did the right thing" in his mill for many young people who wanted to continue their studies. One was his heir, present executor and secretary of the Grundy Foundation, Ed Rummler. Another was Louis B. Whitby, also an heir. Whitby started as an office boy at fourteen, took advantage of the opportunity to have a Grundy scholarship in college textile training and then went into the service in World War I. When he returned he was startled and gratified to be presented by Joe Grundy with the accumulated salary for every day of his service. Whitby became not only a prominent industrialist but also a close friend and confidant of his boss, and, incidentally, a millionaire.

CHAPTER 11

THE ART OF POLITICS

Was Joe Grundy a "king-maker," the man-behind-the-scenes who hand-picked governors of Pennsylvania and at least one president? Facts indicate that he was. A man who has raised more money for a political party than anyone else in United States history would inevitably be in a position of sufficient power to do exactly that. And why not? Grundy's reasoning had common sense behind it.

If a man does the work, raises large sums of money and contributes heavily himself to any cause, he is understandably interested in seeing that the funds are used for the purpose he has in mind, whether it involves building a hospital or a political administration sympathetic to industry. Grundy was sincere in his belief that such an administration was best not only for the employers but also for the wage-earners. In other words, what was good for business was good for the state and the country.

In the 1950's, the late Charlie Wilson, former General Motors Executive, while serving in the cabinet as a dollar-a-year man, got into difficulties by making just such a statement in reference to the automobile industry. Later as the problems of that industry affected the whole national economy, the truth of Wilson's statement was recognized, if not admitted.

Grundy judged all political candidates by the same standards. He believed that, if they favored industry, they would probably do a good job for the state or the nation. He appraised potential candidates by one major test—did they regard "manufacturing as an honorable business" with the manufacturers having "as much right to urge our opinions upon legislators as have the people who work *for* us and those whose agitating livelihoods seem to be dependent upon their work *against* us."

Grundy believed in the citizen's right to lobby and, in his eyes, the chief reason for lobbying was the need of a protective tariff. This viewpoint, considered old-fashioned during the past three decades, has gained some support under the surprising banner of labor. An item in *Time* magazine of February 3, 1961, states:

"When the conservative, protectionist Nationwide Committee on Import-Export Policy met last week in Washington, some twenty labor unions were represented. Breaking away from basic A.F.L.-C.I.O. policy, which remains free trade, the unions joined the committee's trade-association membership in recommending legislation to the new Congress to encourage higher tariffs and more import quotas . . .

"The stand of the newly protectionist unions is put simply and forcefully by Amalgamated Clothing Workers President Jacob Potofsky, an oldtime free-trader himself: 'Do we have to stand by idly while our jobs are destroyed? Do our cutters have to continue to cut fabrics made in Japan?' Potofsky's answer: a resounding 'No.' The clothing workers voted to take direct action against imported goods . . ."

Grundy would have welcomed Potofsky's answer! The Pennsylvanian's high tariff dedication back in 1912 explains his behind-the-scenes activities throughout Woodrow Wilson's terms as president. They led up to that famous caucus in the Blackstone Hotel in Chicago when Wilson's successor, Warren G. Harding, was nominated for president on the Republican ticket. Whenever questioned about his political maneuvering in that historic, smoke-filled meeting on Friday, June 11, 1920, Grundy always smiled that tight-lipped shy, but knowing smile and deprecated his role in the selection of the nominee.

The facts indicate otherwise. To evaluate them, the reader must keep in mind the attitude of Grundy toward Wilson, the theorist. The Pennsylvanian had little respect for the professorial type in public office. He regarded the former Princeton professor as a "swivel chair economist."

Grundy's antipathy to the professor was of long standing. Wilson, Professor of Jurisprudence and Political Economics at Princeton and a prominent Democrat, had published several articles on the benefits of free trade. This point of view horrified Grundy, but impressed "the English free-traders." They invited Professor Wilson to an important dinner at the exclusive London Cobden Club, whose members were interested in achieving lower tariff rates in the United States. Throughout his life, Grundy remained convinced that the theoretically-minded educator was impressed by the compliments of the suave Britishers and deluded by their basically competitive motives.

In spite of his English background, Grundy was a jealously devoted American. With many family ties in England and years of business and travel there behind him, Grundy had an intimate knowledge of the English tariff position and the motive behind the compliments so pleasant to the Princeton professor.

All of these facts Grundy discussed with his good friend, Boies Penrose, United States Senator from Pennsylvania. Of this long-standing friendship, Grundy said, "My relationship with Boies Penrose, was over such a period and so intimate as to create an admiration and respect which amounted to a deep and abiding affection."

According to Senator Grundy, "Penrose never went back on Pennsylvania."

It might be well at this point to take a fresh, objective look at Penrose, one of the most disparaged figures in Pennsylvania's political history. People are apt to condemn the name of Penrose without having the slightest idea why. The uninformed think of him as a tough, cigar-smoking illiterate political boss. Old timers remember him with a huge panama hat on his head driving around Philadelphia in a red Winton with the top down. Cigar-smoking political boss he was, one who was tough and often ruthless, but the picture ends there. He was first of all a physically impressive man, being over six-feet-four-inches in height and weighing some three hundred pounds. He had dark hair, piercing dark eyes and an aristocratic profile. Far from being uneducated and illiterate, he had, according to columnist Mark Sullivan, "one of the best minds that ever functioned on the Senate floor."

In Senate debate he invariably defeated his opponent by the directness of his thinking and his speech. He never compromised and never winced from the frequent blows that came his way. His reaction to insurgents and reformers was not hatred—rather he considered them weak and hypocritical.

Penrose was no poor boy who starved and worked hard for an education. Born in upper social circles, he was prepared for college by private tutors. At Harvard he was an honor man in a class of more than two hundred, and one of five selected to deliver commencement orations. His scholarship stood him in good stead in Senate debate and in the sparring bouts he enjoyed with members of the press.

Here was a politician who was fond of reading Latin authors in the original and whose libraries in both Washington and Philadelphia were extensive. His vast knowledge of his state and his country was based on historical research and his study of the development of the municipal institutions of Philadelphia, read as a paper before the Historical Society of Pennsylvania, still is regarded as a definitive work. Penrose's first love was the Republican organization and he was constantly working to maintain its leadership and strength. The extent of his devotion to it was revealed one evening as he walked along Pennsylvania Avenue with a friend. A platoon of soldiers from Fort Meyer, with flags flying and band playing, swung into the avenue from Fifteenth Street and the friend exclaimed how the sight aroused his admiration and patriotism. Penrose agreed enthusiastically but added, "One other thing that excites my unbounded admiration and my deepest emotion is a well-drilled body of voters marching in perfect and obedient order to the polls."

Such bluntness on the part of any man in public or even semi-public life is always subject to attack. George Wharton

Pepper, the distinguished Philadelphia lawyer, provided a lucid explanation on this point when he stated in his autobiography, *Philadelphia Lawyer*:

". . . Cautious men in political office are careful to hedge on public questions. Some, of course, are more honest and have the courage of their convictions. Senator Penrose was of this sort. He spoke out bluntly and took the consequences. He once remarked that he was so used to being kicked on the backside that he never turned around to see who did it."

The comment might easily have applied to Grundy except that the Quaker would never have used the indelicate term, "backside."

Joe Grundy and Boies Penrose had many things in common besides their love of the Republican organization and their suites at the New Willard in Washington, D. C. Both had distinguished backgrounds, education, polish, and both were teased considerably about their bachelorhood. On the latter subject, Penrose would say, "I am not at all adverse to marriage and shall be glad to consider any candidate the Republican organization may care to recommend."

Much scandal was spread about Penrose in connection with his alleged associations with women. Unfavorable public reaction to the man stemmed largely from an article in *Collier's* weekly in 1931, ten years after his death. It described a scene on the Senator's yacht and pictured Penrose's appearance before his guests, entirely nude, ready for a dip in the ocean. His former secretary, Leighton C. Taylor, Esq., answered this allegation in an article on Penrose in *The Gettysburg Times*. He wrote: "The truth is Senator Penrose never entertained anyone of the opposite sex on his yacht, not even a relative, nor did he entertain women in his various places of abode without a third person present. Not because he didn't admire women, but being a bachelor, he knew that political enemies with frustrated ambition for leadership were watching his every move ready to take advantage of the slightest opportunity to place him in a compromising position and injure him politically."

A true Penrose yacht story is told by the Bristol lawyer, J. Leslie Kilcoyne. He recalls that when as a young man he and a friend were bathing and fishing near Beach Haven, New Jersey, their boat became stuck on a sand bar in an isolated area. Suddenly a large white yacht anchored nearby and two tall men came ashore by dinghy. As the one man stepped out of the boat, young Kilcoyne recognized the tall, frequently photographed Boies Penrose. The famed politician noticed the two boys and their plight, and called out in his booming voice, "What's the matter there, young fellow?"

Kilcoyne replied and asked if the questioner were not Senator Penrose.

Penrose, surprised, said yes and in turn asked, "Where are you from?"

Kilcoyne said, "Bristol."

That was all the big man needed. "Then you are from Joe Grundy's town," he replied.

Kilcoyne said he and his father knew Mr. Grundy.

"A great man," said Penrose, "I will do anything at all to help one of his friends," and the two men proceeded to help push the boat off the sand bar. Penrose explained the point of their anchoring in this isolated location. He said he enjoyed buck bathing and this was a good spot for it.

It is curious that at the same time the defamatory piece was appearing in *Collier's*, articles vilifying Joe Grundy were appearing in the same publication. This was 1931 and one surmises that, with a presidential campaign in the offing, there may have been some opposing political sentiment behind these attacks. Penrose, dead for ten years, could not deny the allegations; and Grundy, the modest Quaker who avoided publicity, never attempted to refute his critics. About these attacks, he said, "When you're paying all your own expenses and supporting the industrial development of Pennsylvania, you don't need to pay attention to what people say about you."

Both Grundy and Penrose were dedicated to the cause of manufacturing in general and Pennsylvania's industries in particular. They were both blunt, Grundy even more so than Penrose, and certainly less tactful. Penrose is quoted as saying of Grundy, "He was the best fund raiser in the history of politics and the worst politician since Julius Caesar."

And yet in dealing with political adversaries, Grundy was in many ways more subtle than Penrose who carried on long-standing feuds including one with Woodrow Wilson. In his reactions, the President was no less childish than Penrose. After his election, Wilson had stated: "I am going to give the people of this great republic a chance to forget Boies Penrose for a while. It will do them good and me good."

Penrose said of Wilson, "This man has brains . . . [but] he won't have anybody around him who isn't a weak reflection of himself. I don't like Wilson—don't like his breed."

There are many examples of the child-like behavior of the two politicians. One is pathetic as well as humorous. Both men had been stricken about the same time and each used a wheelchair. Occasionally when automobile riding, the two chose the same trip, a popular route to Fairfax Court House in Virginia. When during the course of a drive it became necessary for the two cars to pass, Penrose would look the other way, and Mrs. Wilson would cover the President's face with a newspaper or magazine so that the Senator could not see him.

A final exhibition of their deep antipathy took place on Inauguration Day, March 4, 1921. According to custom, Wilson, the outgoing, and Harding the incoming president, rode together from the White House to the Capitol. Because Wilson was partially paralyzed he was unable to make the customary walk with Harding up the Capitol steps and into the Senate Chamber.

On this occasion Harding alighted at the Senate entrance, and Wilson was driven around to the ground floor entrance midway between the Senate and House chambers. There he was lifted from his car and carried inside that part of the Capitol which was closed to visitors. Only a few employed in the building witnessed Wilson's discomfiture.

It was a long walk from this central part of the Capitol to the President's room in the Senate wing. Those present felt it would be too exhausting and far too much of a strain for Wilson whose one leg and arm were practically useless. It was only with the greatest effort and with the help of his aides that he was able to walk at all.

Leighton Taylor, Penrose's secretary, whispered to one of the secret service men in the Wilson party that a wheel-chair was available and that he would be glad to get it. The secret service man agreed and Taylor hurried to Penrose's office where the Senator, Marshall, the outgoing Vice President; Uncle Joe Cannon of Illinois; Senators Brandegee, Knox, Watson, and others were waiting for the arrival of the President so that the inaugural ceremonies could begin.

Breaking in upon this group, Taylor told Penrose that Wilson was out in the corridor having serious difficulty getting to the President's room, and suggested that he lend the President his wheelchair.

Penrose agreed and Taylor rushed to the Wilson party with the chair, but Mr. Wilson's mind was still functioning notwithstanding his impaired means of locomotion. He knew that Senator Penrose, like himself, was using a wheelchair, and when offered the chair by Taylor, he asked a member of his party whose it was. Upon being told it belonged to Penrose, Wilson refused to use it, and delayed the ceremonies by twenty minutes as he laboriously made his way to the President's room.

Penrose could afford to be gracious. He, together with his Quaker friend, Joe Grundy, had triumphed over the professor from Princeton. The election of Harding was, in their opinion, a victory for Pennsylvania and the high tariff that would protect its industries.

Wilson knew that Inauguration Day was a triumphant one for Senator Penrose and for Joe Grundy, the Pennsylvanian who fought steadily, without title, in legislative halls and out, for the protective tariff Wilson repudiated. The President also knew what important roles the two had played in the nomination of his successor, Warren G. Harding.

Harding's inauguration was the end of a long trail. Both Grundy and Penrose had discussed the genial senator from Ohio as a presidential possibility. He had a number of surface qualifications. He was good-looking, pleasant, with a warm personality and a genuine love of people. His newspaper experience gave him a good sense of public relations, and he was honest with a clean record for integrity—a man of his word. What is more, he was an avowed friend of the manufacturing interests. He believed in high tariff. Of this, Penrose and Grundy were sure. On this point, he was the strongest on a long list of presidential hopefuls.

Who first suggested Harding as a candidate—Grundy or Penrose? We do not know. It was Penrose, though, a fellow-Senator, who first approached Harding on the subject.

On a hot afternoon in the summer of 1919, Penrose and his secretary, Taylor, were finishing some tasks in the Senator's apartment in the New Willard Hotel. Penrose was working at his desk when he asked Taylor to telephone Senator Harding at the capitol and ask him to come over.

Harding arrived and Penrose said, "Take off your coat, Senator, and sit down."

Harding did so and Penrose shot out the next question with dramatic suddenness: "Harding, how would you like to be president?"

Harding was startled. He managed an uncertain, "Why, Penrose, I haven't any money and I have my own troubles in Ohio; in fact, I'll be mighty glad and lucky if I can come back to the Senate."

Penrose replied, "You won't need any money. I'll look after that. You will make the McKinley type of candidate. You look the part, you can make a good front-porch type of campaign like McKinley did and we (meaning, undoubtedly, Joe Grundy) will do the rest."

From this point on Penrose and Grundy talked Harding at every opportunity. The big moment for the opening gun of his candidacy was planned by Grundy. It was to be a reception for the Ohioan held at the Pennsylvania Manufacturers Association in Philadelphia and followed by an elaborate dinner. No one could handle such an affair as effectively as Joe Grundy. One of the many contradictions of this self-effacing Quaker was his gourmet's taste and success as a host. He knew how to plan exactly the right foods, the appropriate wines, the music and the general tone of such an affair. His hand was in every detail from the cut of the filet mignon to the seating arrangements.

The big night arrived. Penrose, ill at the time, could not attend but he knew Joe Grundy could be depended upon for such an occasion. A capacity crowd turned out to honor PMA president Grundy. At the auspicious moment, Grundy introduced Harding who made a speech. The Senator from Ohio was apparently trying to emphasize his small town boyhood and community interests for he dwelt at length on his activities as a member of a local band.

Grundy, as usual, kept his observations to himself, but Taylor has given us Penrose's reactions. Taylor took down the speech in shorthand and, as soon as Harding finished speaking, rushed to Penrose's home with his notes. He read the speech to Penrose who listened intently, then volunteered, "He isn't as big a man as I thought he was; he should have talked more about the tariff and not so much about playing the cymbals in the Marion Brass Band."

There is no doubt that, after the speech in Philadelphia, both Grundy and Penrose were somewhat disappointed in Harding, and they kept on looking over the field for candidates. Penrose is known to have attempted to persuade the able Senator Philander Chase Knox of Pennsylvania to be a candidate. But Knox refused to push his own candidacy.

Senator McCormick of Illinois tried to boost the candidacy of Senator Hiram Warren Johnson of California, but neither Grundy nor Penrose approved the choice. In Grundy's judgment, California was a long way from the Keystone State!

During the fall of 1919 Penrose's health failed and he went to Florida, remaining there until April, 1920. However, this undisputed political boss of the regular Republican organization at both state and national levels left the reins in the capable hands of Joe Grundy. The Pennsylvanian, loyal to his trusted political associate, kept the senator informed as to developments and never once attempted to usurp Penrose's power or turn the situation to his own advantage. He was busily making plans for the Republican National Convention of 1920. Penrose was not able to participate in the programming because, on his return from Florida, he was still seriously ill and ordered to stay in bed. His various henchmen, however, kept flooding his home with messages and requests for his advice.

If this seems shocking to present voters, let them remember that this was still the day of the openly acknowledged political boss and that the rule of political leaders of the majority party in Pennsylvania had been dominant in national Republican politics since the days of Simon Cameron, United States Senator from Pennsylvania and Lincoln's Secretary of War. Cameron's mantle fell on Matthew Stanley Quay who became Senator in 1887. Quay's principal lieutenant was Boies Penrose, then a member of the state Senate.

It was in 1897 that Penrose became junior United States Senator from Pennsylvania. Penrose later shared his "boss" mantle with Joe Grundy, but few of the rank and file voters knew this at the time. The influence of the two men was legendary. Both realized that some of this attributed power was mythical. Penrose once said, "There's a lot of fiction connected with the power and influence these fellows say I have, but it will answer our purpose so long as they don't know any better."

Penrose could not wield this power in person at the Republican Convention of 1920 in Chicago because he was too ill to be present. Although General Atterbury, then vice-president of the Pennsylvania Railroad, offered to handle his train arrangements to the convention and Marshall Field volunteered his home as Penrose's headquarters, the senator's physician decided that he could not make the trip. As a matter of fact, throughout the convention week, Penrose was so ill from a complication of diseases that a doctor was in constant attendance; he was not permitted to have any visitors or even talk on the telephone except on two occasions.

Private telephone and wire connections had been set up between his Spruce Street house and the Chicago headquarters of the Pennsylvania delegation. The cost—$4,800 for the six days of the convention—was borne, as usual, by Penrose personally. His secretary, Taylor, manned the Philadelphia end of the telephone.

The idea of Penrose, bedridden in Philadelphia, dictating the nomination of Harding in Chicago, is dramatic and still popularly prevalent in the public mind. But as usual, the quiet Quaker, Grundy, was the man who, more than any other, engineered the nomination of the "high tariff" candidate.

In Chicago the Pennsylvanian was busier than he had ever been in his life. He faced a real challenge because rarely had so many political aspirants been so eager and campaigned so actively for the Republican presidential nomination. Grundy was in an exceedingly difficult position. He had gone to Chicago as the Pennsylvania delegate representing Senator Penrose, the most powerful figure in the Republican party. Penrose's support had long been sought for Governor Sproul who was to be a favorite son candidate of the Pennsylvania delegation.

For some time before the convention, Sproul's Lieutenant Governor, E. E. Beidleman, and W. Harry Baker, Secretary of the Republican State Committee, had been urging Sproul's candidacy on Senator Penrose. They knew better than to urge it on Grundy. He was known to feel that Sproul was weak and susceptible to the viewpoint of the last person with whom he talked. Penrose summed it up, "He won't stay hitched." Grundy was not convinced that he could be depended upon to act for the manufacturing interests of Pennsylvania. Sproul had succeeded Governor Brumbaugh and apparently inherited the latter's animosity toward Grundy.

At any rate, Sproul had many enthusiastic backers. Grundy and Penrose were willing to allow him to play the favorite son role until they were ready to throw the nomination to the selected nominee at just the right moment, but they wanted to be sure that his candidacy would never materialize. Therefore Grundy saw to it that the leading Sproul backers among the Pennsylvania delegates were carefully omitted from meetings with the most powerful figures in the party at the national level.

Meanwhile, the band played on in the Chicago Coliseum where packed galleries eyed the assembling delegates. There were the old faces—Senators Henry Cabot Lodge and Murray Crane from Massachusetts; Slemp of Virginia; and a powerful contingent from Pennsylvania—Knox, Mellon, and the two bitter antagonists, Grundy and Vare. Still older were the wrinkled faces of a few feeble Civil War veterans who stared at the many eager young veteran delegates, fresh from World War I.

Other new faces marched to the floor—two young men of the New York delegation—Fiorello La Guardia and Ogden Mills. After the chaplain prayed and the band played the "Star Spangled Banner," Albert Brown, Director of Community Singing of the Republican League of Massachusetts, rose. He shouted, "Now give three cheers . . . for the greatest country on earth—the United States of America!"

Three times the cheer rang through the Coliseum: "Hurrah for the United States!"

At this point Will H. Hays, of the Republican National Committee intoned, "The next order of business is the reading of the call for the convention."

The seventeenth national convention of the Republican party was under way. Senator Lodge, chosen to be Convention

Chairman, was escorted to the dais by a group of distinguished delegates. None carried the experience and influence of the aristocratic senator from Massachusetts. For thirty years he had served as Convention Chairman or Chairman of the Committee on Resolutions. Friend and advisor of three presidents—McKinley, Taft, and Theodore Roosevelt—he was the implacable enemy of a fourth, Woodrow Wilson.

For an hour, the articulate senator, immaculately clad in gray tweeds, poured condemnation on Wilson and his League of Nations. Lodge was a hero to almost everybody at the convention. One of the few who did not share in the general admiration was another Republican intellectual, Nicholas Murray Butler, who never approached Lodge's popularity. Butler penned this estimate of Lodge in his book, *Across the Busy Years*, ". . . [He] was egotistical and provincial. For him Pittsfield, Massachusetts, represented the Farthest West, except on the quadrennial occasions when he was willing to cross the state boundary to attend a Republican National Convention, at Cleveland, . . Chicago, or St. Louis."

On that hot July 8th in 1920, the audience loved the authoritative rumble of Lodge's words. They shouted and cheered, stamped and hooted according to the unmistakable instructions in his voice.

After Lodge's opening address, several figures, familiar to Republican conventions for more than half a century, made appearances—Chauncey Depew, the witty Philadelphia orator, and Uncle Joe Cannon who had helped to nominate Lincoln.

The Committee on Resolutions, like every Resolutions Committee before and since, wrangled for hours trying to formulate its declaration on foreign policy. But behind the scenes, other voices were working in other ways. Grundy was rushing from one caucus to another, whirling through a constant series of behind-the-scenes meetings and putting in a subtle word here and there for Harding. Yet all the while he was waiting—waiting —for just the right moment to put over his candidate.

He was aware that the ticket of Senator Knox of Pennsylvania for President and Senator Johnson of California for Vice President was favored by many. He felt confident, however, that Johnson would never run in second place. And Grundy was right; Johnson insisted that he would be the presidential nominee and nothing less.

Grundy knew it would be a mistake to show his hand too clearly just yet. It was unfortunate that he could not talk with either Penrose or his secretary except by public telephone because the pro-Sproul Pennsylvania delegates were in control of the private line and Grundy could not use it with any assurance of privacy. He did not communicate with Penrose throughout the entire convention week.

It was a promising year for the Republicans. Various prominent ones were bitten by the presidential bug, and showing startling symptoms. One was Samuel B. Vauclain, president of the Baldwin Locomotive Works. So convinced did he become that he should be the selected nominee that he caught a midnight train to Philadelphia and tried to see Penrose early the next day. Penrose's secretary deflated his ambitions as gently as possible and assured him that under no circumstances could he see the seriously ailing Penrose.

Of all the 1920 Republican presidential hopefuls, Harding was the least known, the darkest of dark horses. Few delegates had ever heard of him. He had served only one term as United States Senator from Ohio and had not been identified with any national issues. But at least four men at the convention were his backers: Grundy, delegate from Pennsylvania; James Watson, a close friend of Penrose and delegate from Indiana who had presidential aspirations of his own; John T. King of Connecticut, a member of the Republican National Committee; and Senator Brandagee from Connecticut. Brandagee was an able and powerful politician who believed that the time was ripe for a Republican victory and did "not require a first-rater."

Most of the delegates were convinced that either of the two leading candidates, Governor Lowden of Illinois or General Wood, was a first-rater. Frank Lowden was a conservative and an extremely wealthy man, dubbed the "poor little rich boy" by the press. The other leading contender, General Leonard Wood, had been nationally known for two decades. His most ardent backer was W. C. Proctor, the head of Proctor and Gamble, the well-known soap firm. Wood was a hero of the Spanish-American War, the former commanding officer of the United States Volunteer Cavalry Regiment known as the "Rough Riders." Directly under Wood had been Lieutenant Colonel Theodore Roosevelt who rode from San Juan Hill into the presidency.

Another 1920 possibility was Will Hays, the energetic chairman of the National Committee. Hays had one very important backer, George Harvey, a prominent publisher, journalist and speaker. Harvey had been president of the publishing firm of Harper and Brothers from 1900 to 1915, a Democrat and a strong supporter of Woodrow Wilson in the presidential campaign of 1912. Later Wilson relied on some gossip to the effect that Harvey was propagating the views of certain financial interests through his publications. Wilson turned against his old friend and Harvey became bitter. In the *North American Review's War Weekly* which he founded in 1918, he expressed sharp criticism of Wilson's second administration and of the proposal for United States entry into the League of Nations.

Harvey was not a delegate to the convention. His position in the inner circle at Chicago was accomplished by personal ambition and more publicity than any of the real Republican leaders would have sought. He turned his suite at the Blackstone Hotel into a general headquarters. It is probable that 100 per centers such as Joe Grundy and Henry Cabot Lodge, Sr., looked askance at Harvey's apostasy.

The list of candidates stretched on and on—Senator Knox from Pennsylvania, Senator Johnson from California with his booming backer, Senator Borah, Governor Sproul of Pennsylvania, Governor Coolidge of Massachusetts, Herbert Hoover with his brilliant record of humanitarian service in World War I, Senator LaFollette from Wisconsin, Senator Charles Curtis of

Kansas, and the party's perennial intellectual, Nicholas Murray Butler, head of Columbia University.

The nominating speeches droned on throughout that stifling June 11th, curiously similar accolades for General Wood, Governor Lowden, Senator Johnson, Governor Sproul of Pennsylvania, Goverenr Coolidge of Massachusetts, Herbert Hoover, and many "also rans."

Congressman Frederick Gillett, Speaker of the House, rose to lyrical heights as he nominated "Silent Cal." Cried Gillett: "Coolidge is . . . as patient as Lincoln, silent as Grant, diplomatic as McKinley with the political instinct of [Theodore] Roosevelt."

Yet the Coolidge demonstration lasted less than a minute. It ran only two minutes for Warren G. Harding after Senator Wilks of Ohio asked, "Why not name the man whose record is the party platform?"

The two top candidates, Governor Lowden and General Wood, received tremendous ovations; Lowden's lasted forty-six minutes and Wood's a rousing forty-two. But it was 5 P.M. that Friday afternoon before the balloting began. Ordinarily such a time is zero hour for any convention and the weary delegates are on their way home. Now in the late afternoon, tempers reflected the heat, caucuses were getting nowhere, and it appeared that no agreement would ever be reached. Most Republican leaders were deeply worried. They had waited too long and too anxiously for this opportunity to have it lost in a stalemate.

As the balloting began, the convention chairman, meticulous Henry Cabot Lodge, Sr., must have wondered whether the past eight years of working and waiting for this day would be thrown away in futile disunity. At least one very determined delegate was confident that they would not. Joe Grundy had been waiting for decades to get a high tariff man elected to the highest office in the land. This explosive situation might provide him with the best opportunity for accomplishing his purpose. He smiled his shy, yet knowing smile, waved to a friend, and waited.

CHAPTER 12

"THERE COMES A TIME . . ."

In 1920 such uncertainty as to the presidential candidate was in direct contrast to the basic agreement within the Republican party itself. In a negative sort of way, Woodrow Wilson had himself forged the Republican party into strength and unity.

Wilson's idealistic fourteen points for world peace provided shrewd European diplomats with a powerful weapon. It was unsheathed in the celebrated Article X of the League of Nations: "The members of the League undertake to respect and preserve as against external aggression the territorial integrity and existing political independence of all members of the League." In the judgment of Joe Grundy, and many other Americans, of 1918, this enmeshed us in the "foreign entanglements" Washington had warned us about in his Farewell Address.

Wilson, who in the opinion of many was ascending farther and farther into the stratosphere of his own ego, saw to it that not a single Republican senator was made a member of the Peace Commission. This was construed as an unjustifiable exclusion from the making of the peace treaty.

Senator Lodge, the intellectual leader of the Republicans in the Senate, announced that in treaty making the Senate had equal power with the President and should make its wishes known in advance of the negotiations. He set forth his idea as to the sort of peace which ought to be made, one radically different from President Wilson's. Lodge wanted Germany disarmed, saddled with huge reparations and, if possible, dismembered. Although Lodge had originally supported the idea of a union of nations, he saw in the League, as planned by Wilson, a threat against American sovereignty. Critics pointed out that the British Empire was given six delegates to our one in the League assembly. Joe Grundy foresaw that under the League such matters as the tariff would be subject to still more European interference. The Republican majority of the Foreign Relations Committee followed Lodge's leadership and rejected the League.

President Wilson decided to carry his message directly to the people on a transcontinental tour. Not far behind him were Senators Borah, Johnson and McCormick, who denounced the League at every stop. The average citizen went along with the senators. The Republican Congressional victory of 1918 had been a general repudiation of the Wilson administration and the defeat of the League forecast the defeat of the Democratic party in 1920.

People were tired of idealistic theories, college professors in government and British diplomacy. As Penrose had observed, they were ready for "normalcy and a man-next-door type of president."

This was the background for the voting on that first ballot in the late afternoon of Friday, June 11, 1920. The voting lined up as follows: General Wood—287 votes; Governor Lowden—211; Senator Johnson—113; Governor Sproul—84; Nicholas Murray Butler—68; Senator Harding—65; Governor Coolidge—34; Senator LaFollette—24, and Herbert Hoover—5½.

On the second ballot Coolidge lost two votes and Butler 30 while Wood and Lowden gained. On the third Coolidge dropped to 27, Wood climbed to 302 and Lowden to 289.

At this point adjournment was attempted, but a fourth ballot was pushed through. Harding had dropped to 61, Lowden had stopped at 289 and Wood had climbed to 314. The delegates were hungry and tired. Now the finesse of the presiding officer worked to the advantage of the Pennsylvanian. On the platform he whispered to Joe Grundy's friend, Senator Reed Smoot, of Utah. Smoot then said, "I move that the convention do now stand adjourned until ten o'clock tomorrow morning."

At first there was shocked silence. The delegates of the two leading contenders, Lowden and Wood, were still fighting, still confident of victory. Adjournment was the last thing they wanted. Yet there was Senator Lodge putting the motion with the scholarly Harvard manner that seemed curiously out of place at a political convention. "Those in favor of the motion to adjourn will signify by saying 'Aye.'"

There was only a smattering of Aye's. Lodge intoned, "Those opposed 'No.'"

A roar of No's swept over the auditorium—and here a strange metamorphosis took place. Lodge the scholar was lost in Lodge the politician. He turned calmly from his desk, announcing as he walked away, "The Aye's have it and the convention is adjourned until tomorrow morning at nine o'clock."

Every delegate in the room knew that the No's had far outnumbered the Aye's, yet they accepted the chairman's decision calmly, almost with admiration. Smoot was later asked why he and Lodge forced the adjournment.

Senator Smoot replied, "Oh, there's going to be a deadlock and we'll have to work out some solution, we wanted the night to think it over."

Was Grundy, a close friend of Smoot, behind the move? Probably. It is certain that he was delighted to have this break in the tense proceedings because the balloting was getting nowhere and it appeared that the voting might run into a second week. In such a case many of the delegates would have spent most of their money, and, anxious to be on their way, would leave before the voting ended.

The Pennsylvanian, the lifelong politician, knew that the situation, swiftly and properly handled, could be used to give Harding's type of candidate the nomination. To do this, it would be necessary to keep the Pennsylvania delegation plugging for Sproul until just the right moment to put over Harding. Grundy and the ailing, absent Penrose were confident that they could, through the power of putting Harding in office against great odds, undoubtedly influence his actions in office in favor of the manufacturing interests.

However, the Ohio candidate was probably unaware of

these possibilities. By this time he was an unhappy and disillusioned man who said he could no longer afford to keep his headquarters at the Auditorium Hotel, was sure he would not be nominated and did not even plan to run again for the Senate. Instead he intended to devote his time to his Marion, Ohio, newspaper and give up politics for good.

To practically everyone at the convention except Grundy the situation looked hopelessly deadlocked. To him it was a dangerous but exciting challenge. How did it happen to work out this way, the only way by which Harding could possibly have been nominated? Was the quiet Quaker somehow behind the general uncertainty? Probably no one will ever know. At any rate, the situation played into the hands of the determined Pennsylvanian who had launched the campaign of the unknown Senator from Ohio.

Harding's very lack of money and zealous backers proved to be in his favor. General Wood's situation was weakened by the zeal and extravagance of his supporters. It appeared that in their efforts to nominate him they had spent large sums to buy the election of delegates favorable to his nomination. The same situation with even more scandal involved existed in the case of Governor Lowden. Furthermore, Mayor Thompson of Chicago was vigorously opposed to his candidacy.

The Pennsylvania delegation met in caucus and adopted a resolution to support Sproul on Saturday. With the two leading contenders now weakened, such support might result in the nomination for Sproul in the morning. Grundy, alone, dared to urge the switch to Harding. Arrayed against him were the majority of Pennsylvania delegates and their powerful leaders—W. W. Atterbury, then president of the Pennsylvania Railroad and chairman of the state's delegation; W. Harry Baker, Secretary of the Republican State Committee, and State Senator William E. Crow, Chairman of the Republican State Committee. Crow and Grundy indulged in bitter words over Grundy's position. The Pennsylvanian was well aware that he was making powerful and probably lifelong enemies but this did not deter him. He was no compromiser then, or ever.

At this point it would be logical to wonder why Grundy would exhibit such devotion to a candidate of mediocre ability. The explanation was quite simple. He was convinced that at this particular time, genial, good-looking Harding of Ohio was a potential winner with the best chance of beating the probable Democratic nominee, Governor Cox of Ohio.

To understand fully Grundy's position on Harding's candidacy, one must keep in mind those Wilson years during which Penrose and Grundy endured, plotted and planned for his defeat and for the election of a man who could be counted upon to encourage high tariffs and the protection of industry. Harding was the one candidate whom they could, at least on this point, trust implicitly.

On Friday evening when Grundy was pondering Harding's chances, Senator Lodge telephoned his suite and said, "Come to the Blackstone Hotel at nine o'clock." He suggested that the decision had already been made to have Coolidge for Vice President. Grundy agreed to meet Lodge at the Blackstone.

Now the Quaker did a political end run around his powerful Pennsylvania delegates and was the lone Pennsylvanian at an historic caucus held late that Friday night after the Pennsylvania caucus had broken up in bitterness and frustration. There were only about a dozen men in the Blackstone suite of Colonel George Harvey. These included Lodge, Brandagee of Connecticut, Smoot of Utah, Watson of Indiana, William Calder of New York, James W. Wadsworth, Murray Crane and Grundy. Despite some reports to the contrary, Harry Daugherty was not present.

How did these particular men come to serve as party elders? There was nothing sinister about their presence in the smoke-filled room in the Blackstone. They had no formal function or extraordinary power. They were merely men who, as individuals, had either held office or worked for the party over long periods of time. Most of them were senators or members of the Republican National Committee. One of them held neither post. The Pennsylvanian, Joe Grundy, was the only man present without benefit of party office. However, everybody knew that he was, as they called it, "the brains of the Pennsylvania Manufacturers Association"—and the biggest fund raiser the party had ever known.

Several of the group have already been identified. Others were Senator Charles W. Curtis of Kansas who later became Vice President, James Wolcott Wadsworth, United States Senator from New York who served two consecutive terms in the Senate from 1915 to 1927, and Joseph Medill McCormick, the wealthy publisher of the *Chicago Tribune*. McCormick had worked on the newspaper after his graduation from Yale, became its publisher in 1908. Four years later he was instrumental in the formation of the Progressive or "Bull Moose" party which nominated Theodore Roosevelt for re-election to the presidency. Between 1912 and 1916 he was elected successively to the Illinois state legislature, the United States House of Representatives and the Senate.

Murray Crane, a United States Senator from Massachusetts, pictured as "the only one left of the real Old Guard," was still flourishing in 1920. Mark Sullivan said of him, "[He] was one of the wonders of the Senate. He never made a speech. I don't remember that he ever made a motion. Yet he was the most influential member of that body. His wisdom, tact, sound judgment, encyclopaedic knowledge of public affairs and public men made him an authority."

One of the most powerful figures in the small group was Smoot, who had been very active in Mormon affairs. He served in the United States Senate from 1903 to 1933. There he was Chairman of the Senate Finance Committee and a member of other important committees as well. He was a recognized authority on finance and government expenditures. Smoot came from a wool growing state and Grundy was especially attracted by the senator's interest in a protective tariff.

In that crowded room at the Blackstone, this small group of men discussed the stalemate. The dominating intellect was undoubtedly that of Lodge. Of him the famed author-speaker Chauncey M. Depew said, "The Senate still has the statesmanship, eloquence, scholarship, vision and culture of Senator Lodge of Massachusetts."

In the hotel room there were frequent intervals of silence, punctuated by various comments on possible nominees. The Harding suggestion kept bobbing up. It stirred neither enthusiasm nor conviction and frequently aroused opposition.

Sullivan, the columnist closest to the group, wrote in his book, *Our Times—The Twenties*:

"Finally, and dubiously, they discussed Harding . . . and reluctantly, some of them, though not all, decided Harding was the most available . . . Curtis was the most confident they had best take Harding. Energetic and competent, Curtis started out to call on state leaders and arrange to have delegates vote for Harding in the morning. . . . The others remained in Harvey's suite. From time to time during the night, Curtis came back to the room; he brought other leaders with him; yet other leaders dropped in. On each, as he came, the Harding suggestion was tried out. Some opposed the notion; none had any enthusiasm or conviction for it. From time to time they renewed their discussion of other possibilities . . .

". . . In the end . . . [they] came to a kind of indifferent, tired unanimity—more a negation of other candidates than an affirmative agreement on Harding . . .

"Any history of the nomination of Harding which should depend on current newspaper accounts would say that a large part, ... was taken by Senator Boies Penrose of Pennsylvania . . . I was interested to observe that neither in my own early draft, nor in any of the some fifty letters that gave me information about the convention, did the name 'Penrose' appear. The nomination of Harding was no better than one Penrose might have made, but it happened that Penrose did not make it. Penrose during convention week was ill at his home in Phila-

delphia, much of the time in coma. From his sick room two wires
. . . were installed at the instance of an inferior henchman to Penrose, . . . John T. King [of Connecticut]. King's purpose was
the double one of pleasing and flattering the sick Penrose, and
giving himself an appearance of importance. From time to time
King took Republican leaders, old acquaintances of Penrose,
into the room to send messages and gossip . . . But none of the
messages had any bearing on the vital part of what the convention was doing. Penrose did not on this occasion control the
Pennsylvania delegation, it was controlled by Governor William
C. Sproul; and even if Penrose had had control, he was too sick
to exercise it. In truth, Penrose was a burnt-out man, shorn of
his power and destined soon to die."

The extraordinary night was described some years later by
Senator Wadsworth who wrote: "It was a sort of continuous
performance. I was in and out of that room several times that
night. They were like a lot of chickens with their heads off.
They had no program and no definite affirmative decision was
reached. If they came to any decision at all, it was to let the
Harding suggestion go through, the fact being that they did not
have anyone else to propose."

Grundy's own account of the memorable night was given
nine years after the event, during the Senate lobby investigation.
It is not surprising that Grundy's inquisitors, in their attempts to
discredit him, should rake up the scene in the Blackstone Hotel.
Senator Walsh asked about the publicized conference that
resulted in Harding's nomination. Joe Grundy was candid as
usual: "Why, Senator Lodge opened the proceedings and
stated that he as the presiding officer of that convention had
watched the proceedings with great interest—that is just a condensed statement, as near as I can get it—that he had come there
in the interest of Leonard Wood, and the developments in the
convention during that week were such as to convince him that
the nomination of Leonard Wood would be ill advised; that the
nomination of Governor Lowden for like reasons was ill
advised."

Senator Caraway kept on probing: "Those reasons were that they had put up too much money?"

Grundy's reply was careful: "Their friends had, apparently. It was then Friday evening. It had been a tremendously hot week, the hottest week I had ever spent anywhere . . . The delegates were pretty well tired out. Their money in many instances had run out . . . and [Lodge] doubted if he could hold that convention there over Sunday, and he believed there should be an effort made that evening, between then and the convening of the convention next day, to agree on a candidate, and that in looking the picture over he was satisfied that the most available man was Senator Harding. Whether the Senator's friends would or would not have spent a large amount of money such as had been spent by the others was not open for discussion, but they apparently had not spent it. But, moreover, the Republican Party had never elected a President without the vote of the State of Ohio, and it looked as if Governor Cox, who had carried the State twice for governor, would be the Democratic nominee for President, and therefore he deemed it especially important that the vote of Ohio should be secure, and for this and divers other reasons he believed it was our business to go out and do what we could to bring about the nomination of Warren G. Harding early Saturday morning. That was the statement as near as I can recall it; and, of course, Senator, it was late Friday, because the convention adjourned on Saturday afternoon, as you may recall. I believe you were there. In fact, I know you were there."

Senator Walsh of Montana commented dryly: "The papers issuing at 4 o'clock in the morning declared Harding would be nominated the next day."

Grundy's only comment was: "Well, I guess they knew what they were talking about."

On Saturday morning by the ninth ballot Wood held only 249 votes. Connecticut, Indiana, and the south joined the bandwagon to give Harding a lead of 374 votes. Pennsylvania was still waiting for the decisive moment when its electoral votes could swing the nomination.

Demonstrations started popping as the roll call went on. The galleries screamed with delight. Former Governor Bailey, head of the Kansas delegation, grabbed the state standard, attached a picture of Harding to it and started marching around the hall. Delegates from other states as well as Kansas, bearing flags and pictures, followed in gay pursuit. Pandemonium broke loose and reverberated across the nation's air waves. The country became aware that the Republican candidate for the presidency of the United States was about to be nominated. It was a moment of triumph for Lodge, the Republican leader of the Senate, whom everyone knew, and for Grundy, the quiet Quaker, known by few outside of legislative halls and his home town.

On the tenth ballot Wood's count had fallen to 156. The others now were Johnson 80, Lowden 11, Hoover 9, and Coolidge 5. At just the right moment the Keystone State's electoral votes clinched the nomination for the Ohioan. In the Pennsylvania delegation somebody's timing had been perfect. Warren Gamaliel Harding was the Republican candidate for President of the United States. Who was responsible for this master-timing? Probably the man who never took credit for it—Joe Grundy.

It was after six when the final shouting started. While the last roll call was proceeding, just as an exultant roar echoed behind the platform, a Michigan delegate ran into a tiny room backstage. In it were seated Harding, Lowden and Butler. The delegate shouted, "Pennsylvania has voted for you, Harding, and you are nominated."

Harding rose, choking with emotion, he said, "If the great honor of the Presidency is to come to me, I shall need all the help that . . . friends can give me."

We shall probably never know whose judgment on that long night of Friday, June 11, 1920, persuaded the convention to back Harding. Grundy, the genuinely modest Quaker, never admitted to any dominant role. It is logical to assume that the man who planned the opening gun of Harding's campaign in

Philadelphia made an effective case for his own preference, and succeeded in putting him over as a compromise candidate.

Was Harding a satisfactory choice at the time? It is unfortunate that the disgraceful Teapot Dome Scandal makes it difficult to evaluate the decision made in June of 1920 and to judge objectively the other aspects of Harding's short term as President. There have been scandals in many otherwise good administrations.

In the eyes of the Pennsylvanian, Harding was the man who could be counted upon to be a winner in the fall of 1920, to protect thereafter the interests of the manufacturers and thus insure the prosperity of the country. And, regardless of gossip and scandal, understandably capitalized on by political opposition, Harding's years were among the most prosperous in America's history. As Grundy had expected, immediately after his inauguration Harding called the Sixty-Seventh Congress in special session and demanded higher tariff rates. The rates were granted promptly on May 27th. Joe Grundy liked a man who kept his word!

CHAPTER 13

THE BIGGEST FUND RAISER IN THE LAND

Just four years after that hot summer afternoon when Harding had been asked by Penrose whether he would like to go to the White House, the unhappy and duped President died suddenly in August. Grundy was relieved that in Harding's successor, Vice President Calvin Coolidge, the manufacturers had a man who believed in them. The Quaker admired Coolidge's moral character and the admiration was probably mutual because soon after he succeeded to the presidency, Coolidge requested Grundy to pay a visit to the White House.

He did so with alacrity. The Pennsylvanian was anxious to see Coolidge run for the presidency in 1924. Neither man would comment on matters discussed during the conference but developments indicated that Coolidge wanted to test his strength in the coming Pennsylvania primaries. Naturally, he turned to Grundy.

It is likely that Grundy told Coolidge of a plot which Pennsylvania's Governor Pinchot was hatching, supposedly secretly, with Senator Hiram Johnson of California to swing the nomination for Johnson at the next Republican Convention. Grundy did not favor this now any more than he had in 1920 and he resented Pinchot's efforts to pull off something which he knew was not acceptable to him. Although Pinchot had achieved the governorship primarily through Grundy's efforts, apparently he felt no necessity for loyalty toward his benefactor's convictions. He was now trying to institute social legislation which Grundy continued to oppose.

Senator Johnson objected to a tax reduction plan advocated by Secretary of the Treasury Andrew Mellon. The plan admittedly was more favorable to wealthy individuals and big corporations. "Andy" Mellon was an old friend of Joe Grundy. In fact, it had been Grundy who made a special trip to Harding's Ohio home to submit Mellon's name for the treasury post. Grundy hoped that Mellon might follow in the footsteps of the "greatest Secretary of the Treasury, Alexander Hamilton."

One of the country's wealthiest men, Mellon came from an influential industrial family that was associated with several leading industries such as the Aluminum Company of America and the Gulf Oil Company. His name had first been raised as a possible selection for Secretary of the Treasury while Penrose was recuperating in Atlantic City after his serious illness in 1920. Penrose was considering various potential candidates for the post. His friend, King of Connecticut, telephoned to suggest Mellon. Penrose's secretary, Taylor, relayed the message to Penrose who said, "Tell King the Mellon suggestion is out of the question, that he is too old and he wouldn't want it anyway."

Here was the master politician, although fatally ill, still clinging to his power. Secretly annoyed that the suggestion had arisen from a Connecticut politician and not from himself, Penrose had immediately decided Mellon would be ideal but this he had no intention of telling King. No sooner had King hung up the telephone than Penrose called Mellon and asked how he would like the job. Mellon was delighted and went to Atlantic City to talk it over with Penrose. It was after this meeting that Grundy carried the word to Harding.

Mellon had served faithfully under Harding and was to continue in the post through the next two presidencies as well. Throughout his years in office, Mellon stuck to his tax reduction plan, considered a boon by the manufacturers and by President Coolidge, but not by Johnson and Pinchot. The Mellon programs were frequently opposed and sometimes modified as a result of the opposition of Republican liberals in the Senate led by Senator Robert LaFollette, Senior, of Wisconsin.

In May, 1924, just a month before the convention, the Republican National Committee needed funds desperately. Naturally, the committee turned to Joe Grundy and William L.

Mellon, Andy's nephew, to raise $600,000 in Pennsylvania. Grundy's eastern half of the state comprised fifty-three counties, Mellon's western half, fourteen.

At the convention, LaFollette grew hostile over the drafting of the platform, declaring that it ignored the interests of the western farmer. For these reasons, he accepted the Progressive party's nomination for the presidency, an action which Grundy considered disloyal and unforgivable since it weakened the Republican party's chances to win the presidency.

While angry at LaFollette's move, all the while attempting to raise money for the campaign, Grundy wrote a letter—addressed to the citizens of Pennsylvania. In it he foolishly referred to LaFollette as a "Lenin" and to Democrat Senator Burton K. Wheeler, LaFollette's running mate, as a "Trotsky." The Pennsylvanian, in anger, was indiscreet. Many able politicians have been similarly guilty.

Grundy's references in this letter, no matter how ill advised, must be considered in the light of the general apprehension about Communism at the time. After the Bolshevik Revolution, the Soviets carried out an intensive campaign against the western nations. The Communist party "high command" and the workers were not then as sophisticated or as subtle in their infiltration here as they later became. The party, then usually called "The Workers," had recently been established in the United States. During the previous fall, the Department of Justice, under the direction of Democrat A. Mitchell Palmer, had made mass arrests of political and labor agitators.

These were the days when public sentiment, undiluted by the tears of both professional and politically naive "do-gooders," was strongly against such offenders. On December 22, 1919, 249 of these anarchists were deported on the U.S.S. *Bufort*. Included in the group were Alexander Berkman, who had served a prison sentence for shooting and stabbing Henry Clay Frick during steel strikes in Pennsylvania, and Emma Goldman, the Communist who had planned the assault. On January 2, 1920, government

Joe Grundy with Governor John S. Fisher and William L. Mellon.

agents carried out raids in twenty-three cities and took twenty-seven hundred into custody. The raids ended in May. Various state criminal syndicalist laws were invoked against the radicals.

Joe Grundy was one of many responsible political leaders who openly condemned the Communist efforts to penetrate the United States government through labor agitators. He also fought ambitious politicians who would follow the welfare state ideology to further their own political ambitions. Grundy considered both LaFollette and Wheeler in the latter category.

Wheeler's platform advocated government ownership of railroads and water power resources and the abolition of injunctions in labor disputes. Such programs were condemned by many as "state socialism," a type of government alien to the principles of our free Republic. At this period, one of the leaders of the Socialist Party, in fact, its candidate for President, was Eugene V. Debs, who had been sentenced to jail for ten years for having engaged in seditious activity.

When Grundy made the unfortunate references to LaFollette and Wheeler, he was angry about LaFollette's desertion of the regular Republican ticket. To the Pennsylvanian this was disloyalty of the rankest sort. It was the kind of thing of which Joe Grundy was never guilty. No one in the Republican party had more bitter disputes within the organization. However, when it came to the election itself, whether he lost or won, whether his preferred candidate or the one he fought most bitterly in the primary was the nominee, Grundy backed the Republican ticket with his all-out efforts and his own money.

He sincerely believed that the aims of the "progressives," a broad welfare program and efforts to redistribute the wealth were progressive, all right—but in the wrong direction—toward Socialism and Communism. He felt that way in 1924 and he still held the same view at his death in 1961. By that time his fears had proven to be far from groundless. No less an authority than Nikita Khrushchev has said that Americans cannot be expected to jump from Capitalism to Communism, but that

Communists can assist our elected leaders by giving us small doses of Socialism until we suddenly awake to find we have Communism.

In 1924 LaFollette saw an opportunity to make a big issue of Grundy's letter. He got enthusiastic help from the Democrats. The Wisconsin presidential hopeful said that Grundy was an enemy of organized labor and of legislation for the protection of women and children. Senator Borah, Chairman of a Senate Committee, investigating campaign expenditures, scheduled hearings. LaFollette could not hope for vast sums to help his candidacy but he could make it hot for those who were raising them for Coolidge. LaFollette charged that the Republican National Committee was planning to buy the election through solicitation of large funds to be sent west and used in doubtful states. He urged that Grundy, Mellon and other Pennsylvania leaders be subpoenaed to appear and testify.

Grundy, the Chairman and Treasurer of the Ways and Means Committee of the Republican State Committee, was one of the first called. His answers were straight-forward. He said that 70,000 letters, at an expense of $10,000, had so far yielded a total of over $300,000 of which $280,000 had been turned over to the National Committee and $20,000 to the State Committee. The paragraph in this Grundy letter which so disturbed La-Follette seems frank and direct. It was: "Our [Pennsylvania's] thirty-eight electoral votes may be safe for Coolidge and Dawes, but our money and energy must be given to help carry doubtful states and doubtful Congressional Committees."

Has there ever been a campaign of either party in which this had not been the situation and a suggested solution? But LaFollette was fighting for the nomination and trying to use adverse reaction to Grundy as a means of winning.

Estimates of what Grundy personally raised in this campaign hover around $800,000 with his own contributions estimated from a low of $50,000 upwards. Certainly Grundy's fund raising was a big factor in Coolidge's election, but there were no criminal practices or frauds connected with any funds ever handled by the Pennsylvanian. Even his enemies admitted this. Grundy always openly expressed his belief that money, properly expended in a political campaign, was justifiable.

On the national scene with Coolidge in office, Grundy was reassured, but at the state level he had continuing problems. In 1926 the governorship and senatorial posts were up for election. Grundy had one—and only one—man in mind, his old friend whom he had favored four years before, John S. Fisher. The Mellons were usually given credit for Fisher's nomination, but it was Grundy who made the decision and persuaded the Mellons to go along.

They were favorably disposed toward William S. Vare's vote-getting machine in Philadelphia, a machine never palatable to either Penrose or Grundy, but they learned that Vare was backing Lieutenant Governor Beidleman for the governorship. They, like Grundy, believed that Beidleman favored the removal of the manufacturers' exemption from the capital stock tax. This realization may have discouraged the Mellons from trying to back Beidleman for the governorship. At any rate they did finally unite with Grundy in backing Fisher.

The incumbent U. S. Senator, George Wharton Pepper, agreed to run and after some differences, both Grundy and the Mellons backed him for the senatorial post. In the primary Fisher won the gubernatorial nomination over Beidleman but Vare defeated Pepper and Pinchot ran a poor third. Vare's choice for Lieutenant Governor, Arthur H. James, of Luzerne County, also won.

Once again, newspapers had a field day with alleged campaign expenditures and a United States Senate Committee started an investigation of expenditures in the Pennsylvania Republican primary. Back went Grundy to the witness stand and explained that he had arranged a loan as chairman of the Fisher-Pepper Citizens Committee—for some $300,000, and that an additional sum of $90,000 was used to pay watchers at the polls. That watchers were badly needed was evident from the results in South Philadelphia.

There was no proof that the Pennsylvania Manufacturers Association contributed any money to the campaign. The investigators thought they had something when they found that William Folwell, president of the Association's insurance companies, had a share of the Grundy note. They assumed that Folwell was to be reimbursed by the Association but were disappointed to learn that Grundy personally would reimburse him. However, the combined expenditures of the three factions made the total cost of this primary over $2,500,000.

All three factions were questioned for excessive campaign expenditures, but the Vare group was accused of a more serious charge—corrupt balloting procedure. Pepper had been leading both Vare and Pinchot by a large plurality when the count began in Philadelphia. Thanks to Vare's machine-controlled South Philadelphia votes, Vare gained an 81,000 vote plurality in the city. A somewhat similar situation took place in the 1960 presidential election when Richard Nixon's plurality in the state was 210,000 until a Philadelphia majority of an incredible 331,000 was counted.

Following the Vare nomination in 1926, the balloting procedure charge was not pressed. However, on the basis of the general election six months later, outgoing Governor Pinchot, bitter toward Vare, would not issue the traditional Certificate of Election in behalf of the Senator-elect. Instead he sent a Certificate of Doubt to the United States Senate with the words "appears to have been chosen" on it. The Senate Committee on Privileges and Election found there was not sufficient evidence of fraud and corruption in the general election to deny Vare his seat. However he was barred from the Senate on the basis of the Committee's earlier inquiry into his primary campaign expenditures.

The Senate, by its three-year deliberation on Vare's qualifications, denied Pennsylvania its right to full representation. Many suspected that the western coalitionists were behind this

184

injustice. Finally, on December 7, 1929, the decision was reached that Pennsylvania was entitled to have its second senator seated.

The inconsistency of the Senate's position is illustrated by an article in the *New York Times* of December 9, 1929, which asked, "How far will concern for the dignity and honor of the Senate carry its champions? The ingenious Mr. Nye has already devised a new qualification. The Governor of Pennsylvania will have to appoint as Senator 'one far removed from affiliation with the Mellon-Grundy-Fisher machine' or Mr. Nye will try to bar the appointee from the Senate doors. The arrogance of the Senate is not surfeited with another victory over the Constitution."

At the same time, Joe Grundy was hitting the headlines as a national figure in the tariff investigation. Suddenly at the age of sixty-six, after a lifetime of behind-the-scenes manipulation, Joe Grundy found himself in the limelight, a new kind of American hero. Almost forgotten for the moment were his wealth and decades of political power. He was just another citizen who, alone, had faced a battery of badgering senators and had the courage to tell them exactly what he thought of them. He was thus realizing a popular American dream.

Even some western newspapers had a good word for him. *The Times* at Oklahoma City, Oklahoma, took a realistic view:

"Grundy may think some of the western states are backward. He may be rough and tough. He may be for protection higher than a cat's back. He may be the most powerful lobbyist of his generation, yet he represents Pennsylvania."

The Davenport, Iowa, *Leader* stated:

"Grundy is perhaps the most interesting character who has come before the Senate Lobby Investigating Committee. He is a rich Pennsylvanian who believes that the sun rises and sets in the protective tariff. He is a lobbyist for it from conviction—has been for years. He is glad to pay his own expenses for the privilege of buttonholing congressmen and telling them why the tariff rates should be raised to the ultimate ceiling.

"Before the investigating committee he had the courage to

declare that the senators from the little-populated non-industrial western states, like Montana, and Idaho, were making entirely too much noise about the tariff. Their Senators, he did not hesitate to say, should keep still—he plainly meant 'shut up'—and let Senators from industrial states like Pennsylvania and Massachusetts frame a high tariff bill and pass it. 'Backward' states, he called those commonwealths which sent Borah and Walsh and Wheeler and other combative Senators to Washington to take up too much of the time—in his view—talking about the tariff."

Yet Grundy was making some powerful enemies including the articulate "western progressives," prominent southerners and even the President-elect of the United States. These men eyed the candid Pennsylvanian's new-found fame with a certain amount of discomfort and foreboding.

Newspapers began at once to speculate on the possibilities of Grundy's appointment to the long-empty post of Junior Senator from Pennsylvania. Senator Nye let it be known that he had formed the nucleus of a bloc to prevent the seating of the Pennsylvanian.

Governor Fisher, annoyed by the threats of Nye and other coalitionists said: "I would be failing in my duty as governor of this state if I allowed a threat from any source, by any United States senator or whoever he might be, to dictate the action of Pennsylvania in the selection of a United States senator."

Great pressure was now put on Grundy to accept the appointment. At first he was not at all receptive to the suggestion. Throughout his career he had avoided all public office except that of serving as councilman of Bristol borough, his home town. This he regarded as a duty to his community. He had always refused any other public office, saying, "A man with my ideas loses influence by being a candidate. It is a duty I owe my country to render services proportionate to the interest and advantages I receive under this government—and I prefer to serve otherwise than in a public office."

The general attitude toward Mr. Grundy's appointment as

United States Senator from Pennsylvania was favorable. Mark Sullivan wrote in the *New York Herald Tribune*:

"The immediate favor Mr. Grundy enjoys in Pennsylvania arises from the feeling that the coalition senators tried to bully him, that he fought back, and that he won the contest and will continue to win it. As it was put at the time by an admiring Democrat, 'Every time the coalition Senators tried to bite Grundy, they broke a tooth.'

". . . If the country has been led to assume by fragmentary accounts of recent events that Mr. Grundy is a lobbyist in the ordinary sense, that is a mistake. He is as far as possible from the professional 'recommendation maker,' who lobbies for a favor . . .

"Those who know [him] feel that his political efforts are less in the interest of his own wealth which is inherited and ample, than in the interests of the employees who work for him and for the manufacturers associated with him. Several Pennsylvania industries including textiles, some parts of the steel business, and coal, are in a distress as acute as that of the farmers. Some of these industries are even more dependent on the tariff for prosperity than are the farmers of the west.

"Pennsylvania has come to feel, in the later stages of the tariff discussion, and in the Senate coalition attitude toward Mr. Grundy, that their state is being 'kicked around' by the Senate, like Champ Clark's hound dog. Mr. Grundy and the interests he represents are prefectly willing to let the farmers have what tariff they think they need. The late development in which the farm senators try to deny any tariff increases to industry have caused resentment. Thus sectionalism started from one section, grows by what it feeds upon, and arises in another section.

"An essential element in the esteem for Mr. Grundy is his courage, both his personal courage and his courage of conviction. He believes in the protective tariff as earnestly as any farm senator believes in farm relief, and more than some. His tariff activities are to him and to most of Pennsylvania a case of strongly held principle advocated in a courageous way.

". . . His personal tariff views are rather extreme. He doubts, for example, whether there should be any flexible tariff provisions whatsoever. He thinks a general tariff should be written by Congress and that it should remain stable and unchanged for several years until another general revision is called for.

"The number of Republican Senators who are as extreme on the tariff as Mr. Grundy is quite small. All that can be said at the present is that Mr. Grundy will be a courageous spokesman of a definite point of view which he is able to express and argue for with a high quality of intellectual substance."

Such favorable comments and the persistent urging of his friends and political associates finally convinced the cautious Pennsylvanian that he should accept the appointment. Governor Fisher's announcement that Grundy would fill the seat denied to Vare stated the reason behind his choice, "There is no question before the Senate of greater importance to Pennsylvania than the tariff. The person most able to carry on the fight for the protection of the state's industries is Mr. Grundy."

On December 11th, just twenty-four hours before Grundy was to be sworn in as a senator the coalitionists reluctantly admitted that their lobby investigation had turned up nothing which might serve as grounds for denying Grundy a Senate seat. On December 12th, Nye of North Dakota, determined once more to raise the issue of 1926 campaign funds solicited by Grundy, introduced a resolution declaring the appointment invalid. The debate on the Senate floor lasted three hours. The redoubtable Senator Borah, who probably would have given anything to have prevented the appointment was, after all, a political realist. He recognized that Nye's attempt to challenge Fisher's authority was not within the Senate's jurisdiction. He moved that the oath of office be administered to Grundy.

On that day, December 12th, Joseph R. Grundy became the Junior United States Senator from Pennsylvania. Nothing could have been more ironic to the protesting senators because Grundy, the man chosen by Fisher to fill Vare's unexpired term, had, in his 1926 campaign to defeat Vare, spent more than twice the amount expended by Vare! The Grundy-Mellon vs. Vare fight had been lost in the state campaign in 1926. However now, three years later, Grundy's appointment amounted to victory at the national level, over the city politician whom he had opposed for many years. The Pennsylvanian now became undisputed leader of the party within his state. He would also, for the first time in his life, be forced to remain in the steady glare of national publicity.

Senator Norris was infuriated by the turn of events. He did admit, however, that even if the Governor of Pennsylvania insulted the Senate by the Grundy appointment, there was nothing in the Constitution that said he could not do it. In a burst of bitter eloquence he shouted, "There is nothing in the Constitution that says that the Governor of Pennsylvania cannot make a damn fool of himself if he wants to do it." He might appropriately have added that senators enjoyed the same privilege.

The *Herald Tribune* stated: "From the standpoint of Republican party politics, he (Grundy) is doubtless a bad choice as he is extremely tactless. Let us assume the incredible, that he will be as poor a senator as Senator Caraway; even so the State of Pennsylvania would still have the constitutional right to name him as long as representative government exists in the United States."

The *Washington Post* described the swearing-in ceremony: "No one ever walked into the body more quietly or more unobtrusively and yet the effect was like that of the wild colts of the western prairies when an express train rushes past."

The ceremony did nothing to halt the flow of denunciations from the coalitionists, especially Senator Bronson Cutting, Republican from New Mexico, and from the Democrats with Senator Alben W. Barkley, of Kentucky, one of Grundy's most bitter assailants. Barkley's antagonism lasted even as late as the July 1948 presidential nomination when Grundy was eighty-five years old and no longer a big power in Pennsylvania politics. In Barkley's keynote address to the Democratic convention at Philadelphia, he plunged into an eloquent indictment of Grundy-ism when he recited a slightly blasphemous parody of Charles Wesley's well known hymn: "All hail the power of Grundy's name, let Republicans prostrate fall; Bring forth the royal diadem! And crown him lord of all!"

On that December 12th in 1929 when Grundy took his seat in the Senate of the United States, there was wide agreement with the sentiment expressed in the Philadelphia *Evening Public Ledger*: "The Senate needs men who, whatever their convictions may be, aren't mere shouters of sentimental platitudes . . . Proceeds of big business in the United States are the foundations of the higher general standard of living which the people in general have developed for themselves. Assaults against big business aren't assaults against capital alone. They are assaults against people in general and against people who work for wages in particular."

On the night following Grundy's swearing-in ceremony, he was the guest of honor at a formal dinner held at the Union League in Philadelphia. Joe Grundy was gracious and smiling, very handsome in white tie and tails.

At last, the Pennsylvanian became openly a key figure in the national scene. The most determinedly "behind-the-scenes man" in United States politics had landed in the center of the stage. The spotlight was bright and warm!

CHAPTER 14

THE PENNSYLVANIAN TAKES HIS SEAT

At the famed Gridiron dinner, given annually by the press in Washington, the most heartily applauded refrain of early 1930 was:

> "Old Joe Grundy
> Lobbied on Monday
> Subpoenaed on Tuesday
> Sworn on Wednesday
> Questioned on Thursday
> Threatened on Friday
> Welshed on Saturday
> A Senator on Sunday
> And that is just the beginning
> of old Joe Grundy."

Editorial comment on the seating of the Junior Senator from Pennsylvania was mostly favorable. Typical is the article in the *New York Herald Tribune* of December 12, 1929:

"Whatever else the Senate Lobby Investigating Committee may have done or fallen down trying to do, it made Mr. Joseph R. Grundy immensely popular. The public likes fair play. It likes to see the tables turned on an arrogant and pestiferous bully. When Mr. Caraway and the other senatorial hecklers bore down on Mr. Grundy, he did not flinch. He gave them back as good as he got and a little more. The hypocrisy and ulterior motives of the investigation were transparently clear to everybody. Equally so were Mr. Grundy's candor and intellectual integrity as a witness. He could not be intimidated; he was perfectly willing to show his hand. He had no secrets from the committee. He talked on the stand as he talked off it. He met the bumptious and menacing Mr. Caraway on the latter's ground and worsted him . . . So the Constitution wins a temporary victory.

"The Junior Pennsylvania Senator is a man of marked characteristics. He is a guileless Quaker. He thinks aloud. His yea is yea and his nay is nay. He lacks neither self-respect nor intellectual integrity. If he believes ardently that protection is to Pennsylvania's interest, he also believes ardently that it is to the interest of the whole country . . .

"Mr. Grundy is not a politician in the customary sense. He is not a trimmer or compromiser, and says things which an experienced politician is expected to avoid saying. He lacks conciliation and tact. He is disturbingly outspoken. Yet the Senate has more than its due quota of statesmen of the other school, whose thoughts are concentrated on the short and politic view exclusively, on doing or saying nothing which may require positiveness or give offense. What is needed in the Senate is more intellectual and moral courage, more serious conviction one way or another, more willingness to work out opinions and then stick to them. The upper house is at present ruled by a coalition of groups which do not agree on anything except the hope of temporary political advantage, which live by trading views and votes. To such a Senate, Mr. Grundy, the steadfast Quaker, ought to be a real acquisition."

As expected, many of the southern and western newspapers viewed Grundy's appointment with disfavor. The Cleveland, Ohio, *Plain Dealer* reported:

"A veritable high priest of protection . . . The chief of high tariff states will be represented by the chief of high tariff lobbyists . . .

"If Pennsylvania sees in Grundy its ideal senator—if Massachusetts once idolized Webster and Kentucky clung to Clay—why, that is Pennsylvania's affair. The rest of the country can stand it if Pennsylvania can . . . Grundy, of course, believing any revision is good so long as it is upward, regardless of its effect on the consumer's breakfast table, moves in majestic disregard of his critics."

The Press of Pella, Iowa, quoted Senator Norris as characterizing it a "stench in the nostrils of the country." But Norris's own state of Nebraska repudiated its senator's view and upheld the Pennsylvanian's cause as did many of the other grain-belt states. They evidently believed Grundy when he said:

"There is nothing sectional, provincial, or narrow in my viewpoint. I am convinced that anything that is good for the producing interests of Pennsylvania, whether it is a mill, a mine, or farm, is good for the whole United States. Prosperity is like the waves of the radio. Its impulses are going out in every direction. A man produces something in Pennsylvania, and upon the sale of it, receives a certain sum. Then he in turn needs something, and he buys it. The thing he purchases, in all probability, will have been produced in some other state and of materials from states still farther away. So that's why I feel that if I can promote the industrial greatness of Pennsylvania, I shall be in turn helping the entire nation."

A few days after taking the oath of office he closed his lobby headquarters and moved its equipment to his new office in the Senate Office Building. In early January, the Senate coalition lost its fight to prevent raising wool yarn rates. Grundy refused to vote on the issue because of his own yarn mills. The *Washington Post* stated:

"If gestures of this kind were more frequent in the Senate, that body would find itself gaining in self-respect and public esteem."

The *Star Enterprise* in Poughkeepsie, New York, reported on January 4th:

"This [Senator Grundy's refusal to vote] was in excellent taste . . . but it probably sets a standard considerably too high for the Senate."

The Pennsylvanian resigned from his posts as president of the Pennsylvania Manufacturers Association and vice president of the American Tariff League. He hired Leighton C. Taylor, Senator Penrose's former secretary, and kept in his employ

Warren F. Doane, one of the tariff experts from the former "American Tariff News Bureau." In an interview Grundy said,

"My job in Washington is to promote the interests and the prosperity of the people of Pennsylvania . . . If I can do that, I know I shall be doing something for the whole United States, for anything that helps the industrial or the economic interests of one commonwealth must, as a natural sequence, be of benefit to the others.

"In the years I have put in trying to do what I considered the right thing for Pennsylvania, I have had to take a good many hard knocks. I have learned that the best thing to do is to take it all with a smile and then forget it.

"When I have views of my own, I feel that I have the right to express them, and I accord that right to everyone else.

"I've got to buckle down here and do a lot of hard work . . .

"I had been going along so many years doing what I could for Pennsylvania without holding any public office that I never visualized myself in this position."

The newly appointed senator, so dedicated to Pennsylvania, turned the tables on one occasion when a great deal of wrangling was taking place on the Senate floor. As the legislators argued about the separate and various needs of their respective states, the Pennsylvanian brought an end to the examples of self-interest by saying, "Gentlemen, should we not be attending to the nation's business?"

In spite of Senator Grundy's devotion to his senatorial duties, he was sharply criticized by Senator Patrick Harrison, Mississippi Democrat. Harrison charged that Grundy freely admitted that he was having frequent visits from several who were, in fact, serving the Tariff League. For this reason alone, the Senate Lobby Investigating Committee once more jumped at the opportunity to harass the imperturbable Quaker. One of the first to testify was his employee, Warren F. Doane, tariff expert and editor of *The Manufacturer*, publication of the Manufacturers Club of Philadelphia. He stated that he received a monthly wage of $500 and had been on Grundy's personal payroll for nearly seven years.

Once again the Pennsylvania Senator spoke frankly on his own behalf. The people to whom he had given office space were his own employees. As for assistance in gathering background material for his speeches, he pointed out that few, if any, senators did not rely upon such assistance and that such activities were essential to help him "serve the industries of Pennsylvania." Grundy added that his only regret was that his office was too small to permit Doane to have a more comfortable place in which to work to assist him in the duties which he had been specifically appointed to do and intended to fulfill. Again the candid Quaker proved that he was acting for his state and paying for such work from his own pocket. The committee, at the conclusion of its investigation, found no grounds to warrant action against Senator Grundy.

Soon after taking his seat the Pennsylvanian was permitted a privilege rare for a new senator. He was appointed on no less than four standing committees, manufacturing, banking and currency, naval affairs, and civil affairs. Although he devoted himself conscientiously to all of his duties, the subject upon which he spent the most time was, as might be expected, the tariff question.

The coalition members had been unsuccessful in their efforts to degrade the fighting Pennsylvanian during their tariff lobby investigation but now, in view of President-elect Hoover's attitude on tariff, they were making headway in the Senate. While some increases, as in the case of mine tariff rates, had been gained for industry, further prospects were not bright.

The running battle between the Republican coalitionists and the regulars continued. On a number of occasions, the vote was deadlocked thus requiring the vote of Vice President Curtis of Kansas. Fortunately, from Grundy's viewpoint, this vote was always cast with the regular Republicans. However, before this time the coalitionists had succeeded in lowering many tariff rates under consideration in the Smoot-Hawley bill. Senator Grundy was uncompromisingly antagonistic toward these alterations.

The coalition appeared to be dominating by a slim majority. How could this be overcome? Suddenly, on March 5, 1930, an unexpected event bolstered Grundy's position. Or was it unexpected? For several months the Pennsylvanian, who knew more about end runs than many a younger politician, had been aware that a former critic, Senator Harrison, was anxious to have the tariff on sugar rates continued. On March 5th, Senator Smoot, often the spokesman for Grundy, introduced an amendment proposing an increase in sugar duties. The amendment passed 47-39.

Senator Caraway expressed the opinion that a secret deal had been made involving a trade of support. By this time the Smoot-Hawley bill was known as the "Grundy" bill. The *Baltimore Sun* had stated:

"The present tariff bill should be called the 'Grundy' tariff bill because Grundy had more to do with writing it than did Hawley."

The Junior Senator from Pennsylvania had consolidated a group to defeat the coalition and just two days after the sugar duty increase, the important issue of cement schedules came up for consideration. Grundy won a real victory when cement was removed from the free trade list by a vote of 45-37.

By this time the coalitionists were accusing the Pennsylvanian of being the directing genius behind the new effort to overthrow them; however, they felt confident that their three major issues, lumber, oil, and aluminum would remain on the free list, unchallenged. Amazingly, this did not happen. Lumber was removed from the free list. Senator Nye frantically attempted resolutions to remove the recently restored sugar and cement duties but both were beaten by the identical vote of 47-38. However, when the oil and aluminum rates were reintroduced, the coalition prevailed and these two products did remain on the free list.

The western "progressives" and southern Democrats had generally lined up to defeat the Smoot-Hawley Tariff Bill and the regulars to pass it. Careful estimates indicated that each side had mustered an equal number of votes. Grundy insisted that his own vote was in doubt. In the end he did, in fact, vote reluctantly in favor of the bill. On June 22,1930, it passed the Senate 44-42. Grundy's statement concerning his doubts about the bill belied the charge that it was a masterpiece of Grundyism Grundy said the bill was "unfair to the east" because almost ninety-four per cent of the increased duties was on agricultural products. Furthermore, he declared that the increased rates were largely directed toward the interest of the western farmer. Grundy also pointed out, "This is the first time in the history of tariff legislation that the administrative professions have been subject to party politics."'

He was referring to a change in the function of the Federal Tariff Commission. This body was originally a fact-finding one with the function of recommending rate changes to the President. Although the Senate had failed in its attempt to seize the flexibility power vested in the President, it had succeeded in transferring this power to the Federal Tariff Commission which no longer "recommended" to the President, but now "directed" him.

Grundy also criticized the fact that the bill, like the Fordney-McCumber tariff before it, was based upon a system of foreign evaluation. He and other leaders in industry, labor and agriculture had long been urging a system of American evaluation. Moreover, the Smoot-Hawley bill deprived the United States of new means of obtaining correct information about foreign evaluations. This country could no longer place an embargo on products of the foreign manufacturer who refused to inform our treasury agents abroad concerning his retail prices.

At least Grundy had made a courageous fight to protect industrial interests and to fulfill that promise in the tariff plank of the Republican platform of 1928. In spite of the insidious attempt of the coalition to prove that Grundy's efforts were *against* the welfare of agriculture, it never succeeded in doing so.

Grundy's interest in agriculture had ever been a part of his belief in the American economic system. He objected to the original Smoot-Hawley tariff not because it was favorable to agriculture but as unfair to industry. His efforts were aimed toward the welfare of the industry which accounted for the tremendous growth and power of the United States during the preceding decades. Had it not been for these efforts, the bill would have been a complete victory for agriculture and a total loss for industry.

The Pennsylvanian, as United States Senator from Pennsylvania, faithfully served the industrial economy of his state, promoting, in his own words, "the interests and the prosperity of the people of Pennsylvania."

CHAPTER 15

"I'LL GO IT ALONE"

In view of the national acclaim which marked the beginning of Grundy's activities as a senator from Pennsylvania, it is ironic to see how quickly clouds gathered in his own state. This surprised Joe Grundy because he was a man of his word and to the day of his death at the age of ninety-eight, he so remained. Even though he had learned that many others might not be counted on to hold to this principle, he persisted in a childlike belief that they would. In December, 1929, he had the word of Governor Fisher and other leaders of the Pennsylvania Republican organization that he would have their unqualified support in the spring primaries. That was the condition upon which he had reluctantly assumed the office of United States Senator on December 12th.

However, an old story repeated itself. Vare's cohorts in Philadelphia decided that their leader could recoup power in the coming primaries. Mellon, long a Grundy friend and backer, remained strangely uncommitted for the Senator. The explanation for this probably lies in his position as Secretary of the Treasury under President Hoover, a post he had held under the two previous administrations. Mellon may have been influenced by President Hoover who had been embarrassed by Grundy's pounding away at "unkept campaign promises." Hoover, wanting a second term, was up against Grundy's openly declared intentions to line up "protection delegates" early for the 1932 convention.

The situation was further complicated by the fact that Grundy's attitude on friendship was the same as his viewpoint on campaign promises. He had a long memory for those who helped or hindered his projects. An old favorite was Samuel S.

Lewis of York County. Lewis, a tough-talking politician and former state treasurer who could be counted upon to work hard in an election and "get out the votes," was Grundy's choice for governor. In a hard fought race, Lewis had served as campaign manager for the Fisher-Pepper ticket in 1926 and his performance was, in Grundy's opinion, a decisive factor in Fisher's triumph.

Nevertheless, the Pennsylvanian's preference for Lewis was anathema to Governor Fisher and, even though the Mellons apparently granted approval at first, they later showed such antagonism toward Lewis that rumors of his and Grundy's withdrawal from the race began to circulate. It was evident that Lewis was about to give up but Joe Grundy issued this statement, "Lewis is running his own campaign and I am running mine."

Early in February of 1930, General Wallace W. Atterbury, president of the Pennsylvania Railroad and a close friend of Vare, suggested that if Grundy would go along with Judge Francis Shunk Brown, a Vare man, for the governorship, Vare would retire from the senate competition and a Brown-Grundy ticket would be formed. The Mellons suggested that such a ticket would harmonize the major forces within the state, but Grundy refused to be a part of the Vare political machine. Vare tried to persuade Grundy that if he would go along with Brown, his election to the Senate was secure. Grundy turned down the offer, saying calmly to his intimates, "By this refusal, I have just lost the primary race."

From that point on, he had few illusions about winning, but he was not one to run from a fight. Despite threats to run with Brown, Vare withdrew and announced the candidacy of Hoover's Secretary of Labor, James J. (Puddler Jim) Davis for the Senate.

Mellon had not yet declared for any of the candidates. He invited a number of Republican leaders to a dinner party on March 24 at his home in Pittsburgh. Neither Vare nor Davis was invited although Davis, a Pittsburgher, was a friend of the host and a fellow member of the Hoover cabinet. Mellon, who knew that Davis had Hoover's blessing in the senatorial race, was in a difficult position. He naturally wanted to continue in the President's good graces, yet he remembered that it was Joe Grundy who had recommended him to Harding for the treasury post. Furthermore, it was to Grundy that they would all turn for the fund raising needed to put the whole party over in the next election!

This Mellon dinner, ostensibly to celebrate "Andy" Mellon's seventy-fifth birthday, would be, in fact, a political gathering of great importance. Grundy laid his plans as he rode on the overnight train to Pittsburgh. He arrived there early on the morning of the 24th, was greeted at the station by several western Pennsylvania friends, and conferred with them at the Duquesne Club. At noon W. L. Mellon met Grundy and accompanied him to the Mellon mansion at Schenley Park. Governor Fisher arrived from his home in Indiana, Pennsylvania. At the sumptuous dinnner Grundy lost little time in stating flatly that he was "in the fight to the finish." He reminded all present of the promises made to him when he had agreed to accept the senatorial appointment in December. To Grundy, then, as ever—a promise was a promise.

Efforts were made to reach a compromise between Grundy and the Vare machine. Grundy refused to compromise. The dinner was superb and it catered to every aspect of Grundy's gourmet taste, but if Andy Mellon had expected to "soften up" his old friend at the affair, he was doomed to disappointment. Joe Grundy returned to Washington as determined as ever to stay in the race.

It was a spectacular race. One of the long shots, Gifford Pinchot, making a bid for a second try at the governorship, pledged all kinds of welfare legislation efforts—old age pensions, help for unemployed, relief for servicemen and an "all-out fight to break the power of the utilities."

By March 28, 1930, Grundy had little time left in which to

file his petition for the senatorial post. The Pittsburgh *Post Gazette* declared: "The people of Pennsylvania have no intention of permitting Grundyism to dominate state politics."

Fisher tried patiently to explain to Grundy why Lewis would not be a good candidate for Governor, but Grundy refused to listen. This obstinacy was the Pennsylvanian's weakness as well as his strength.

The writer became acquainted with the late Sam Lewis when he was Secretary of the Department of Forests and Waters of Pennsylvania. He was the old line type of politician, tough, probably able, certainly loyal to his political associates; but lacking in many qualifications desirable for a gubernatorial candidate. This did not seem important to Grundy. He had agreed to back this man and could not be budged from his position. At any rate, Lewis, realizing that neither Fisher nor Mellon would back him, withdrew.

It is probable that Mellon and Hoover both secretly wanted Davis. In view of their friendship with Grundy, the Mellons were hopeful that he would withdraw so that they could back Davis without incurring Grundy's displeasure. They had counted on Grundy's pulling out as soon as the Lewis withdrawal was announced but on the following day the fighting Quaker decided to stay in the race anyway.

His friends were flabbergasted. His cause looked so hopeless that many of the members of the Pennsylvania Manufacturers Association and others wise in the ways of politics urged him to withdraw. Aligned against him were many of the men such as General Atterbury and former Mayor Moore of Philadelphia, whom he had helped to place in power. Moore, successfully backed by Grundy against the Vare candidate in 1919, was now the Philadelphia manager for the Vare ticket.

Two men remained faithful to Senator Grundy, State Chairman Edward Martin and Governor Fisher. This forced the hand of the Mellons who, although they kept silent for another month, finally did announce their open support of Judge Brown for Governor, and Grundy for Senator, thus straddling the issue.

202

It was an exciting primary for Pennsylvania. There were no fewer than six candidates, including two wets, Thomas W. Phillips and Francis H. Bohlen, Professor of Law at the University of Pennsylvania. Another candidate, running independently to regain the office for which Grundy had supported him in 1922 was former Governor Pinchot.

Grundy was fighting alone. Many overtures were made to assuage his feelings and he could have had any of the other candidates as his running mate for the governorship, but Grundy had wanted Sam Lewis and no other. He never was a compromiser. With many battles behind him, he knew that a good offense is the best defense so he geared offensive action against no less an adversary than the powerful General Atterbury. Screaming headlines reported his comments on the attempts of the Pennsylvania Railroad to dominate the political scene.

George Wharton Pepper said, "Grundy's theory was . . . that political control in the state had at one time been held by the railroads but they had misused their power in their own interests and that at a later date the liquor interests had similar power. He maintained that political control could be more beneficently exercised in the name of business. This was plausible enough, but he was never able to prove that it meant an appreciable rise in ethical or governmental standards."

Grundy was equally blunt in his attack on the Vare machine which he called "a corrupt and degraded coterie of professional politicians . . . men who have been living on the taxpayers for years. Their system is one of mismanagement and corruption [as] they stretch out itching palms for a wholesale raid on the state treasury." Grundy continued, "Their program is trading political offices and an exploitation of public funds as they loot the people of the entire state."

When reporters besieged Grundy as he travelled between Bristol, Philadelphia and Washington, they speculated that he would withdraw any moment. He said, "I am running alone and without strings of any kind. This is the way it will be to the finish."

One technique used by Grundy was a potentially effective one. He declared that probes for election frauds after elections were stupid and meaningless. The time to probe a situation was before it happened. He demanded an investigation of the Philadelphia political machine's use of bribes, extortion, etc., *before* the election.

The 1930 campaign rolled into high gear. "Grundyettes" blossomed forth—young women of Philadelphia and vicinity who had decided to cast their first vote for Grundy. The chairman, Miss Marian T. Beans, said: "There is a strong sentiment among the young women voters of Philadelphia for Mr. Grundy. They feel he is out to protect their economic future."

The Woman's Trade Union League of Pennsylvania issued pamphlets and two-foot placards reading: "Pennsylvania womanhood must defeat Grundy." For copy the pamphlets quoted the *North American* stories described by Grundy.

Grundy was "Assailed as Foe of Labor." A union leader charged he equipped his mill "solely with English machinery." In the *Public Ledger* Grundy answered that the matter of machinery was irrelevant, but that when he outfitted his mills, American machinery was not available and that, at least, since its installation, the American standard of wages had always been paid.

One of the strongest units in the labor movement of Philadelphia was the International Union of Elevator Constructors, Local No. 5. At a May meeting in Bricklayer's Hall, 700 elevator constructors rose to their feet as Senator Grundy finished speaking to them and gave him a tremendous ovation. This was all the more remarkable because certain elements within the Philadelphia labor movement had, in the words of the May issue of *The Progressive Labor World*, "sought insidiously to paint Senator Grundy as a 'foe of labor.' "

However, no one knew better than Grundy that his chances were very slim. He was also aware that he was sure to be elected if he merely gave the nod to the able gubernatorial candidate,

Francis Shunk Brown, but Grundy would not compromise with the Brown backer, Vare. It was a matter of principle. The Pennsylvanian had fought the Vare city machine all his life and he was not going to accept it now even for his own victory.

Defeat did not surprise him. Davis won by about 240,000 votes. There has been speculation about the fact that everyone running on the Brown-Davis ticket except Brown won. He was defeated by the long shot gubernatorial nominee, Gifford Pinchot. Did Grundy, knowing that he would lose, help Pinchot even against his own candidacy? We shall never be sure but we are certain that Pinchot's victory provided Grundy with the opportunity he wanted.

He was the first to come out for Pinchot in the November election. Helping Grundy in the Pinchot campaign were State Chairman Martin, Sam Lewis, and State Representative John M. Flynn who soon thereafter became president of the PMA. The Mellon-Vare combination supported the Democratic liberal nominee, John M. Hemphill, but Grundy commented that a good Republican would stick to the choice made at the primaries whether his choice won or not. Grundy's action was as good as his word. Although none of the present candidates including Pinchot had been favorable to him in the primary effort, Grundy contributed his senate salary of $10,000 to the whole ticket.

Many of Pinchot's original backers deserted him in deference to the Mellon-Vare move. So powerful were the efforts of these two, both backed by millions and powerful city political machinery, that it seemed inconceivable that Pinchot could win. But Pinchot had something behind him besides Senator Grundy's money; that was Grundy, the man. Against overwhelming odds, Grundy's power and efforts won the election for Pinchot.

This was a strange alliance, one that had been formed in an earlier battle in 1922. Although allied at the time, a breach between the two men occurred later. This estrangement, for the moment, had been ended. The alliance between Grundy, the conservative, and Pinchot, the reformer, has been called a political marriage of convenience. Pinchot was a dry, a dreamer, a liberal and idealist. Grundy was a wet and a hardhearted practical businessman. Yet even after the election the extraordinary alignment continued to hold together during the 1931 session of the legislature. Pinchot's declaration that it was "no time for the imposition of additional tax burdens" was gratifying to the Manufacturers Association and Pinchot stood by his word.

However, during the following year conflict between Grundy and Pinchot broke out once more. Grundy had backed Pinchot because he was fighting for the necessary control best to serve the manufacturing interests of the state. He tolerated Pinchot's titular leadership in the state, but he would not back him for federal office. He was appalled by the Governor's presidential aspirations because Pinchot was a staunch "progressive" and among his close friends were three men whom Grundy had good reason to dislike, United States Senators LaFollette, Nye, and Norris.

The fact that in 1932 Grundy did not run as a convention delegate from Pennsylvania is significant. He even refused to attend as a member of the Republican State Committee. It was the first time he missed a national convention in more than a quarter of a century. His absence can probably be explained by the fact he already had figured out that a great majority of Pennsylvania's delegates, under the leadership of Chairman of the Delegation, Vare, would back Hoover's reelection.

Pinchot and Grundy broke openly the following year. The Governor sent a letter to both houses demanding a full scale reform program, including the establishment of old age pension, compulsory unemployment insurance, a minimum wage for women and children and ratification of the child labor amendment to the federal constitution, which had been rejected in 1931. None of these proposals passed because of the powerful PMA lobby. Grundy triumphed over the Governor, but the Governor's wife was another proposition altogether.

Mrs. Pinchot's energy was boundless. She took it upon herself to be a publicized champion of the working classes. She dashed around the state encouraging labor leaders, then picketing with strikers in attempts to force union recognition by the manufacturers. A special committee was called to investigate charges that sweat shops existed in many of the mills throughout the Commonwealth. It is easy to understand that one of the first investigated was, of course, the Grundy mill at Bristol.

Anonymous letters came to the committee describing dismal conditions under which employees worked, with special attention to Grundy's mill where it was claimed, "you work until you drop." Grundy angrily declared the report completely untrue. It was brought out during testimony that several complaining witnesses not only lied but had been planted in factories and misrepresented themselves as laborers. Mrs. Pinchot and a man from the Department of Labor and Industry were implicated in a plot to produce false witnesses. That was the end of the Grundy-Pinchot alliance.

In the fall of 1932 the Roosevelt power was sweeping across the country and Pennsylvania went Democratic for the first time since 1890. Even Grundy's home town of Bristol, to which he had given over half a million dollars, voted Democratic.

Pinchot's welfare program followed the trend and Grundy and the PMA were feeling the results. The Association had a sad story. Its president Flynn reported that of the more than 7,000 Pennsylvania manufacturing corporations which filed income tax reports with the Bureau of Internal Revenue for each of the years, 1932, 33, and 34, less than 2,000 each year showed any net income.

Grundy placed much of the blame on Pinchot's welfare program and when the Governor made another try for the United States Senate in 1934 Grundy worked hard for David A. Reed, his opponent in the primaries. Reed and William A. Schnader, who ran for the governorship, also backed by Grundy, won the nomination. Vare, whose political power had already begun to decline, died shortly thereafter, and the man who held the reins in Pennsylvania, late but firmly, was now Joe Grundy.

The bulk of the program of Pinchot's successor, Democratic

Governor Earle, including a levy on corporate net incomes and the five mill capital stock tax, passed the legislature. One prominent Democrat opposed this type of corporate taxation. It was Grundy's critic of earlier years, Senator Hiram G. Andrews. He said: "If manufacturing is to be taxed, the place to impose the levy is upon income. As a general principle, taxes should represent the benefits received from government. Most certainly they should not be imposed for the purpose of increasing operating deficits. A manufacturing corporation pays the same tax at the present time upon its capital stock when it is operating in the red as it pays when it is making millions."

In 1936 Govenor Earle called for taxes to yield $55,000,000 for unemployment relief. The Republican majority in the Senate limited this program by $20,000,000 and the Governor, dissatisfied, urged Republican Mayor Wilson of Philadelphia to confer with Grundy and Joseph N. Pew, Jr., a millionaire executive of Sun Oil Company whom Joe Grundy was introducing to the political scene. Earle hoped that with the help of these two powers he could get either the full $55,000,000 or a compromise of $45,000,000 from the legislature. Finally in desperation the Governor sent four telegrams to the state's four leading Republican businessmen; they were Grundy, Pew, Mellon, and Ernest T. Weir, the latter being chairman of the National Steel Corporation. The telegrams were identical; each read: "The Republican senators are controlled by you body and soul because they know they cannot win the election this year without the campaign funds you give them."

Ultimately, with the help of the four, a $45,000,000 tax program was agreed upon and passed by the state legislature. Earle had pulled off a new electioneering stunt for Roosevelt by the statements in his telegrams but they were undoubtedly true ones. The national campaign of 1936 with its second Democratic victory was a bitter pill for Grundy to swallow. In the national sweep of Landon's defeat, Grundy saw the Democrats elected to the majority in both the senate and the house at Harrisburg.

This overwhelming Democratic victory in Pennsylvania in November carried Senator Grundy's own county with it for the first time since the Civil War. The blow was undoubtedly a factor in the lessening of his political activities, but it did not affect the astonishing social life of the seventy-three year old Pennsylvanian. During that very fall of 1936, he decided to give a party in honor of his young friend, Attorney Jim MacIntosh and his recent English bride, Daphne, at the Lancaster Country Club. All the Grundy ingredients were in evidence—a superb dinner, irresistible music and other carefully planned touches, with a representative selection of his many friends in the Lancaster area. By three a.m. the guests of honor were weary and asked that they might be excused. The Senator escorted them gracefully to their waiting car, which he had provided, and cheerfully wished them a very happy good night. They expressed warm appreciation for the gala evening and inquired if he would not accompany them back to the home of the friends with whom they all were staying. Grundy laughingly declined, executed a few dance steps and said, "Retire? Goodness, no. The night is still young; I'm going back to the party. Just ask the driver to bring the car back when you are through with it."

And back he went!

As expected, after such a smashing victory in 1936, the taxes passed by the Democratic legislature in 1937 were the highest in Pennsylvania's history. The Workmen's Compensation Law was even fifteen per cent higher than that of New York, in second place. In addition a forty-four hour law had been passed, a situation then existing in only three other states. By the end of the Earle administration there was an alleged deficit of $50,000,000 in the state budget, and the major state taxes on industry had been increased nearly eight hundred per cent in the previous three years.

Grundy's political activities were ending and the general public was beginning to regard Joseph Pew as the new leader of the Republican state organization. In 1938 Pew declared his choice for governor was Arthur James. Grundy, still interested, if not active, was not particularly partial to James. He wanted to see Sam Lewis elected Lieutenant Governor and State Senator Mason Owlett in the United States Senate. Eventually the James-Owlett compromise ticket was agreed upon. James and Lewis were successful but Owlett was defeated by incumbent Senator James Davis who had beaten Grundy just eight years earlier.

At the Republican National Convention in Philadelphia in 1940 Grundy did not understand the enthusiasm for Wendell Wilkie. He was puzzled when enthusiastic political amateurs shouted "Wendell Wilkie" until they were hoarse. One of Grundy's friends, who had hopped on the Wilkie bandwagon, became infuriated as she listened to the convention proceedings on the radio. It seemed that everyone at the convention or listening to it on the radio was fully aware that the convention was swinging to Wendell Wilkie but the Pennsylvania delegation was apparently altogether overlooking the trend. Its leaders were holding a special caucus off the floor, desperately trying to keep the dissenting Pennsylvania delegation in line for Governor James, who had not the slightest chance of being nominated. During the caucus Wilkie gained the nomination on the sixth ballot; thus Pennsylvania lost the opportunity to keep up with the enthusiastic pitch of the nomination.

The Grundy friend was so angered by the stupidity of this situation that she sent a long and angry telegram to Grundy at Convention Hall. She did not know that he was not there. Mason Owlett had been acting for him. When the woman next met Grundy, she tried to think of some appropriate comment. By that time she was somewhat embarrassed by her boldness, even her rudeness to the seventy-seven-year-old Pennsylvania leader. She wondered how he might react to her telegraphed condemnation. From that day to his death the Senator greeted her as cheerily as ever and never referred to the incident. Many times, as in the Wilkie nomination, he was blamed for actions made by subordinates, frequently without his knowledge.

Although he slowly withdrew from political activities, the last two decades of Grundy's life were busy ones. The aged Pennsylvanian devoted more attention to the management of his own business affairs. His sense of timing, famed throughout his career both as lobbyist and businessman continued to function perfectly even in advanced age. One instance occurred when he was eighty-two years old. He had then decided that the wool market was permanently damaged by the developments in synthetics and that he would sell his Bristol plant. He handled the transaction personally and, in a declining market, picked up two million dollars from the deal.

Of course the final day of this critical negotiation was planned by the incomparable host Grundy—a perfectly catered luncheon at his Bristol home, with an astonishing supply of champagne. One of the young lawyers attending said it was his "first business luncheon where champagne was served."

In the impressive dining room with its broad view of the Delaware, there were timely jokes and toasts that warmed the heart—and loosened the purse strings—of the shrewd New England buyer. By the end of the luncheon Grundy had the two million in cash and the buyer the old Bristol mill.

Although the Pennsylvanian was attempting to withdraw from the political scene, a few more lively feuds were inevitable, and one of the most notorious was that with James H. Duff. The Duff story is another in the seemingly endless list of situations involving people whom Grundy had befriended personally, ofttimes financially, and who had initially obtained their positions through his efforts. Once in power they inevitably proceeded to disregard the opinions of the man who made their success possible.

Many believe that Jim Duff owed his high place as attorney-general in Governor Edward Martin's cabinet to Joe Grundy. Although wealthy at one time, Duff had been left in debt by the depression. Grundy encouraged Owlett to help him by obtaining a sizable retainer from a Pittsburgh corporation. Duff later asked Grundy and Owlett to assist him in procuring the post of attorney-general and they apparently persuaded Martin to give Duff the appointment. Martin, not at first enthusiastic over his new attorney-general, went along with him for the sake of his prominent sponsors.

Once in office, Duff took at least two steps opposed by the Pennsylvania Manufacturers Association—efforts for pure stream legislation, and liberalization on the status of workmen's compensation and unemployment. When time for the 1946 primaries arrived, Martin had come to admire Duff's abilities. Grundy and Owlett, protective as always for the manufacturers, viewed Duff with considerable skepticism. They favored Weldon Heyburn for the governorship but Pew had still another man in mind. This caused the stalemate Governor Martin had counted on and he proposed Duff as a compromise choice. Pew sided with Martin and Duff became the candidate. It should be noted that by this time Owlett was frequently acting for Grundy because the Senator was now personally attending only the most important conferences. Owlett, however, could never compare in appearance, personality or ability with his boss, Joe Grundy.

When on January 21, 1947, Duff's liberalism replaced Martin's conservatism, the struggle between two uncompromising leaders, Duff and Grundy, began in earnest. Pennsylvania's levy upon industry's capital stock was higher than that of any other state except Massachusetts. Grundy had a point in arguing that this situation explained the slowing up of industrial growth in Pennsylvania and the loss of many industries to other states. Governor Duff, however, needed funds for public improvements that he considered vital to Pennsylvania's welfare.

Duff's particular interest in pure stream measures provided an issue dear to the heart of anyone who lives near or loves the Pennsylvania streams. Duff argued with reason that industry had made additional profits during the war and so could stand the present tax burdens. The Duff-Grundy break was now complete. The exemption of manufacturers from the multimillion dollar capital stock tax had been suspended by successive Legislatures

The late Robert A. Taft with Grundy, who said, "When we lost Senator Taft, we lost the best that the Republican Party had to offer."

for a number of sessions and, although the proposed restoration of the exemption in 1947 was supported by the Republicans in the campaign in which Duff was elected and had been advocated by Duff as a member of Martin's cabinet, following his election he reversed his position. In his budget message of March 11, 1947, Governor Duff stated, "It would be unfair to give tax exemptions to any group when it is necessary to expand the tax base during this abnormal period to provide the absolutely essential funds to operate our Commonwealth." He succeeded in controlling the state legislature in the 1947 session and putting over his public works program.

The first round went to Jim Duff but eighty-five-year-old Joe Grundy was still fighting. When the 1948 Republican convention rolled around, Grundy was there in person to lead the battle against Duff's candidates Vandenburg or Taft. Grundy backed ill-starred Thomas E. Dewey who won the nomination.

During the next few years Grundy withdrew from active participation in the management of the PMA and spent more time away from his beloved Bucks County. The Grundy name persisted and Duff made Grundyism one of his campaign issues. The opposition stated that Duff and his backers were spendthrift, new deal type social reformers who ought to be listed as Democrats. Duff said: "For the Grundyites there is and can be no compromise with their basic philosophy. That which helps industry to prosper helps the state to prosper."

Duff, like most Grundy detractors, recognized the basic truth of this guiding principle of Grundy's life, yet he, like all the rest, managed to suggest that it held sinister implications. Although Duff made political capital of the term Grundyism, he was anxious to get Grundy's financial support. John S. Fine, running for governor, is reported to have asked: "Jim, if you could win by 200,000 without Grundy's support or 400,000 with his support, would you want me to go (to him)?"

Duff replied, "Yes."

Although in 1950 Duff won the United States senatorship and Fine the governorship, the break between Duff and Grundy was widening. In the Republican National Convention of 1952 Jim Duff was a prominent figure. He had been one of Gen. Dwight D. Eisenhower's foremost champions. Strangely enough Duff's elderly adversary, Grundy, was now the devoted champion of the man to whom Duff had been committed four years earlier, Robert A. Taft. By this time Grundy was avoiding all political activity and had no illusions about the possibilities of winning the Pennsylvania delegation over to Taft. Governor Fine was for Eisenhower and so were most members of the Philadelphia delegation led by Duff's old friend and former Philadelphia sheriff, Austin Meehan. Duff managed to keep the Grundy faction uninformed as to Governor Fine's position.

When Owlett eventually learned that Fine was backing Eisenhower, it was too late for the Grundy followers to switch and share in Eisenhower's triumph. However, it is unlikely that Senator Grundy would have switched if he could. He explained this in private conversations with his friends. Grundy regarded Dwight D. Eisenhower as a great general, an able man with a warm personality, but to Grundy he could never give the type of Republican leadership the party needed after so many years of Democratic reign.

To the Pennsylvanian the late Robert A. Taft typified the highest type of Republican leader. Grundy frequently commented, "When we lost Senator Taft, we lost the best that the Republican party had to offer."

Although now in his nineties, Grundy had still another momentous business transaction ahead of him. For years he had fought what he called the "invasion" of larger banks into Bucks County. He had opposed this trend back in 1950 when the Girard Trust Company was interested in absorbing the Morrisville Bank, and led the protest when bankers in Montgomery and Delaware Counties "sold' out" to Philadelphia banks.

In the early fifties when United States Steel Corporation and Levittown brought thousands of new residents into Bucks County, Grundy frequently commented on the entry of both

Bristol banks into new banking fields, such as automobile financing and consumer installment buying. He was uneasy about the extent to which the resources of both banks, in which he was the largest stockholder, had been committed to these new fields and viewed developments with deep concern. In 1956 he was alarmed by the fact that his Delaware Valley Bank and Trust Company had approximately 11,000 depositors' accounts, but at the same time held outstanding approximately 9,000 loans to such depositors.

The Senator felt that a business recession or labor difficulties might "tie up" a substantial portion of the resources of each bank and thereby strain the banks' credit. Even he finally became convinced that this strain would be avoided if the Bristol banks were merged into larger Philadelphia banking institutions.

In the case of the Farmers National Bank Grundy felt the additional personal responsibility stemming from the long roots of family connection. In this case the subject of merger was first broached to his fellow directors and a negotiation committee and special counsel, Morgan, Lewis and Bockius, was appointed to negotiate with one or more banking institutions. Detailed financial data was assembled and submitted to the six largest such institutions in Philadelphia. June 27, 1956 was fixed as the date for the submission of sealed proposals. At the appointed hour representatives of the six Philadelphia banks assembled in the office of Morgan, Lewis and Bockius and bids were opened.

After an analysis of them it was announced that the Fidelity-Philadelphia Trust Company had, to quote the *Evening Bulletin*, "captured the prize."

Subsequently a merger agreement was negotiated between the Delaware Valley Bank and Trust Company and The Philadelphia National Bank on somewhat similar terms. And, by these two transactions, Grundy added approximately one million dollars to the value of his holdings. Age did not dim the extraordinary business judgment of the Pennsylvanian.

CHAPTER 16

THE NASSAU YEARS

The beat of the popular orchestra at Nassau's exclusive Bahamian Club was irresistible. Well-dressed partners crowded the dance floor, but most eyes strayed from their elegance and lingered on one particular couple. The woman, tall, sixtyish and still glamorous, was the most famous figure in the islands, Lady Eunice Oakes.

The stoop of the man's shoulders indicated great age. Yet his thick white hair, china-blue eyes, and pink, almost unlined complexion denied the years. Could this man in impeccable evening clothes actually be ninety-seven?

Joe Grundy was one of those people who at sixty, looked sixty, and thereafter never appeared any older except for posture in the very last years.

Gradually the other dancers withdrew, leaving the floor to Lady Oakes and Grundy. When they found themselves alone, and, surprised, stopped dancing, the others broke into sustained applause. Joe Grundy looked startled, self-conscious and shyly pleased as he escorted Lady Eunice to his table. He whispered, "I hope thee is not embarrassed by all this fuss."

He glanced across the table at his hostess, Mrs. Charles Stauffer. The trim, brown-eyed widow returned his smile. Mrs. Stauffer, known in Nassau as well as Lancaster County, Pennsylvania, for her wit and infectious gaiety, was recalling the first time she had looked across a dinner table at Joe Grundy. It had been his special table at the Mayflower Hotel in Washington. It was 1928 and Grundy was the most powerful political figure in Pennsylvania. She had already established her position as one of the smartest politicians in her influential county. Feminine charm softened but could not hide a keen mind and an unerring ability to size up people and situations with astonishing accuracy.

As vice-chairman of the Republican State Committee, she had been advised to consult the powerful Pennsylvanian about the rumor of an unacceptable appointment by Governor Fisher. Several women had protested the naming of a certain person as head of the Women's and Children's Bureau. As vice-chairman Mrs. Stauffer went directly to Fisher with the protests of her constituents. The Governor told her that the appointment had been recommended by Joe Grundy and if she wanted to protest it, she should go directly to him.

Although her husband had been acquainted with Grundy for some years, Mrs. Stauffer knew him only slightly. Now, facing a conference with him, she remembered with misgivings a remark by William L. Mellon, the Pittsburgh industrialist. It was made during a discussion with Mellon about her becoming vice-chairman of the Republican State Committee. She made it clear that she didn't want the job unless all those active in the party, such as the powerful Grundy, were behind her nomination. Mellon said he had discussed the appointment with Grundy and that although he was not too enthusiastic about women office holders, he had said to Mellon, "If we must have a woman vice-chairman, it might as well be a woman from a county like Lancaster that gives a real Republican majority."

Mrs. Stauffer, known to her friends and political associates throughout the state as Gertie, now decided that she should see Mr. Grundy who was in Washington at the time. She telephoned to arrange for a meeting. He was polite but said that the particular day which she suggested was filled with scheduled appointments—could she talk with him at dinner? This she agreed to do.

The following week, as she neared the Mayflower Hotel at the arranged time, she became increasingly nervous. After all, this famous bachelor was known to take seriously the women's vote, but not their political thinking. She straightened her black velvet dress, carefully chosen for the occasion, and readjusted her new, matching velour tricorne hat.

Mr. Grundy in his customary perfectly-tailored blue serge

suit was waiting in the lobby. Gravely he escorted her to his table in the main dining room as respectful waiters bowed along the way. He spoke not a word until he had ordered, as a ritual, a full course meal with all the suitable wines. Then, settling back in his chair, Grundy asked, "Now what does thee have on thy mind?"

Gertie plunged into the objections to the rumored appointment. The Pennsylvanian listened, expressionless and without comment. When she had finished, he was silent for a few moments. She wondered whether she had said too much or perhaps, too little to this enigmatic politician. Suddenly he smiled. "Thee states thy case well and thee comes from a good Republican county, so it shall be as thee wishes."

He did not refer to this conversation again but talked at length about Lancaster County politics and the importance of its farm vote. "Greatest farm county in the state," said the Pennsylvania manufacturer who happened to be a farmer as well. "What is more, the farmers know the value of manufacturing to their own pockets, just as the manufacturers know the value of the farm market. In our state we work together. That is why Pennsylvania is so prosperous and some of the industrially backward states are envious of us."

He could not then possibly imagine how that term "backward states" would, within a year, make headlines in leading newspapers and rock a nation from coast to coast.

Grundy eventually became a close friend of the entire Stauffer family, including the two children, Sarah Ann and Charles, Jr. He enjoyed the superb parties in the Stauffer townhouse in Lancaster and the family's warm friends both in the city and among the Lancaster farmers throughout the county. When Charles Stauffer died in 1933 Grundy felt a deep sense of loss. His friendship with the family lasted until the day of his own death twenty-eight years later.

It was Gertie who introduced Joe and Meta to the Bahamas,

Grundy celebrates his ninety-sixth birthday with Lady Eunice Oakes in Nassau.

Grundy and good friends, Mrs. Charles Stauffer and daughter, Sarah Ann (Sally), in early Nassau years.

years before the Islands became popular as a vacation resort. In traveling here Grundy again demonstrated that he kept up "with the lastest." Just as he was one of the first telephone users, he now became one of the first regular winter airline passengers, flying from Miami to Nassau by Pan-American clipper or seaplane. The only new developments in which "Uncle Joe" as he was called in his last years, showed little interest were those in outer space travel. Of these he said, "Can't get concerned about another planet—I'm having enough trouble struggling to stay on this one."

He spent increasingly long winter vacations in the Bahamas and enjoyed warm friendships with many of the prominent Bahamian residents, among them the delightful Archibald Higgs; Mrs. Higgs' sister, Mrs. Arthur H. Sands; the Episcopal Dean of the Bahama Islands, Frederick Ellis, and his witty wife, Helen.

Grundy had a far-reaching reputation as a host in Pennsylvania as well as Nassau, and one of his most memorable parties occurred in June, 1939, when he entertained at a dinner before a benefit performance of *George Washington Slept Here* at the Bucks County Playhouse in New Hope, Pennsylvania. The authors, Moss Hart and George S. Kaufman were unable to attend; however, Beatrice Kaufman, George's first wife, accepted. She was an able writer and wit in her own right, and at the time was associated with the ultra-liberal newspaper, *P.M.* Curious about the famous politician, she went to the Grundy dinner armed with a stock of prejudices in her mind and a batch of unfavorable newspaper clippings on her controversial host. Among the other guests were Major and Mrs. Charles J. Biddle of Andalusia and Governor Arthur H. James of Pennsylvania. Beatrice Kaufman was surprised to find her host both genial and charming. She whispered to a guest, "But I thought this man hired small children and practically beat his mill hands!" The guest, unaware of Mrs. Kaufman's newspaper affiliations said, "You must read only the tabloids."

By the end of the evening Beatrice Kaufman was under the spell of the Pennsylvanian. Upon leaving she said, "I really must be going or you might even turn me into a Republican."

"At that rate," was Grundy's quick reply, "thee must return as soon as possible."

After the death of his sister in 1952, Senator Grundy asked Gertie Stauffer and her charming sister, Myrtle Neff, to be his Nassau hostesses in the magnificent house, Jacaranda, which he rented each season.

In their later years most people withdraw into the lonely quiet of old age—not so with the Pennsylvania Quaker. In his last nine years, from the age of eighty-nine to ninety-eight, Joe Grundy lived more glamorously and more luxuriously than he had throughout his entire life.

Jacaranda was as opulent as its multimillionaire owner, Lady Eunice Oakes, the widow of fabulous Sir Harry, whose murder in 1935 was an international sensation. Although she owned several houses on the Island, Jacaranda was her much-loved townhouse. There she spent seven months of the year and rented it to Senator Grundy for the other five.

Jacaranda was situated two long blocks above the center of Nassau, across the street from the Royal Victoria Hotel. A beautiful wrought iron gate guarded its entrance, the black filigree contrasting pleasantly with the faded pink walls that surrounded it. Once inside the grounds, the hum of Nassau's hub abruptly ceased and the excitement of the city seemed far away. A quietness enveloped the visitor—a balminess that was more than a type of weather. It was a mood, a mellowness, a sense of timelessness.

The house was large though low and rambling. Its inevitable fading from the constant sunshine increased the beauty of the well-preserved pink stucco walls. For contrast, the porch was painted a sea-green. On it, soft green and gold cushions added comfort to the white wrought iron furniture. The steps, of native stone had a time-swept appearance and the long veranda overlooked cocoanut palms and breadfruit trees. To the south of the patio was the large drawing room and kitchen wing, with a charming guest apartment above. Carved in stone on the patio wall were the familiar lines:

"A kiss of the sun for pardon;
The song of the birds for mirth—
You are nearer God's heart in a garden
Than anywhere else on earth."

In the wide center hall hung a large portrait of Nancy Oakes. Three other paintings, all French, lined the walls. To the left was the drawing room with beige wall-to-wall carpeting, eighteenth-century French provincial furniture and comfortable cretonne-covered pieces in soft tones of rose and blue. Above the sofa was a famous painting of the five Oakes children and Lady Oakes, painted in 1934 by Kenneth Forbes.

For Joe Grundy this was a gracious winter home to which many friends flocked. Each found warm hospitality whether it was a neighbor from Bristol, or one of Grundy's old political cronies such as Republican former Speaker of the House, Joe Martin.

All arrivals were met either at the ship or the airport by Adam Munro, Lady Oakes' butler. Each year when Joe Grundy rented Jacaranda in December, he also took over Eunice Oakes' domestic staff, headed by the able Munro, who combined the dignified bearing of the English butler with the gentle charm that is native Bahamian.

The writer's visit in 1959 was typical. The S.S. *Nassau* was three hours late in anchoring at Nassau harbor. Strong head-winds throughout the night had slowed the ship. Shortly before we anchored, a sudden heavy cloud formation brought a downpour. It was over quickly and in the immemorial manner of passengers, we watched the native boys dive for coins from battered rowboats.

Tourists started trotting purposefully around the decks—bandanas, Nassau hats, Bermudas, short shorts, men in socks,

221

whose knees looked as embarrassed as their faces. There were baskets, bags, and the inevitable cameras.

About twenty-five of us were disembarking. The tender "Lady Moore" pulled up beside us and we got aboard. Ahead of us, the island shone in the noonday sun. The lighthouse on the tip of Hog Island, facing Nassau, looked like a toy. The pink British Colonial Hotel dominated the shore line. Buildings were low and painted pastel shades. We saw few windows, only Bahamian shutters and jalousies. The docks were colorful and artistically dilapidated. The sun was hot.

The startlingly blue waters sparkled as the fishing boats bobbed about lazily. Native boys, perched on the tender, put on self-consciously Bahamian acts, tunes and comment, strictly for the tourist trade. As we approached the dock, several on it waved to arriving friends. We felt that sense of loneliness one always feels when one arrives, a stranger at a strange destination.

Then, all at once, we saw a face that was vaguely familiar. It was Munro, Lady Oakes' butler. His tall, commanding figure towered above the crowd, his dark skin contrasting with a light blue suit. A man standing beside him was smiling. He moved toward the boat and called to us, "Hello, how are you?"

My husband and I were startled and delighted to see Eddie Rummler, Senator Grundy's affable secretary who was, we thought, in Philadelphia. They had been waiting all morning for us because the Senator had been worried about the lateness of the ship.

Grundy guests differ as to which aspect of their visits was the most fabulous—the breakfasts served so daintily on trays placed on the individual verandas that overlooked the city and Nassau harbor, the gay cocktail hours with their memorable drinks and exotic hors d'oeuvres, or the regular meals themselves, served punctually at 10 a.m., 2 p.m., and 8 o'clock. Joe Grundy always gave his arm to the woman guest of honor, escorted her to the dining room and himself seated her at his right—this even at ninety-eight years of age! The long, highly polished mahogany table under the expert eye of Gertie Stauffer was always a picture in itself. Each year she carried some of her own beautiful antique silver to Jacaranda. There it gleamed next to a solid silver epergne, a gift from her good friend, Lady Oakes.

The flower arrangements were always conversation pieces. Another was Munro's highly acclaimed ingenuity with finger bowl decorations. These included varied figures made from vegetables, such as a carrot with toothpick legs, tiny onion eyes, and sprigs of parsley for ears; an olive head with clove eyes and celery body; or intricate designs of tiny blossoms with petals floating in the crystal bowls.

Guests were always curious about Grundy's eating habits. The diet of any man whose skin is still fresh and firm in his nineties and who continues to eat with obvious relish is well worth noting. Breakfast was hearty—a whole grapefruit, frequently orange juice as well, three slices of bacon, one soft-boiled egg, one piece of cracked wheat toast, one pat of butter. In later years Grundy carefully divided the butter, half-a-pat on toast, half on his egg. He always used cream and saccharin in his coffee. Some mornings he substituted a large bowl of hot cereal for the egg.

During the last twenty years of his life, his health routine began when he got out of bed, around 6 a.m. He drank at once, on doctor's orders, a small glass of whiskey and ice water. Then he dressed slowly and enjoyed fruit juice and coffee before reading the newspaper. Near the breakfast hour of 10 a.m., he made his way downstairs and walked the length of the porch ten or twelve times.

After breakfast he read his mail, and settled down to enjoy current periodicals or a favorite book. Every Friday morning was reserved for going over accounts. Each household item was checked and every quarter accounted for. The methodical habits of the young Grundy persisted throughout his life.

In Nassau, luncheons were simple. They usually featured soup, frequently conch with its oyster-like taste, or the host's favorite green turtle soup, seafoam crackers and cheese, with fruit for dessert.

Throughout his earlier years in Bucks County, Grundy frequently had lunch at his townhouse in Bristol. There his lunch usually consisted of lamb chops with several vegetables, especially fresh asparagus in season, and fresh fruit and cookies for dessert. Another favored dish was creamed dried beef.

For his noonday meal at the Union League in Philadelphia, the Senator preferred Chincoteague oysters on the half-shell, green turtle soup, coffee, and a baked apple for dessert. Other favorite foods, according to Curt Lauterbach of the Union League staff, were braised sweetbreads on Virginia ham, lobster thermidor, and all types of fruit, including figs and Pride-of-Wisconsin melons. He reported that the Senator never used much seasoning, but liked cream in his coffee and on his beloved baked apple. Before luncheon and dinner he enjoyed one drink— "Old Granddad" on the rocks.

Grundy was a gourmet all his life and his tastes persisted through the Nassau years. Dinners at Jacaranda were uniformly delicious, varying from fillet of sea bass, sauteed, to turkey and roast chestnuts, cornish hen and wild rice, or larded tenderloin. For dessert he often chose vanilla ice cream with guava slices and guava sauce. One gay guest startled him by remarking that this was a very "sexy" dessert. Grundy looked at her for a moment, his eyes twinkling, and said, "I suppose then thee might say that when thee gets too old for sex, thee can have guava jelly."

After dessert, in true Victorian fashion, the women retired to the drawing room for after-dinner coffee, often enhanced by Tia and Maria Brandy, while the men remained at the table as host Grundy handed out imported cigars and led off with an entertaining and perhaps slightly risque story. Soon the men joined the women for cordials and stories that were amusing and more discreet. Eventually the group played bridge or bonanza, while the Senator took on all comers at casino and, as his astonished guests soon learned, beat them all roundly. There was no need to try to "be kind to the old gentleman." Right up to the time of his death he won decisively and on merit.

Grundy's good health throughout his advanced years was undoubtedly due in large measure to his inheritance. "I picked out the right Mother," he would say. He escaped all serious illness; however he had numerous close scrapes in automobile accidents. He drove a car as he had driven a bicycle—with wild abandon and a reckless disregard for red lights. It is said that many newspapers acting on the law of averages, carried obituary notices of "death by accident" for the Pennsylvanian.

At sixty-five, while driving in his Owens Magnetic, he had a serious accident near Torresdale, a section of northeast Philadelphia. While driving, he leaned out to close the car door and ran into a telegraph pole. His jugular vein was severed, in fact, he was almost decapitated. A nearby resident carried him into the house and by prompt first aid, saved his life. Grundy's blood ruined the furnishings in the front room and Grundy paid for the complete redecorating of the entire house in appreciation.

After the age of eighty-five, Joe Grundy began listening carefully to medical advice. His ninetieth birthday found him in general good health but suffering from an eye infection. On July 13th of that year, 1953, he entered the University of Pennsylvania Hospital for a losing battle with both the infection and advanced glaucoma of one eye. He was under the care of Dr. Harold G. Scheie, the internationally renowned ophthalmologist. Throughout the long four-and-a-half month stay at the hospital, genial Joe Grundy was an ideal patient who enjoyed the attention of the hospital staff and the visits of his friends.

Dr. Scheie was surprised and touched by the extent of the Senator's confidence. To the doctor's suggestions that he have a consultation with another eye specialist, the Pennsylvanian always demurred and retold a favorite story about "Old Abe" who kept having a five-dollar bill changed into nickels, counting them carefully, and then a short time later, exchanging the nickels for a five-dollar bill. When asked why he did this so often, Old Abe replied, "Well, if I keep this up long enough, somebody's going to make a mistake—an it ain't goin' to be Abe." Then the Senator would add smilingly, "Now, I'm going to do everything you say and I'll not make any mistakes. See that you don't make any, either!"

Two years later on October 22nd the Senator returned to the hospital for removal of the infected eye. Dr. Scheie succeeded in preventing the infection from reaching the other eye of the ninety-two-year-old patient. After the operation Grundy remarked, "At my age it is better to be seen than to see." He did see from the one eye for the rest of his life—reading until twenty-four hours before his death.

Impressed by both the skill of his surgeon and his department, the Senator made a bequest of $1,000,000 to the University of Pennsylvania, to be under the direction of Dr. Scheie, Professor of Ophthalmology, as long as he is on the school staff, and after that, as directed by succeeding departmental chairmen.

Dr. Scheie and his charming wife and two children became yearly visitors at Jacaranda. The doctor never ceased to be amazed by the freshness of Grundy's skin and by the way the aged man trotted about. "He always, even when stooped, walked briskly, never slowly," commented Dr. Scheie.

Many have wondered about the secret of Grundy's unwrinkled skin and amazing energy. He did pursue a regular schedule during his last years, retiring at eleven o'clock each night, when he was given a half-grain of phenobarbitol and a small glass of "Old Granddad" or "Jack Daniels" on ice. He then slept soundly for six or seven hours and awoke refreshed. He never, even at ninety-eight, took afternoon naps.

Walking was Grundy's only exercise and he did it regularly on verandas, indoors, and, in his last summers, at Ocean City, New Jersey. There at the age of ninety-five he purchased a charming house near the boardwalk. Daily in good weather he sauntered for about five hundred yards south on the boardwalk and back. One evening in the summer of 1960 he took the walk with a friend fifty-four years of age who had suffered a heart attack some months previously. At the end of the five hundred yards, the two men paused and the ninety-seven-year-old Pennsylvanian said firmly, "Thee had better rest awhile," and remained standing while insisting that the younger man sit on a bench nearby.

Grundy was almost ceremonial about one health notion—propping his feet on a stool whenever he sat down. He always explained carefully how much work the heart had to do to pump the blood up through the legs and into the feet and how much easier it was for the heart if the legs were elevated. He considered reference to the toes somewhat indelicate and so explained that the blood went "down through the feet and whatever embarrassment there is there."

The Senator was always ready to take advice from competent authorities on any subject except tariff and politics (and surely few were better qualified on these). He showed the same loyalty to his lawyers as to his doctors. The law firm handling his large estate was that of Morgan, Lewis and Bockius one of Philadelphia's largest and best-known legal firms. The association developed through a senior partner, W. James MacIntosh, who as a young lawyer, made the acquaintance of Joe Grundy. The meeting occurred in 1933 in connection with the reorganization of a Pennsylvania coal company in which Grundy had a substantial investment. At that time Morgan, Lewis and Bockius represented other bondholders whose interests were similar to those of Senator Grundy. Senator Grundy was impressed by MacIntosh's work on the case and sought his help in connection with some of his own estate matters.

Grundy persuaded the younger man and his friend, Orus J. Matthews, to accompany him on one of his many trips to Europe. Forever after, in referring to this crossing, Grundy said that the young lawyers were so busily involved with the attractive ladies on board that he saw very little of them!

Jim MacIntosh remained a close personal friend throughout

the Senator's lifetime and frequently visited at Walnut Grove and Jacaranda. In later years a junior member of the law firm, Oscar M. Hansen, became closely associated with the Senator during the sale of his woolen mills in Bristol. Hansen, who was graduated from New York University in 1932 and received his Master's Degree in 1933, served as a Colonel in the Ordnance Department of the United States Army during World War II. The young lawyer admired the ability and wit of the aged Pennsylvanian. Grundy returned this admiration and regarded Hansen not only as lawyer but as one of the family.

Hansen always enjoyed one of the Senator's favorite "lawyer" stories. The Pennsylvanian liked to remind his lawyer friends that they had been wise in their choice of a profession. "Lawyers," chuckled Grundy, "are just like 'coon traps—they get you coming and going."

In his last years Joe Grundy dined out less frequently. When he did appear publicly in Nassau it was for some benefit and he would always explain apologetically, "Thee knows it is all for charity." One night in 1959 he escorted old friends including the writer and her husband to a charity affair at the Royal Victoria. The Senator was dressed, as usual for dinner, in a well-cut tuxedo, with a cummerbund. At the reserved table the wine steward brought the wines for the ninety-six-year-old host to taste and he did so with the air of a true connoisseur. Grundy ate every course—lobster entree, turtle soup, steak, vegetables, parfait and coffee. A guest at another table recognized him and brought over a visiting celebrity who asked for his autograph. He gave it graciously and with shy, but nevertheless evident, pleasure. All heads turned as he left the table with his beautifully-gowned hostess, Gertie Stauffer, and their guests. It was impossible to believe that this pink-cheeked, courtly, white-haired man had lived nearly a century.

Very occasionally the Senator took a short trip on the yacht he hired for the season and lunched at the exclusive Porcupine Club on Hog Island. Its small membersip list included the names of du Pont and Rockefeller.

Grundy with his young friends, Nancy and Eric, the children of Dr. and Mrs. Harold G. Scheie.

Grundy and his cousin, Mrs. James H. Emack (Sue Campion).

Dr. Harold G. Scheie, head of the Department of Ophthalmology, University of Pennsylvania Medical School, accepts for the university a $1,000,000 bequest contained in the will of Joseph R. Grundy. Presentation was made by Samuel H. Ballam, Jr., right, one of the executors of the Grundy estate.

Left to right: Oscar M. Hansen, Esq., Board of Trustees of The Grundy Foundation; Henry R. Pemberton, Financial Vice President, University of Pennsylvania; Thomas E. Morris, Board of Trustees; Harold G. Scheie, Professor of Ophthalmology, University of Pennsylvania Hospital; Samuel H. Ballam, Jr., Senior Vice President, Fidelity Philadelphia Trust Company; Dr. Gaylord P. Harnwell, President, University of Pennsylvania; W. James MacIntosh, Esq., Chairman, Board of Trustees; Edwin R. Rummler, Secretary, Board of Trustees.

Grundy was a generous host but if, when dining out, a bill was presented, he read every item carefully and checked the addition. He then unclasped an old fashioned purse, removed a rubber band from a roll of bills and peeled them off with deliberate precision. The Pennsylvanian was never one to throw his money around. In the last five years of his life, at least while living at Jacaranda, he indulged in expensive entertaining and brightly lighted rooms. But once back at Walnut Grove he resumed the more cautious habits of earlier years. At night when he left the library to go to the drawing room, he invariably walked over and turned out the light in the room he was leaving.

While Meta lived, she was a gracious and charming hostess, at beautiful Walnut Grove. Her brother was always happy to entertain her friends and those connected with the many projects in which she was interested. The members of the Pennsylvania Society of the Colonial Dames of America and the Pennsylvania Society of New England Women were frequently invited to their home; as were the local Women's Club, Red Cross workers, Needlework Guild members, and many others associated with Meta in civic affairs.

Joe Grundy encouraged his sister's interest in gardening. She grew rare azaleas, delphinium, sweet william, and pansies, the latter the Senator's favorite flower. He loved the old buttonwood trees at Walnut Grove and often pointed out that he had planted every tree on the east side of Newportville Road and everyone had said he wouldn't "live to see them grow up!" He once paid an enormous sum to save one old sugar maple. His sentimental attachment to this tree was prompted by the fact that his Uncle Joseph Knight Grundy, who eventually died from an ailment contracted in the Civil War, helped him to plant it.

Each evening as Grundy returned to Walnut Grove from work his standard greeting was, "Any riots today?" To the latest gossip which Meta invariably recounted to him at dinner, his usual retort was, "Oh, my, my, my!" Lighted candles always brightened the dining room table and Grundy enjoyed blowing these out before leaving the room. His sister's answer to this evening gesture was a smiling, "You're full of wind anyway!"

Meta frequently spent hours preserving fruits and vegetables to his taste, and sometimes an entire morning making his favorite soup. The Senator, recalling the days of lavish entertainment, continued to purchase all foods in large quantities. Even in his last years he followed the practice, at one time buying thirty-two dozen eggs from Lancaster. (A real money saving, too!)

Betty Jamison and her husband, Russell, who worked as cook and gardener for fourteen years said, "I never saw two people get along any better than the Senator and his sister—each of them always thinking of the other."

Many have explained Grundy's bachelorhood in terms of his Victorian sense of responsibility in looking after his sister, burdened with ill health for many years. Several other explanations have been offered. Three possibilities are illustrated by treasured clippings of his favorite light verse. The reader may draw his own conclusion.

LEFT

"I left this humble rustic town,
    Quite eighteen months ago
    To win a fortune and renown
    For Ruth, my own dear one.
"I left her, promised wife and joy
    My hated rival, too—
    Jim Jones, the burly butcher boy,
    Who once my love did woo.
"I left, and now I'm once more home
    To claim my charming Ruth;
    But she's been married just a year
    To Jones. I'm left in truth."

WHAT SHE KNOWS ABOUT IT

"What is flirtation? Really!
    How can I answer that?

Yet when she smiles I see its wiles,
And when he lifts his hat.
"Tis meeting in the ballroom,
Tis whirling in the dance;
With something hid beneath the lid
Besides a simple glance.
"Tis walking in the hallway,
Tis resting on the stair;
Tis bearded lips on finger tips
(If mamma is not there).
"Tis going out for ices,
Tis buttoning on a glove;
Tis lips that speak of plays next week,
And eyes that talk of love.
"Tis tucking in a carriage;
Tis asking for a call;
Tis lifted eyes and tender sighs,
And that is—no, not all.
"Tis parting when tis over,
And one goes home to sleep;
Tra la, my friend, best joys must end—
But one goes home to weep."

   —Ella Wheeler, in Albany, New York, *Times*

From a poem "DRIFTING APART":

"So a sweetness is gone from our lives and the flower
Whose beauty has gladdened us many an hour
Lies dead, and the dream that we might have made true
Like a shading has fled—Who's to blame, I or you?
. . . For the love we let pass unheeded by
Then who is the sadder, you or I?"

In later years on the advice of his doctor, Grundy shunned
any active participation in politics. To his Republican employees
at Walnut Grove, he would point out why they should vote for

the ticket; however, neither he nor his sister tried to influence the ones of Democratic persuasion. The authority for this conclusion was Claudia Maddox who worked at Walnut Grove during the last twelve years of his life. At the time that she was being hired by Meta Grundy, Claudia said to her, "I am afraid you wouldn't want me—I'm a Democrat."

According to Claudia, Miss Grundy replied, "That makes no difference whatever. I do want you." And Claudia moved into Walnut Grove. After Meta's death she looked after the Senator. She recalled the first time she asked him if it was all right for her to register Democratic in Bucks County. "Register Democratic, vote as thee pleases," he said, "and don't ever let it be said that Joe Grundy told thee how to vote."

When his sister died of a heart attack in 1952, Grundy was grief-stricken. Of Meta, who lived an active life until her death at the age of eighty-six, he said, "Thee knows, Meta was never strong." Sue Campion Emack, the Senator's cousin and heir, who had always been close to Meta, followed in her footsteps as the Senator's gracious hostess at Walnut Grove.

Although Sue lived in Philadelphia, she journeyed to Bristol every week to look over the house and check with the servants. Whenever Joe Grundy returned from Nassau in the spring and from Ocean City in the fall, fresh lace curtains brightened the windows and his favorite cookies were on the table. He looked forward to Sue's weekly visits and, when they selected the preferred evening for dinner together at Walnut Grove, he would always say with Victorian graciousness, "I shall await thy visit with fond expectancy."

Sue and the Senator shared many family memories. They enjoyed reminiscing about favorite stories of the days when her father, Richard Campion, in 1876 became a partner of the firm, then called Grundy Brothers and Campion. Sue Emack's mother, Susan Grundy, was the daughter of Joe Grundy's Uncle Ned. When she returned from boarding school a charming young lady, the Grundy partner, Richard Campion, although twenty years her senior, fell in love and married her in 1886.

The couple's only daughter, Susan Campion Emack, who had extensive experience with family papers and records in her work as Registrar of the Colonial Dames of America, preserved family letters and items of furniture for the Grundy Foundation and for Historic Fallsington, Inc., the non-profit organization for which Joe Grundy was the chief benefactor. She continues to serve on the Board of Trustees of this and many other organizations, being also honorary president of the Pennsylvania Society of New England Women.

Only a few have been wise enough to discard the Grundy myth and privileged to know the man. Unlike John D. Rockefeller and certain other millionaires of his time, Joe Grundy was not interested in personal public relations. To those who pleaded with him to contradict some of the harsh stories about himself and to allow some of his many philanthropies to become known, he said, "We Friends don't like that sort of thing."

In the late years, although his political enemies kept his name in campaign issues right up to 1960, he avoided political activities. The Senator did not actively endorse any candidate during the last eighteen years of his life. He could not fully approve of Dwight Eisenhower because, at the Republican Convention of 1952, he had been so strongly in favor of Robert A. Taft. The two men had been friends for years and the Pennsylvanian admired the Ohio Senator.

When Eisenhower became the party's nominee, Grundy, in spite of his preference for Taft, donated heavily as always to the campaign fund. In his beloved Bucks County even in advanced old age, he continued to contribute from $1,500 to $2,000 each year to the Republican Finance Chairman. Grundy believed in 100 per cent loyalty whether it be to political party, family, county, state, or country.

As the debates continued in the Kennedy-Nixon campaign, the last one he was to witness, Grundy fretted. "An 'insider' should never be talked into debating with an 'outsider,'" he kept saying.

The 1960 Presidential campaign pointed up the two vocabularies Joe Grundy had mastered throughout his political life. One was for the polite society in which he moved and the other for his political associations. The only time the writer ever saw him confuse the two was during one of our last discussions. Grundy was referring to a Nixon speech. "The candidate can't be expected to do the heavy firing. He should just be pointing out the administration's good but poorly advertised record. However, Nixon should have key men lined up to 'give 'em h—'!" Then he turned to me with an embarrassed smile, "I *beg* thy pardon."

Another time he forgot himself while chatting with his political protege, Sally Stauffer, who is following in her mother's footsteps in political leadership in Lancaster County and throughout the state. Sally, angered by what she considered a scurrilous newspaper reference to Grundy, asked, "Uncle Joe, why don't you get completely out of politics?"

His reply shot out before he had time to edit it. "Because there's always some s—of—a—b— that has to be licked!"

Grundy expressed his feelings frankly, whether on politics or patriotism. His love of country was not an abstract thing. It was backed by heavy investments in United States bonds, many awards for his work in Liberty Loan drives, substantial donations to historic shrines and a deep reverence for his nation's flag. Whenever he was in residence at Walnut Grove, he saw to it that the flag was flying in front of the house.

Grundy rode to his Philadelphia office in the Fidelity-Philadelphia Trust Building daily. Rain or shine, he was driven to the city by his dependable chauffeur, Joe Glassmire, a World War II veteran who had been with him for his last ten years. Joe was good friend as well as chauffeur to the aged man. He always responded appropriately with a knowing grin to Grundy's invariable comment as he left for the office: it was, "Thee knows a man has to make a living!"

Glassmire relates that in the afternoons the Senator would signal it was time to leave the office by the remark, "Let's go home and see what the neighbors brought in!"

This routine was followed on weekdays even during the fall of his ninety-seventh year. Each morning the Senator got out of the car at the office and walked, head down, to the elevator. To any greeting he responded cordially, but in his last years he was embarrassed by his failing eyesight and memory. He lived in constant fear of not recognizing an old friend and was continually apologizing for "this old head of mine" and "when thee gets to be my age—."

His faithful and competent secretary, Eddie Rummler, who had been with the Grundy firm since his messenger-boy days, was always waiting for him at the office. This simple old-fashioned suite told a great deal about the man. In the ante-room was an engraving of the Penn Treaty Tree, the Great Elm of Shackamaxon (now Kensington), under which William Penn concluded his treaty with the Indians in 1682. The inscription read, "Unbroken faith by deeds of peace."

Other pictures lining the walls were of Pennsbury, Bucks County, the home of William Penn; an old map of Pennsylvania; pictures of 610 Radcliffe Street, Bristol, and Walnut Grove, both the house and the old and new barns. There were also photographs of close friends and political associates—William L. Mellon, Governor Fisher, Senator Martin, Boies Penrose, Governor James, General Daniel Strickler, Gertrude Stauffer, Mrs. Jay Cooke, Gertrude Detwiler, and Daniel Rhoades. Many events were pictured including Pennsylvania Manufacturers Association dinners, a few citations such as one from the Republican National Committee, and mementoes of social affairs.

The objects on Grundy's desk told their own story—a photograph of Gertie Stauffer and her children, six elephants of various sizes in ivory, ebony, bronze, and glass, and campaign pins and ribbons from Republican National Conventions.

Of the hundreds of newspaper articles and photographs available in his scrap book, only one was framed and hung on the wall. It was from the *Derrick*, Oil City, Pennsylvania, and accompanied a picture of Grundy at seventy-seven, surrounded by his co-workers in his own precinct, the Second Ward of the Borough of Bristol.

The clipping read: "We are in receipt of the above photograph from the Honorable Joseph R. Grundy, the same Grundy who for over a generation has been abused like a pickpocket because as a rich man, he takes a deep interest in politics, as every citizen has a right to do—and should do. So persistently has Senator Grundy been pilloried by political humbugs and penny-a-liners that they think the easiest way to defeat any candidate they do not like is to pin the Grundy label on him.

"In the above picture Grundy is seen with a group of his fellow citizens who seem to be proud they are with him. He is the man in the center holding the paper. That group is a fair cross-section of Pennsylvania's citizenry. For fifty-five years, with one exception, the Senator has made it his duty to be at the polls in the Second Ward of the Borough of Bristol, Pennsylvania, from the time they open until they close.

"When an Associated Press photographer asked him to pose on last election day, he at first refused, but compromised by asking the AP man to include the workers who for many years have been associated with him in getting out the vote in the precinct.

"There is no better evidence of any man's character and integrity than the esteem in which he is held by his friends and neighbors. Senator Grundy is in his seventy-seventh year. He is a Quaker and lives up to the tenets of his religion. Even if he is the biggest man in his community, he is not too big to rate a cheery greeting by every man, woman or child who knows him."

During each of his last years Grundy left for Nassau with understandable doubt as to the possibility of his return. On November 30, 1960, the night before he was flying to Nassau, a few friends including the writer and her husband called at Walnut Grove to say good-bye. Grundy sat in the small study that he loved, a twinkle in his eye and several bottles of Bourbon and an ice bucket on a tray for his guests.

He was as genial a host as ever but his parting remarks held a serious note. Referring to the presidential election results, he said: "After living from the time of the Civil War through three more wars and having witnessed a great many things taking place, I'm convinced that the good Lord never intended the younger generation to profit from the lessons of their elders. I believe that they are all meant to make mistakes, suffer, and learn the hard way. It doesn't matter about all of us as individuals, but God help our country."

Grundy never saw Walnut Grove again. He died at Jacaranda after an illness of ten days. In the end his ninety-eight-year-old heart simply gave out. He joked and got out of bed into a chair until some twenty-fours hours before his death, yet there is no doubt that he knew the end was near. Those closest to him—his cousin, Sue Emack, his devoted secretary, Eddie Rummler, who had been, as he said, "like a son to me" stayed with him, and Gertie Stauffer was ever on hand with a cheering word. When the Senator learned that a Philadelphia doctor had been summoned, he asked Rummler, "Is it that bad, Eddie?"

He made no further reference to his condition—not even to the doctor whom he recognized at once. Grundy's only anxiety seemed to be that the doctor enjoy his visit and "get enough to eat." He finally slept into death as quietly and unostentatiously as he would have wished. Mrs. Stauffer, her daughter, Sally, and the Senator's old friend, Mrs. Jay Cooke, then vacationing in Nassau, accompanied the body home.

In accordance with his wishes, his Bristol friend, Republican John Black, handled the funeral arrangements and the simple Episcopal service was read. Floral tributes lined the walls— carnations, roses, orchids, even the pansies that he loved. Old friends from Bristol, Lancaster, distant parts of Pennsylvania and New Jersey, and a surprising number of young friends attended the ceremony.

As requested long before his death, Joe Glassmire, the Senator's long-time friend and chauffeur, drove the hearse. Joe Grundy was buried next to his relatives in the tiny ancient burial ground at Hulmeville.

237

The Pennsylvanian's interest in his town, his county, his state and his country did not end with his death. In the establishment of the Margaret R. Grundy Memorial Library and Museum named for his sister, Grundy's devotion will continue in helping "projects for the benefit of the inhabitants and institutions of the Commonwealth of Pennsylvania and for projects or works designed for the benefit and use of the people generally."

BIBLIOGRAPHY

A Biographical Album of Prominent Pennsylvanians, The American Biographical Publishing Company, Philadelphia, 1888

A Brief History of the United States, A. S. Barnes and Company, New York, 1871, 1885

A Century of the Farmers National Bank of Bucks County, 1814-1914, The Bristol Printing Company, Bristol, Pa., 1914

Allen, Frederick Lewis, *The Big Change*, Harper and Brothers, New York, 1952. *Only Yesterday*, Harper and Brothers, New York, 1957

Archambault, A. Margaretta, *A Guide Book of Art, Architecture and Historic Interests in Pennsylvania*, The John C. Winston Company, Phila., 1924

Bancroft, George, *History of the United States of America*, Little Brown and Company, Boston, 1876

Brookhouser, Frank, *Our Philadelphia*, Doubleday and Company, New York, 1957

Brumbaugh, R. Bruce, *The Grundy Movement in Pennsylvania*, Princeton University, Princeton, New Jersey, 1953

Brunhouse, Robert L., *The Counter-Revolution in Pennsylvania*, 1776-1790, Pennsylvania Historical Commission, Harrisburg, 1942

Butler, Nicholas Murray, *Across the Busy Years*, Charles Scribner's Sons, New York City, 1939-40, Vols. 1 and 2

Bye, Arthur Edwin, *A Friendly Heritage Along the Delaware*, Vantage Press, Inc., New York, 1959

Canfield, Leon H. and Wilder, Howard B., *The Making of Modern America*, Houghton-Mifflin Company, Boston, 1956

Coleman, Elizabeth Tyler, *Priscilla Cooper Tyler*, University of Alabama Press, University of Alabama, 1955

Commager, Henry Steele and Nevins, Allan, *The Heritage of America*, Little Brown and Company, Boston, 1951

Congressional Record, Senate, Address of Senator Grundy of Pennsylvania, January, 1930

Coolidge, Calvin, *The Autobiography of Calvin Coolidge*, Cosmopolitan Book Corp., New York, 1929

Davenport, Walter N., *Power and Glory*, The Life of Boies Penrose, G. P. Putnam's Sons, New York, 1931

Davis, William W. H. *History of Bucks County, Pa.*, The Lewis Publishing Co., New York, 1905. "Early History of Bristol," *Bucks County Historical Society*, Vol. I, The Chemical Publishing Company, Easton, Pa., 1905

De Cou, George, "Mount Holly and Vicinity," *The Historic Rancocas*, The News Chronicle, Moorestown, N. J., 1949

Degler, Carl N., *Out of Our Past*, Harper and Brothers, New York, 1959

Depew, Chauncey M., *My Memories of Eighty Years*, Charles Scribner's Sons, New York, 1924

Eggleston, George Cary, *Life in the Eighteenth Century*, A. S. Barnes & Co., New York, 1905

Earle, Alice Morse, *Home Life in the Colonial Days*, Macmillan Co., New York, 1898

Encyclopaedia Britannica, 11th Edition, New York, 1911

Fink, Leo Gregory, *Buckingham Palisades of the Delaware River*, The Paulist Press, New York, 1960

Garber, John Palmer, *The Valley of the Delaware and Its Place in American History*, John C. Winston Co., Philadelphia, 1934

Gordon, Ernest, *The Wrecking of the 18th Amendment*, The Alcohol Information Press, Francestown, N. H., 1943

Green, Doron, *History of Bristol, Pennsylvania*, C. S. Magrath, Camden, N. J., 1911

Grundy, Joseph R., *Pennsylvania's Relationship to the Protective Tariff Principle*, Statements before the Lobby Investigating Committee of the United States Senate (October 24 to November 11, 1929).

"Highlights of History, Boies Penrose," The Gettysburg Times, Gettysburg, Pa., 1958

Hume, David, *The History of England*, Porter and Coates, Philadelphia, 1876

Hutton, Ann Hawkes, *Portrait of Patriotism*, Chilton Company, Phila., 1959 "The Bristol Story," *The Bucks County Traveler*, Doylestown, Pa., 1956

Jackson, Joseph, *America's Most Historic Highway*, John Wanamaker, Phila., 1926

Langner, William L., *An Encyclopedia of World History*, Houghton-Mifflin Co., Boston, 1940

Lowrie, Sarah D., *Firsts in Pennsylvania and Philadelphia*, Strawberry Mansion Committee, Fairmount Park Commission, Phila., 1952

Macaulay, Thomas Babington, *The History of England*, Vol. I, Porter and Coates, Phila., 1887

Macdonald, William, *Documentary Source of American History*, The Macmillan Co., New York, 1920

MacReynolds, George, *Place Names in Bucks County, Pa.*, The Bucks County Historical Society, Doylestown, Pa., 1942

Montgomery, D. H., *The Leading Facts of American History*, Ginn and Co., Boston, 1894

Morris, Richard B., *Encyclopedia of American History*, Harper and Brothers, New York, 1953

Morrison and Commager, *The Growth of the American Republic*, Oxford University Press, New York, 1942, Vol. 2

Niebuhr, Reinhold, *The Irony of American History*, Charles Scribner's Sons, New York, 1952

Nutting, Wallace, *Pennsylvania Beautiful*, Old America Company, Framingham, Mass., 1924

Oakley, Amy, *Our Pennsylvania*, The Bobbs-Merrill Co., Inc., New York, 1950

O'Connor, Harvey, *Mellon's Millions, The Life and Times of Andrew W. Mellon,* John Day, New York, 1933

Penn, William, *An Essay Towards the Present and Future Peace of Europe,* London, 1694

Pepper, George Wharton, *Philadelphia Lawyer, An Autobiography,* J. B. Lippincott Company, Phila., 1944

Ridpath, John Clark, *A Popular History of the United States of America,* Nelson and Phillips, New York, 1876

Salmon, Thomas, *Modern History; or the Present State of All Nations,* Vol. III, London, 1766

Siegfried, Andre, *America Comes of Age,* Harcourt, Brace and Company, New York, 1927

Stackpole, E. J., *Behind the Scene with a Newspaper Man,* J. B. Lippincott, Phila. and London, 1927

Stevens, S. K., *Pennsylvania, Titan of Industry,* Vol. 1-3, Lewis Historical Publishing Co., New York, 1948

Sullivan, Mark, *Our Times: The United States,* Charles Scribner's Sons, New York City, 1926-1935, Vol. 6.

The Concessions and Agreements of the Proprietors, Freeholders and Inhabitants of the Province of West New Jersey in America, The Burlington Press, Burlington, N. J., 1951

The New Funk and Wagnalls Encyclopedia, Unicorn Publishers, New York, Vols. 18, 22, 23, 35, 1952

Townsend, Virginia F., *Our Presidents,* Worthington, New York, 1889

Tributes to William Penn—A Tercentenary Record, 1644-1944, Pennsylvania Historical and Museum Commission, Harrisburg, 1946

United States Senate Report 43, Pt. 3, 352 Report of the 71st Congress, 1929

United States Senate—*Lobby Investigation,* V. 1-2, Part 2, United States Govt. Printing Office, Washington, D. C., 1929

Westcott, Thompson, *The Historic Mansions of Phila.,* Porter and Coates, Phila., 1877

Wharton, Anne Hollingsworth, *Through Colonial Doorways,* J. B. Lippincott Company, Phila., 1893

White, William Allen, *A Puritan in Babylon* (The Story of Calvin Coolidge), The Macmillan Company, New York, 1938

Wildes, Harry Emerson, *The Delaware,* Farrar and Rinehart, Inc., New York, 1940

Wilkinson, Gen. James, *Memoirs of My Own Times,* A. Small, Philadelphia, 1816

Wood, Clement, *A Complete History of the United States,* The World Publishing Company, New York, 1941

World Scope Encyclopedia, Universal Educational Guild, New York, 1948, Vols. 6, 10, 12

Young, John Russell, *Memorial History of the City of Philadelphia,* New York History Company, New York, 1895